THE PSYCHOLOGY OF SUGGESTION

A RESEARCH INTO THE SUBCONSCIOUS NATURE OF MAN AND SOCIETY

BORIS SIDIS

SSEL

CONTENTS

SOCIETY

INTRODUCTION BY
WILLIAM JAMES

I am glad to contribute to this book of Dr. Boris Sidis a few words of introduction, which may possibly gain for it a prompter recognition by the world of readers who are interested in the things of which it treats. Much of the experimental part of the work, although planned entirely by Dr. Sidis, was done in the Harvard Psychological Laboratory, and I have been more or less in his confidence while his theoretic conclusions, based on his later work in the Pathological Institute of the New York State Hospitals, were taking shape.

The meaning of personality, with its limits and its laws, forms a problem which until quite recently had to be discussed almost exclusively by logical and metaphysical methods. Within the past dozen years, however, an immense amount of new empirical material had been injected into the question by the observations which the "recognition" by science of the hypnotic state set in motion. Many of these observations are pathological: fixed ideas, hysteric attacks, insane delusions, mediumistic phenomena, etc. And altogether, although they are far from having solved the problem of personality, they must be admitted to have transformed its outward shape. What are the limits of the consciousness of a human being? Is "self" consciousness only a part of the whole consciousness? Are there many "selves" dissociated from one another? What is the medium of synthesis in a group of associated ideas? How can certain systems of ideas be cut off and forgotten? Is personality a product, and not a principle? Such are the questions now being forced to the front—questions now asked for the first time with some sense of their concrete import, and questions which it will require a great amount of further work, both of observation and of analysis, to answer adequately.

Meanwhile many writers are seeking to fill the gap, and several books have been published seeking to popularize the new observations and ideas and present them in connected form. Dr. Sidis' work distinguishes itself from some of these by its originality, and from others by the width of its scope.

It is divided into three parts: Suggestibility; The Self; Man as One of a Crowd. Under all these heads the author is original. He tries by ingenious experiments to show that the suggestibility of waking persons follows an opposite law to that of hypnotic subjects. Suggestions must be *veiled*, in the former case, to be effective; in the latter case, the more direct and open they are the better. By other ingenious experiments Dr. Sidis tries to show that the" subliminal" or "ultra-marginal" portions of the mind may in normal persons distinguish objects which the attentive senses find it impossible to name. These latter experiments are incomplete, but they open the way to a highly important psychological investigation.

In Part II, on "The Self," a very full account is given of "double personality," subliminal consciousness, etc. The author is led to adopt as an explanation of the dissociations which lie at the root of all these conditions the physiological theory of retraction of the processes of the brain cells, which in other quarters also seems coming to the front. He makes an elaborate classification of the different degrees of dissociation or amnesia, and, on the basis of a highly interesting and important pathological case, suggests definite methods of diagnosis and cure. This portion of the book well deserves the attention of neurologists.

In Part III the very important matter of "crowd psychology" is discussed, almost for the first time in English. There is probably no more practically important topic to the student of public affairs. Dr. Sidis illustrates it by fresh examples, and his treatment is highly suggestive.

I am not convinced of all of Dr. Sidis' positions, but I can cordially recommend the volume to all classes of readers as a treatise both interesting and instructive, and original in a high degree, on a branch of research whose importance is daily growing greater.

WILLIAM JAMES
HARVARD UNIVERSITY
November 1, 1897

INTRODUCTION

The study of the subconscious is becoming of more and more absorbing interest. The phenomena of hysteria and of hypnosis are now studied by the French psychologists with remarkable acumen and with an unrivalled fertility of ingenious devices, and the results obtained thus far form almost an epoch in the history of psychology. Although the French psychologists work independently of one another and disagree among themselves on many important points, still their method and general line of investigation are pretty nearly the same. They all care for clinical cases more than for minute, detailed laboratory experiments—the present hobby of the Germans—and their chief work falls within the domain of the subconscious. The French psychologists seem to be on the track of a rich gold vein. Without closely formulating their method, they have all, as if by a mutual tacit understanding, chosen the right way that leads to a better and deeper insight into the nature of mind. For the mechanism of consciousness is hidden deep down in the depths of the subconscious, and it is thither we have to descend in order to get a clear understanding of the phenomena that appear in the broad daylight of consciousness.

The German school, with Wundt at its head, at first started out on similar lines, but they could not make any use of the subconscious, and their speculations ran wild in the fancies of Hartmann. The reason of this failure is due to the fact that the concept of the subconscious as conceived by the German school was extremely vague, and had rather the character of a mechanical than that of a psychical process. An unconscious consciousness that was their concept of the subconscious. In such a form as this the subconscious was certainly meaningless—mere nonsense—and had to be given up. The German psychological investigations are now confined to the content of consciousness in so far as the individual is immediately conscious of it. But as this form of consciousness is extremely narrow and circumscribed, the results arrived at, though remarkable for their thoroughness, are after all of a rather trivial nature. It is what Prof. James aptly characterizes "the elaboration of the obvious." We may therefore, with full right, assert that it was the French psychologists who made proper use of the subconscious and arrived at results that are of the utmost importance to psychology, although it were well if the French were to conduct their investigations with German thoroughness.

It is not, however, the French alone who work along the lines of the subconscious, but the English and Americans, too, have a large share in the work. Gourney, James, Myers, and others, have done much toward the elucidation of the obscure phenomena of the subconscious. Psychology is especially indebted to the genius of Myers for his wide and comprehensive study of the phenomena of the subconscious, or of what he calls the manifestations of the subliminal self. The only drawback in Myers's concept of the subliminal self is that he conceives it as a metaphysical entity, as a kind of a cosmic self. Now, while Myers may be right in his belief, the phenomena under investigation do not warrant the hypothesis of metaphysical entities. I have therefore avoided the use of the term "subliminal self," however excellent it might be in itself, in order not to entangle the reader in the metaphysical considerations that cluster round that concept, and also because my point of view of the subconscious widely differs from that of Myers.

The study of subconscious phenomena is of great interest from a purely practical standpoint, because of the use that call be made of it in the state of health and disease. A knowledge of the laws of the subconscious is of momentous import in education, in the reformation of juvenile criminals and offenders, and one can hardly realize the great benefit that suffering humanity will derive from a proper methodical use of the subconscious within the province of therapeutics.

The study of the subconscious is especially of great value to sociology, because nowhere else does the subconscious work on such a grand, stupendous scale as it does in the popular mind; and the sociologist who ignores the subconscious lacks a deep insight into the nature of social forces. For the practical man who takes part in social affairs, in so far as they concern his own interests, the knowledge of the subconscious can hardly be overestimated; and this knowledge becomes an imperative necessity to him who lives in a democracy. The object of this book is the study of the subconscious, normal or abnormal, individual or social, in its relation to suggestion and suggestibility; and let me hope that the thoughtful reader will find my work not only interesting, but stimulating to thought and useful in practical life.

SUGGESTIBILITY

1
SUGGESTION AND SUGGESTIBILITY

PSYCHOLOGICAL investigators employ the term "suggestion" in such a careless and loose fashion that the reader is often puzzled as to its actual meaning. Suggestion is sometimes used for an idea bringing in its train another idea, and is thus identified with association. Some extend the province of suggestion, and make it so broad as to coincide with any influence man exerts on his fellow beings. Others narrow down suggestion and suggestibility to mere symptoms of hysterical neurosis. This is done by the adherents of the Salpêtrière school. Suggestion, again, is used by the Nancy school to indicate the cause which produces that peculiar state of mind in which the phenomena of suggestibility become especially prominent.

This vague and hazy condition of the subject of suggestion causes much confusion in psychological discussions. To free the subject from this confusion of tongues, we must endeavour in some way or other to give a strict definition of suggestion, and rigorously study the phenomena contained within the limited field of our investigation. "We must not follow in the way of those writers who employ the terms suggestion and suggestibility in all possible meanings. Such carelessness can not but lead into a tangle of words. In order to give a full description of suggestion and make its boundary lines clear, distinct, and definite, let us take a few concrete cases and inspect them closely.

I hold a newspaper in my hands and begin to roll it up; soon I find that my friend sitting opposite me rolled up his in a similar way. This, we say, is a case of suggestion.

My friend Mr. A. is absent-minded; he sits near the table, thinking of some abstruse mathematical problem that baffles all his efforts to solve it. Absorbed in the solution of that intractable problem, he is blind and deaf to what is going on around him. His eyes are directed on the table, but he appears not to see any of the objects there. I put two glasses of water on the table, and at short intervals make passes in the direction of the glasses-passes which he seems not to perceive; then I resolutely stretch out my hand, take one of the glasses, and begin to drink. My friend follows suit——dreamily he raises his hand, takes the glass, and begins to sip, awakening fully to consciousness when a good part of the tumbler is emptied.

To take an interesting and amusing case given by Ochorowitz in his book Mental Suggestion:

"My friend P., a man no less absent-minded than he is keen of intellect, was playing chess in a neighbouring room. Others of us were talking near the door. I had made the remark that it was my friend's habit when he paid the closest attention to the game to whistle an air from Madame Angot. I was about to accompany him by beating time on the table. But this time he whistled something else—a march from Le Prophète.

"'Listen,' said I to my associates; 'we are going to play a trick upon P. We will (mentally) order him to pass from Le Prophète to La Fille de Madame Angot.'

"First I began to drum the march; then, profiting by some notes common to both, I passed quickly to the quicker and more staccato measure of my friend's favourite air. P. on his part suddenly changed the air and began to whistle Madame Angot. Everyone burst out laughing. My friend was too much absorbed in a check to the queen to notice anything.

"'Let us begin again,' said I, 'and go back to Le Prophète.' And straightway we had Meyerbeer once more with a special fugue. My friend knew that he had whistled something, but that was all he knew."

A huckster stations himself in the middle of the street, on some public square, or on a sidewalk, and begins to pour forth volumes of gibberish intended both as a compliment to the people and a praise of his ware. The curiosity of the passers-by is awakened. They stop. Soon our hero forms the centre of a crowd that stupidly gazes at the "wonderful" objects held out to its view for admiration. A few moments more, and the crowd begins to buy the things the huckster suggests as "grand, beautiful, and cheap."

A stump orator mounts a log or a car and begins to harangue the crowd. In the grossest way he praises the great intelligence, the brave spirit of the people, the virtue of the citizens, glibly telling his audience that with such genius as they possess they must clearly see that the prosperity of the country depends on the politics he favours, on the party whose valiant champion he now is. His argumentation is absurd, his motive is contemptible, and still, as a rule, he carries the body of the crowd, unless another stump orator interferes and turns the stream of sentiment in another direction. The speech of Antony in Julius Cæsar is an excellent example of suggestion.

All these examples undoubtedly belong to the province of suggestion. Now what are their characteristic traits? What are the elements common to all these cases of suggestion? "We find in all these instances a stream of consciousness that goes on flowing in its peculiar, individual, idiosyncratic way; suddenly from the depths of the stream a wave rises to the surface, swamps the rest of the waves, overflows the banks, deflects for a while the course of the current, and then suddenly subsides, disappears, and the stream resumes its natural course, flowing once more in its former bed. On tracing the cause of this disturbance, we invariably find that it is due to some external source, to some other stream running alongside the one disturbed. Stating the same in the language of Baldwin, we may say that by suggestion is meant a great class of phenomena typified by the abrupt entrance from without into consciousness—of an idea or image which becomes a part of the stream of thought, and tends to produce the muscular and volitional efforts which ordinarily follow upon its presence."[1]

Is this our last say of suggestion? Far from being the case. On closer inspection of our examples we find some more traits which are of the utmost importance. The subject accepts *uncritically* the idea suggested to him, and carries it out almost *automatically*. This can be easily detected in nearly every instance of suggestion, but it stands out especially clear and sharp in its outline in cases of hypnosis.

I hypnotized Mr. F.,[2] and commanded that, after awakening, when he would hear me cough, he should take three oranges on the table and give them to my friends who were present at the *séance*. I woke him up. A few minutes later I coughed; he snatched from the table the oranges, which were, in fact, nothing but ordinary potatoes, and distributed them among my friends. While carrying out this post-hypnotic suggestion he appeared to be in a peculiar automatic condition. His movements were hurried, as if some spring was loosened in his ideo-motor mechanism; his eyes were dull and glassy; it was plain he was in a semiconscious state. On my asking him afterward how the oranges appeared to him he replied: "They seemed to me rather queer; they were too small and heavy for oranges. I thought they were lemons, but I did not attempt to examine them; something impelled me to carry out the order and be done with it."

To take a still better example from the store of my hypnotic experiments: I hypnotized Mr. F., and suggested to him that after awakening, on hearing me cough, he should take the umbrella, open it, and promenade in the room three times. I woke him up. A few minutes later I coughed; up went his legs, but he remained sitting in the chair. I coughed again; once more up went his legs, but he did not carry out my commands. I rehypnotized him, and this time I strongly and authoritatively commanded him he should carry out my post-hypnotic suggestion, taking care to suggest to him he should forget everything that passed during the hypnotic trance. He was awakened, felt well, conversed with his friends. While he was engaged in conversation I went behind his chair and coughed. Up he jumped, opened the umbrella, and walked in the room three times. "When he was through with the suggested promenade the umbrella dropped from his hands on the floor, and, without picking it up, he sat down on a chair and smiled. He remembered very clearly the umbrella affair, and it seemed to him queer and comical. I asked him whether he knew what he was going to do when he heard me cough. "Yes, I knew I must do something—in a general way, though." When I took the umbrella, I do not know how it happened, but I opened it and began to walk." I asked him whether he knew how many times he had to walk, to which he answered: "No, I did not know, but I kept on walking; and when it came to the end of the third turn, the umbrella dropped from my hands."

I could easily bring many more instances of the same type, but I think that those given will suffice for our purpose.

What we find in all these cases is the uncritical acceptance of the ideas or actions suggested, and also the motor automatism with which these ideas or actions are realized. In short, mental and motor automatism constitute the prominent elements of suggestion.

There is, however, one more element in suggestion—an element which must be taken into account, and without which our definition of suggestion will be incomplete. This factor, or element, is the overcoming or circumventing of the subject's opposition. The suggested idea is forced on the stream of consciousness; it is a stranger, an unwelcome guest, a parasite, which the subject's consciousness seeks to get rid of. The stream of the individual's consciousness combats suggested ideas as the organism does bacteria and bacilli that tend to disturb the stability of its equilibrium. It is this opposition element that Dr. J. Grossmann has in mind when he defines suggestion as "der Vorgang, bei dem eine Vorstellung sich einem Gehirn aufzuzwingen versucht."[3]

My friend would not have rolled up his paper, nor would Mr. A. have taken the glass and sipped the water, nor would Mr. P. have whistled his airs, nor would the crowd have bought the articles of the huckster or voted for certain political candidates had they been openly commanded to do so. They would have opposed strenuously the suggestion given to them. It was required to devise means in order to circumvent this opposition. The same necessity for circumvention of opposition we find in post-hypnotic suggestion. At first the subject F. opposed the idea of walking with the umbrella. When I rehypnotized him I asked him, "Why did not you carry out my command?" The reply was, "I wanted to see whether I could resist." That this was actually the case we can see from the fact that, while his legs started at the signal and went up to fulfil the order, Mr. F. exclaimed, "I know what you want me to do, but I will not do it." This opposition was overcome only after repeated and insistent injunctions that he must obey my command.

The first stages of hypnosis are especially characterized by this spirit of opposition, which, however, gradually slackens as the subject falls into a deeper state of hypnosis, and completely disappears with the advent of somnambulism. To watch the struggle of the mind in its opposition to the engrafted suggested idea is of intense interest to the psychologist, and of great value to a clearer comprehension of suggestion itself.

I hypnotized Mr. J. F. With one resolute command I made him cataleptic. "Rise!" I commanded him. He rose. "Walk!" He walked. "You can not walk forward!

" He tried to walk, but he could not. " You can only walk backward!" He began to move backward. At the very first sitting he seemed to have fallen completely under my control and to carry out without any opposition all the motor suggestions given to him. This, however, was not really the case. Opposition was there, only it was ineffective. As we continued our sittings (and we had many of them) Mr. J. F. became more and more intractable, my control over him grew less and less, and now it is only after great exertion and repeated imperative commands that I am enabled to bring him into any cataleptic condition at all. The opposition or inhibition kept in abeyance during the first séance asserted itself as the subject became more familiar with the hypnotic condition.

The following experiments are still more interesting, as revealing to us in the clearest way possible the internal struggle——the great opposition which the consciousness of the subject shows to the parasitic suggested idea:

Mr. L. falls into a slight hypnotic condition——into the first degree of hypnosis; he can open his eyes if I challenge him that he is unable to do it. Although his hypnosis is but slight, I still tried on him post-hypnotic suggestions. While he was in the hypnotic condition I suggested to him that after awakening, when he will hear a knock, he will go to the table, take a cigarette, and light it. I suggested to him he should forget everything that passed during the hypnosis.

On awakening he remembered everything. I gave a few knocks in quick succession. He rose from his chair, but immediately sat down again, and laughingly exclaimed, "No, I shall not do it!" "Do what?" I asked. "Light the cigarette——nonsense!" "Had you a strong desire to do it?" I asked him, putting the desire in the past, although it was plain he was still struggling with it. He did not answer. "Did you wish very much to do it?" I asked again. "Not very much," he answered curtly and evasively.

On another occasion I hypnotized Mr. L. by the method of fascination.[4] He seemed to have fallen into a slightly deeper hypnotic condition than usual. The post-hypnotic suggestion was to light the gas, and also complete amnesia. On awakening he remembered everything that passed during hypnosis. He ridiculed the post-hypnotic suggestions I gave him. After a few minutes' conversation, without my giving the suggestion signal, which was to be a knock, I left the room for a few moments——for five or tell seconds. When I returned I found him lighting the gas. "What are you doing that for, Mr. L.?" I asked. "To feel easier," he answered; "I felt somewhat uneasy." Evidently the post-hypnotic suggestion took deep root in his mind. He struggled hard against it, to put it down, to suppress it; and it was due to this fact that he attempted to counteract the suggested idea by ridiculing it. As long as I was in the room he wanted to show the energy of his will, and he struggled hard against the insistent idea, keeping it at bay; but when I left the room one of the motives of resisting the suggestion was removed, and the struggle became an unequal one. The insistent parasitic idea asserted itself with greater force than before, and this time, not meeting with such a strenuous opposition, it gained the upper hand and realized itself completely.

To take one more instance of the many sittings I had with M. L. I hypnotized him once in the presence of two acquaintances of mine, and gave him a post-hypnotic suggestion to take from the table a box of matches and light the gas. This he had to do when hearing me cough. I woke him up, and as soon as he heard me cough he started up from his chair, looked hard at the box of matches, but did not take it. He went up to the window, put his head against the window pane, and seemed to be engaged in a severe struggle against the insistent suggested idea. Now and then one could perceive a slight shudder passing over his entire body, thus making almost palpably evident the inner, restless, contentious state of his consciousness. Again and again the suggested idea cropped up in his mind, and again and again it was suppressed; now the suggestion gained ground, and now once more it was beaten and driven back into the obscure regions from which it came. I then rehypnotized him, strongly emphasized my suggestion, and then awakened him. I slightly coughed. This time the suggested idea got a stronger hold of his mind. Mr. L. rose from his chair, took the box of matches, kept it in hi" hand for a second or two, and threw it resolutely on the table. " No," he exclaimed, "I will not do it!"

Such cases might be multiplied by the hundreds, but I think that the hypnotic experiments made on my subjects L. and J. F. will suffice for our purpose. They show most clearly that the trait of opposition is an ingredient of suggestion. This opposition element varies with the state of mind of the individual. What the nature of this variation is we shall see later on; meanwhile the present stage of our discussion fully enables us to formulate a definition of suggestion and suggestibility.

By suggestion is meant the intrusion into the mind of an idea; met with more or less opposition by the person; accepted uncritically at last; and realized unreflectively, almost automatically.

By suggestibility is meant that peculiar state of mind which is favourable to suggestion.[5]

---

1. Psychology, vol. ii.
2. Let me say at the outset that all the subjects on whom I made hypnotic experiments were never hypnotized by anyone else before. Whatever, therefore, occurred during hypnosis was not due to previous suggestive training unknown to me. Each subject was fully under my observation. I took the precaution of isolating my subjects from extraneous suggestion. During trance I suggested to them that no one should he able to hypnotize them. I ask the reader to hear this in mind.
3. Zeitschrift für hypnotismus, August, 1893.
4. Ordinarily I use the method of Nancy: it is the most convenient and pleasant way of hypnotization, as it requires no strain on the side of the subject.
5. The psycho-physiological state of suggestion I term suggestibility. By "*suggestibility of a factor*" is meant the power of the factor to induce the psycho-physiological state of suggestion of a certain degree of intensity, the suggestiveness of the factor being measured by the degree of suggestibility induced.

2

THE CLASSIFICATION OF SUGGESTION AND SUGGESTIBILITY

ONCE the subject-matter under investigation is defined, we must proceed to a further subdivision of it; we must define and classify the different species of suggestion and suggestibility. Already in our last chapter, in adducing different cases of suggestion, suggestibility in the normal state was tacitly implied. We have now reached a stage in our discussion in which we must state this fact more explicitly. The soil favourable for the seeds of suggestion exists also in what we can the normal individual. Suggestibility is present in what we call the normal state, and in order to reveal it we must only know how to tap it. The suggestible element is a constituent of our nature; it never leaves us; it is always present in us. Before Janet, Binet, and many other investigators undertook the study of hysterical subjects, no one suspected the existence of those remarkable phenomena of double consciousness that opened for us new regions in the psychical life of man. These phenomena were merely not noticed, although present all the while; and when at times they rose from their obscurity, came to light, and obtruded themselves on the attention of people, they were either put down as sorcery, witchcraft, or classed contemptuously with lying, cheating, and deception. The same is true with regard to normal suggestibility. It rarely attracts our attention, as it manifests itself in but trifling things. When, however, it rises to the surface and with the savage fury of a hurricane cripples and maims on its way everything it can not destroy, menaces life, and throws social order into the wildest confusion possible, we put it down as mobs. We do not in the least suspect that the awful, destructive, automatic spirit of the mob moves in the bosom of the peaceful crowd, reposes in the heart of the quiet assembly, and slumbers in the breast of the law-abiding citizen. We do not suspect that the spirit of suggestibility lies hidden even in the best of men; like the evil jinnee of the Arabian tales is corked up in the innocent-looking bottle. Deep down in the nature of man we find hidden the spirit of suggestibility. Every one of us is more or less suggestible. Man is often defined as a social animal. This definition is no doubt true, but it conveys little information as to the psychical state of each individual within society. There exists another definition which claims to give an insight into the nature of man, and that is the well-known ancient view that man is a rational animal; but this definition breaks down as soon as we come to test it by facts of life, for it scarcely holds true of the vast multitudes of mankind. Not sociality, not rationality, but suggestibility is what characterizes the average specimen of humanity, for *man is a suggestible animal.*

The fact of suggestibility existing in the normal individual is of the highest importance in the theoretical field of knowledge, in psychology, sociology, ethics, history, as well as in practical life, in education, politics, and economics; and since this fact of suggestibility may be subject to doubt on account of its seeming paradoxicalness, it must therefore be established on a firm basis by a rigorous experimentation, and I have taken great pains to prove this fact satisfactorily. The evidence for the existence of normal suggestibility I shall adduce later on in our discussion; meanwhile I ask the reader to take it on trust, sincerely hoping that he will at the end be perfectly satisfied with the demonstration of its truth.

The presence of suggestibility in such states as the hysterical and the hypnotic is a fact well proved and attested, and I think there is no need to say a word in its defence. Since the hysterical, the hypnotic, the somnambulic states do not belong to the routine of our experience; since they are but rare and occur under special peculiar conditions; since they unfit one for social life, disable in the struggle for existence, I think the reader will not quarrel with me for naming such states abnormal.

Thus it becomes quite clear that suggestibility must be classed under two heads: (1) Suggestibility in the normal state, or normal suggestibility, and (2) suggestibility in the abnormal state, or abnormal suggestibility.

Turning now to suggestion, we find that it can be easily subdivided and classified according to the mode it is effected in consciousness. Concrete examples will best illustrate my meaning. The hypnotizer commands his subject to walk; the latter walks. He raises the hand of the patient, and it remains uplifted in a contracted cataleptic condition. The hypnotizer tells the subject that after awakening, when he will hear a knock, he will take off his coat and dance a polka, and the subject, on awakening and perceiving the signal, fulfils the order most faithfully. In cases like these the experimenter gives his orders or suggestions *directly*, without beating round the bush, without any circumlocution, without any evasions. In a plain and brusque manner does the hypnotizer give his suggestion, so much so that it partakes of the nature of an imperative command issued by the order of the highest authority from which there is no appeal. The essential feature here, however, is not so much the authoritativeness, for in many cases it may be totally absent, and a courteous, bland way of expression may be used; not so much the authoritativeness, I say, as the plainness, the directness with which the suggestion is given. Such a suggestion we may designate as *direct suggestion*.

Suggestions may also be given in quite a different way. Instead of openly telling the subject what he should do, the experimenter produces some object, or makes a movement, a gesture, which in their own silent fashion tell the subject what to do. To illustrate it by a few examples, so as to make my meaning clearer: I stretch out the hand of the hypnotic subject and make it rigid, and while during this I press his arm with an iron rod. In the next *séance* as soon as the iron rod touches the arm the hand becomes rigid. I tell the subject to spell the word "Napoleon," and when he comes to "p" I stretch out my hand and make it stiff; the subject begins to stammer; the muscles of his lips spasmodically contract and stiffen. Dr.

Tuckey brings a case of suggestion given by him unintentionally in such an indirect way. He hypnotized a physician and ordered him to wake up in a quarter of an hour. He then left the room for about half an hour, being sure that in the meantime the subject would come back to himself. When he returned he was surprised to find the patient still sitting in the chair, and in the most distressed condition possible. The patient could not recover his speech; his jaws were firmly shut. Dr. Tuckey thinks that while hypnotizing he inadvertently passed his hand over the mouth of the subject, and this was taken as a suggestion to keep the mouth firmly shut. My friend who drank the glass of water on account of my suggestive movements; Mr. P., whom Prof. Ochorowitz suggested to whistle certain airs; the crowd that was induced by the politician by means of flattery and talk of business prosperity to vote for the party whose cause he advocated-all these are good cases of this type of suggestion. This mode of influencing the mind plays a great part in the history of humanity, and is therefore of great importance in sociology. Such a kind of suggestion may be properly designated as indirect suggestion.

Suggestion partakes of the nature of reflex action. This truth was implied in our discussion of the last chapter, and in the definition of suggestion we finalJy arrived at. And authorities are not lacking who go to support the same view. "Eine sorgfältige Beobachtung," writes Prof. Forel, "der Bedingungen der Suggestibilität bringt uns immer wieder auf die relativ Ruhe des Gehirns zurück, auf einen plastischen Zustand desselben oder wenigstens eines Theiles desselben, worin die Vorstellungen eine schwächere Kraft oder Tendenz haben sich associiren und deshalb leichter dem von aussen commenden Impuls folgen." "Der Mechanismus (der Suggestion)," writes Dr. Bernheim, "ist ein physiologischer mechanismus dessen Realisation sich mit den Eigenschaften unseres Hirn ganz gut vereinbarn lässt."[1] What Dr. Bernheim means to say here is that suggestion partakes of the nature of the reflex and automatic activity that characterizes the physiological mechanism in general. He makes himself more explicit in another place. "The mechanism of suggestion," he writes in his book Suggestive Therapeutics, "may be summed up in the following formula: Increase of the *reflex* ideo-motor, ideo-sensitive, and ideosensorial excitability."

Gourney tells us in his simple straightforward way that the mechanism of "suggestion is conscious reflex action."[2] As reflex action of consciousness, suggestion has a double aspect: afferent, centripetal, or sensory, and efferent, centrifugal, or motor. This is perfectly obvious, for in suggestion we deal, on the one hand, with the impression of the suggested idea on the mind and its acceptance by consciousness; this is the afferent, sensory side of suggestion; and, on the other hand, with the realization of the accepted idea; this is the efferent, motor side of suggestion. The process of suggestion may therefore be represented in the form of an arc, which may be called the suggestion arc. It is quite clear that in classifying suggestion as direct and indirect, we had solely in view the afferent, the sensory aspect of suggestion. If now we regard suggestion from the other aspect, from the efferent or motor aspect, we find that suggestion is subject to another subdivision. Concrete instances will bring out this subdivision most clearly.

The experimenter suggests to the subject to turn over the chair and sit down near it on the floor. This is faithfully and immediately carried out by the subject. The experimenter raises the patient's arm and bends it immediately the and becomes stiff, rigid, cataleptic. The suggested idea impressed on the brain is immediately discharged into the motor tracts. The same holds true of post-hypnotic or deferred suggestion. The idea suggested or the order given is present in the mind, only there is present a suggested obstacle to its motor discharge; but as soon as some kind of suggested signal is perceived, the obstacle is removed and the idea immediately discharges itself along the motor tracts. I hypnotized one of my subjects, Mr. F., and ordered him that on awakening, when he hears me cough, he should put out the gas. I woke him up. He remained quietly sitting in his chair, waiting, as it seemed, for my signal. He himself, however, was not in the least conscious of it; for when his brother asked him whether he would like to go home, as it was rather late, he answered in the negative. I then coughed, and Mr. F. immediately rushed for the light and put it out. What we find here is the literal carrying out of the suggested idea. This kind of suggestion the realization of which bears a direct and immediate relation to the suggested object or act is, of course, also present in normal suggestibility, as in the case of the buyer who chooses the goods suggested to him by the salesman or huckster, as in the case of the citizen who votes for the unknown candidate suggested to him by the politician. In short, when there is full and complete realization of the idea or order suggested, directly or indirectly, we have that kind of suggestion which I designate as *immediate*.

Instead, however, of immediately taking the hint and fully carrying it into execution, the subject may realize something else, either what is closely allied with the idea suggested or what is connected with it by association of contiguity. A suggestion is given to the subject that when he wakes up he will see a tiger. He is awakened, and sees a big cat. The subject is suggested that on awakening he will steal the pocket-book lying on the table. When aroused from the hypnotic state he goes up to the table, does not take the pocketbook, but the pencil that lies close to it. The buyer does not always choose the precise thing which the salesman suggests, but some other thing closely allied to it. In case the suggestion is not successful, it is still, as a rule, realized in some indirect and mediate way. Man is not always doing what has been suggested to him; he sometimes obeys not the suggested idea itself, but some other idea associated with the former by contiguity, similarity, or contrast. Suggestion by contrast is especially interesting, as it often gives rise to counter-suggestion. Now such kind of suggestion, where not the suggested idea itself but the one associated with it is realized, I designate as *mediate*.

Thus we have four kinds of suggestion:

(a) Direct. (d) Immediate.
(b) Indirect. (e) Mediate.

The classification of suggestion and suggestibility may be represented in terms of the suggestion are in the following diagrammatic form:

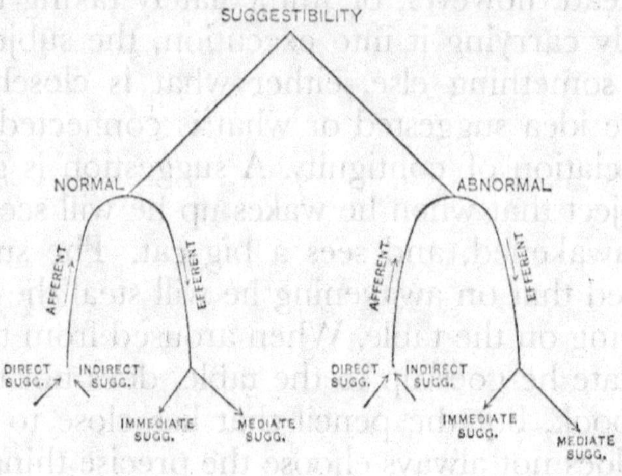

1. Zeitschrift für Hypnotismus, Januar, 1893.
2. Mind, Oct., 1884.

3

THE EVIDENCE OF SUGGESTIBILITY

IN our last chapter we ventured to generalize that every man in his full normal waking state is more or less suggestible. I should not wonder if such a seemingly sweeping generalization should startle many a cautious reader, and should call forth strenuous opposition. We must therefore rigorously demonstrate the fact of the universality of normal suggestibility. Such a proof is of the more importance, as the generalization which it establishes supplies a new principle to sociology, furnishes a key to the comprehension of many a great historical event, gives a deeper insight into the phenomena of political and economical life, and might possibly be of use in education. Is there such a thing as suggestibility in the normal waking condition? The Nancy school, with Bernheim and Liebault at its head, gives an affirmative answer. "Jemanden hypnotisiren," says Bernheim, "heisst nur: seine Suggestibilität künstlich erhöhen." In fact, the hypnotic state itself is induced by suggestion. "Es giebt keinen Hypnotismus: es giebt nur

37

Phänomene der Suggestion," exclaims the Nancy professor. "Als etwas pathologisches, als eine künstliche Neurose betrachtet existirt ein Hypnotismus nicht. Wir schaffen im eigentlichen Sinne mit ihm keinen besonderen Zustand des Gehirns oder des Nervensystems; wir machen uns ganz einfach nur eine physiologische Eigenthümlichkeit des Gehirns—die Suggestibilität—zu Nutze und schaffen die zur Entfaltung dieser Suggestibilität günstigen Vorbedingungen." On closer inspection, however, we find that the great authority of the Nancy school stretches too wide and far the conception of suggestion, for, according to him, "Jede Vorstellung ist eine Suggestion." This, I say, is too far-fetched; for it is to identify the whole field of mental activity with but a part of it, namely, suggestibility. This is, in fact, the obliteration of all traces of the problem itself. If now we turn and ask for facts that go to support his view, we find that Bernheim does not sustain his cause. He limits his instances to but a small class of persons who are easily suggestible in their waking state, but he offers no proof that suggestibility is present in all men. "*Es giebt Menschen* bei denen . . . die einfache Affirmation, ohne Schlaf und ohne vorhergehende ihn begunstigende Manipulationen bei ihnen alle sogenannten hypnotischen Phänomena hervorruft. Durch das einfache Wort schafft man bei ihnen Anästhesia, Contractur, Hallucillationen, Impuls, die verschiedensten Handlungen."[1]

Although the instances Prof. Bernheim adduces do not certainly establish the fact of the universality of normal suggestibility, they are still interesting for us as they show the presence of normal suggestibility in some particular cases at least. "Many subjects," writes Bernheim in his Suggestive Therapeutics, "who have previously been hypnotized may manifest susceptibility to the same suggestive phenomena in the waking state, without being again hypnotized, however slightly might have been the influence of a small number of previous *séances*. Here, for example, is the case of K., one of my patients who is accustomed to being hypnotized, and is subject to light somnambulism. Without putting him to sleep, I say directly: 'Close your hand. You can not open it again.' He keeps his hand closed and contracted, and makes fruitless efforts to open it. I make him hold out his other arm, with his hand open, and say, 'You can not shut it.' He tries in vain to do so; brings the phalanges into semiflexion, but can do no more in spite of every effort. There is in my service a young hysterical girl afflicted with sensitivo-sensorial hemiamæsthesia of the left side, and capable of being hypnotized into deep sleep. In the waking condition she is susceptible to catalepsy or suggestive contraction. I can effect transfer of the hemianæsthesia from the left to the right side without hypnotizing and without touching her. In one of my somnambulistic cases I can obtain all possible modifications of sensibility in the waking condition. It suffices to say, 'Your left side is insensible'; then if I prick his left arm with a pin, stick the pin into his nostril, touch the mucous membrane of his eye, or tickle his throat, he does not move. The other side of his body reacts, I transfer the anaesthesia from the left to the right side. I produce total anæsthesia, which was on one occasion so profound that my *chef de clinique* pulled out the roots of five teeth which were deeply embedded in the gums, twisting them round in their sockets for more than ten minutes. I simply said to the patient, 'You will have no feeling whatever.' He laughed as he spat out the blood, and did not show the least symptom of pain."

Here, as we see, the experiments were carried on with somnambulic and hysterical subjects; the result, therefore, can not prove the facts of suggestibility in normal and perfectly healthy people. Some of my own experiments might possibly prove more conclusive. Mr. W., an acquaintance of mine, who was never hypnotized by anyone, readily took suggestions in his waking state. I told him he could not write his name. He tried, and he did write it. I stretched out my arm, opened my hand and stiffened the fingers, and said, "Try now." He could not write—his hand became cataleptic. I made a whole series of experiments of this kind, but as they interested me from quite a different point of view I shall give a detailed account of them later on. Mean while this one instance will suffice for our present purpose to show the power of suggestion in the waking state. The fact, however, of its rarity and singularity makes it unfit to prove the universality of normal suggestibility.

In the Zeitschrift für Hypnotismus[2] Prof. J. Delboeuf brings cases of suggestibility in normal condition. Thus he made a patient anæsthetic who was not and could not be hypnotized. He told the patient: "Reichen Sie mir Ihren Arm, sehen Sie mich fest an und zeigen Sie mir durch Ihren Blick, dass Sie entschlossen sind, nichts zu fühlen, und Sie werden thatsächlich nichts fühlen." The patient did it. Prof. Delboeuf severely pricked the subject's arm, and the latter felt no pain.

To take another case. An old man of seventy suffered great pain from facial neuralgia for more than fifteen years. "Ich komme zu ihm," says Prof. Deluoeuf, "ziehe ihn heftig am Bart und erkläre ihm, dass er keine Schmerzen mehr hat, dass er auch ferner keine Schmerzen haben wird, und meine Prophezeilmng erfüllt sich." These cases, like the preceding one, are subject to the same objections; they do not prove the universality of normal suggestibility on account of their rarity and singularity. Not everyone can so easily be made cataleptic or anæsthetic in his waking condition. With most people such suggestions are failures even in hypnosis. The only way, then, to test the verity of normal suggestibility is to lay aside all experimentation on hysterical, somnambulic, hypnotic, and extraordinarily suggestible subjects, and start a series of experiments on perfectly healthy and normal individuals. Thanks to Prof. H. Münsterberg and to the admirable facilities afforded by the Psychological Laboratory of Harvard University and the Pathological Institute of the New York State Hospitals, I was enabled to carry out more than eight thousand experiments relating to the subject of suggestion.

The order of experiments taken up first was suggestion of letters and figures. The mechanism of this class of experiments was as follows: A successive series of letters or of figures was introduced through a slit on a white screen, each letter or figure being pasted on a separate slip of cardboard which in colour and position coincided with the background of the screen. Each experiment consisted of a series of nine slips. Each slip was kept on the background for two or three seconds. The interval between the slip and its successor was also two or three seconds. Time was measured by a metronome inclosed within a felt box, with a rubber tube passing close to the ear of the experimenter, so that the subjects should not be disturbed by the ticking of the metronome. For the same reason the experimenter and his movements of inserting the slips into the white screen were all carefully hidden by screens. The ring of a bell indicated that the series came to an end, and it also served as a signal for the subjects to write down *immediately* on paper which they kept ready in their hands anything that came into their mind at that particular moment——letters, numerals, words, phrases, etc.

While looking for evidence for normal suggestibility, an opportunity was also taken to arrange the experiments according to different factors, so that should it be proved that suggestion in the normal state is an indubitable fact, we should be enabled to know what kind of factors are the more impressive and suggestive.

The series of letters and figures were arranged according to the following factors and their combinations:

1. Repetition.
2. Frequency.
3. Coexistence.
4. Last impression.

Great care, of course, was taken not to repeat the same series of letters or figures. As I had many slips at my disposal the series could be easily changed both by permutation and insertion of new slips. The subjects did not and could not possibly suspect the suggested letter or figure, first, because there were so many of them in each series; second, because the factors studied were constantly varied; and, third, because sham series, such as inverted or coloured letters, etc., were introduced so as to baffle the subjects.

I had twelve subjects at my disposal, and experimented with three or four at a time. Recently I made experiments of this kind with thirteen subjects more, so that the total number of subjects is twenty-five.

The results are as follows:

1. REPETITION.——In the middle of the series a letter or numeral was shown three times in succession——e.g.:

B		3
E		6
K		8
M		5
M	or	5
M		5
N		7
O		2
P		9

Of 300 experiments made, 53 succeeded——that is, the subject wrote the letter or numeral suggested by the factor of repetition.

The factor of repetition gives a suggestibility of 17.6 per cent.

2. FREQUENCY.——A letter or numeral was shown three times in the series, and each time with an interruption——e.g.:

B		5
K		3
E		7
K		3
M	or	9
K		3
O		4
R		8
D		6

Of 300 experiments made, 128 succeeded.

The factor of frequency gives a suggestibility of 42.6 per cent.

3. COEXISTENCE.—A letter or numeral was shown repeatedly; not, however, in succession, as it was in the case of the factor of repetition, also not with interruptions as it was in the case of frequency, but at the same time—e.g.:

B		4
E		1
C		2
D		6
R R R	or	7 7 7
M		5
L		3
A		9
F		8

Of 300 experiments made, only 20 succeeded.

The factor of coexistence gives as its power of suggestion 6.6 per cent.

4. LAST IMPRESSION.—Here was studied the suggestibility effected by the last impression, by the last letter or figure. In all our experiments unnecessary repetition was carefully avoided. It is plain that the nature of these experiments of last impression required that not one letter or figure should be repeated twice in the series—e.g.:

A		7
K		9
F		5
L		8
D	or	6
R		2
B		4
E		1
M		3

Of 300 experiments made, 190 succeeded.

The factor of last impression gives a suggestibility of 63.3 per cent.

5. COEXISTENCE AND LAST IMPRESSION.—In these experiments a slip with three identical characters pasted on it appeared at the end of the series, thus combining in one the factor of coexistence with that of last impression—e.g.:

E		2
N		5
C		7
K		1
B	or	9
M		8
Q		4
Z		6
A A A		3 3 3

Of 300 experiments made, 55 succeeded.

The combined effect of coexistence and last impression gives a suggestibility of 18.3 per cent.

6. FREQUENCY AND LAST IMPRESSION.—The letter or numeral repeated with interruptions was also shown at the end of the series—e.g. :

M		5
C		2
B		8
C		2
K	or	4
C		2
P		9
N		6
C		2

Of 150 experiments made, 113 succeeded.

The combined effect of the two factors gives a suggestibility of 75.2 per cent.

Arranging now the factors in the order of their rate of effected suggestibility, we have the following table:

Frequency and last impression.......

75.2 Per cent.

Last impression.................................

63.3 "

Frequency...

42.6 "

Coexistence and last impression...

18.3 "

Repetition...

17.6 "

Coexistence......................................

6.6 "

Comparing now the suggestibility effected by different factors,[3] that of the last impression stands out most prominently. The "*last impression*" is the most impressive. Our daily life teems with facts that illustrate this rule: The child is influenced by the last impression it receives. In a debate he, as a rule, gains the victory in the eyes of the public who has the last word. In a crowd he moves and stirs the citizens to action who makes the last inciting speech. In a mob he who last sets an example becomes the hero and the leader.

Frequency comes next to last impression and precedes repetition. This may be explained by the fact that in repetition the suggestion is too grossly obvious, lying almost on the surface; the mind, therefore, is aroused to opposition, and a counter-suggestion is formed; while in frequency the suggestion, on account of the interruption, is not so tangibly obvious, the opposition therefore is considerably less, and the suggestion is left to run its course.

Coexistence is a still poorer mode of suggestion than repetition; it only arouses opposition. Coexistence is in reality of the nature of repetition, for it is repetition in space; it is a poor form of repetition.

On the whole, we may say that in the normal state temporal or spatial repetition is the most unfortunate mode of suggestion, while the best, the most successful of all the particular factors, is that of the last impression—that is, the mode of bringing the idea intended for suggestion at the very end. This rule is observed by influential orators and widely read popular writers; it is known in rhetoric as bringing the composition to a climax. *Of all the modes of suggestion, however, the most powerful, the most effective, and the most successful is a skilful combination of frequency and last impression.* This rule is observed by Shakespeare in the speech of Antony. Be these rules of the particular factors what they may, one thing is clear and sure: these experiments unquestionably prove the reality of normal suggestibility; they prove the presence of suggestibility in the average normal individual.

From suggestion of ideas I turned to suggestion of movements, of acts. The first set of experiments was rather crude in form, but not without its peculiar interest and value.

The experiments were carried on in the following way: On a little table I put a few objects, screened from the subject by a sheet of white cardboard. The subject was asked to concentrate his attention on a certain spot of the screen for about twenty seconds. On the sudden removal of the screen the subject had immediately to do something—anything he liked. It was, of course, also under6tood that the subject should keep his mind a blank as much as it was in his power, and, at any rate, that he should not beforehand make up his mind what to do. The subjects, I must add, were perfectly trustworthy people—coworkers in the Psychological Laboratory.

Now, while the screen was removed I at the same time loudly suggested some action—such as "Read!" "Write!" "Cut!" "Strike!" "Ring!" etc. On the table were objects appropriate to such actions—a book, a pen, a knife, a hammer, a bell. The subjects very frequently carried out the commands, the suggestions given to them.

Of five hundred experiments made, about one half succeeded; that is, the subject carried out the suggestion given to him during the removal of the screen. Allowing ten per cent for chance, there remains about forty per cent in favour of suggestibility.

On interrogating the subjects of their state of mind at the moment of action, many of them told me that they felt no desire nor any particular impulse to carry out the act suggested, but that they complied with my order out of sheer politeness. (I should say, though, that the fact of the order being realized so many times, be it even from mere politeness, indicates the presence of suggestibility.)

Some of the subjects became totally unfitted to do anything at all. It seemed as if all activity was for the time being under some powerful inhibition.

In the case of one subject—Mr. S., one of the ablest men in the Psychological Laboratory—I found that my order was carried out in a reflex way; so much so that a few times, when I called out "Strike!" " Hammer!" the hand went down on the table instantaneously and with such violence that the table was nearly shattered. Mr. S. felt pain in his hand for some minutes. On one occasion I called out, "Look there!" Quick as lightning Mr. S. turned round and looked hard. On another occasion I commanded, "Rise!" Back moved the chair and up went Mr. S.

Now this set of experiments, if regarded alone, certainly does not carry conviction as to the presence of suggestibility in all perfectly normal and healthy persons; but along with other experiments—with those that relate to suggestion of ideas, and with those in relation to choice suggestion, of which I shall soon give a detailed account—this last set of movements' and acts' suggestion certainly contributes its mite of evidence. It is not, however, on account of their positive side that I value these movement experiments, but on account of their negative side. I shall resume this subject further on in its proper place. Interesting as that last line of investigation was, I still had to abandon it, because the experiments could not possibly be expressed in precise quantitative terms. Except in the case of Mr. S., I could not precisely know how far the experiment succeeded and how far it failed. The different factors remained unanalyzed, and the whole mechanism was extremely crude and primitive. Thanks to the advice of Prof. H. Münsterberg, I was enabled to continue my research further and penetrate deeper into one of the most obscure, most mysterious, but also most promising regions of human nature. The experiments which I am about to describe were carried out with great care and minuteness of detail. The new factors studied were carefully analyzed and separated. I must confess that at first I did not fully realize the import and value of these experiments; I saw in them nothing else than a further test and affirmation of the fact of normal suggestibility, especially on its efferent or motor side. The highest I thought of their value was that along with the preceding experiments they would carry to the mind conviction——perfect certitude as to the universality of normal suggestibility. But later on, when I summed up the results and thought the matter over, I was glad to discover that the results had a profounder meaning than the one I put on them; that they pointed to something beyond, to something deeper and wider than the problem they were intended to solve.

To pass now to the experiments themselves. The experiments were carried on in the following way: Six small squares (30 X 30 mm.) of different colours were placed on a white background. The white background with the six squares on it was again covered by a black carboard. The subject was told to fix his attention on the black cardboard for five seconds (time being measured by the metronome). At the end of five seconds the black cover was removed, and the subject had immediately to take one of the coloured squares, whichever he liked.

The subjects were nineteen in number. No subject was allowed to take part in these experiments more than one hour a week. Precautions were also taken that the same series of colours should not be repeated in the experiments with the same subject. For this purpose Bradley's colours were used, which give an endless combination of different colours. At the beginning of each week the colours were rearranged in new series of six squares each; no series containing the same colour, the squares were all of different colours. Precaution was also taken to hide the arrangement of the experiments from the suhjects.[4]

In these experiments on suggestion of choice the following six factors were studied:

1. Abnormal position.
2. Colored cover.
3. Strange shape.
4. Colour verbally suggested.
5. Place verbally suggested.
6. Environment.

1. ABNORMAL POSITION.—One of the coloured squares was placed in some abnormal way, thus:

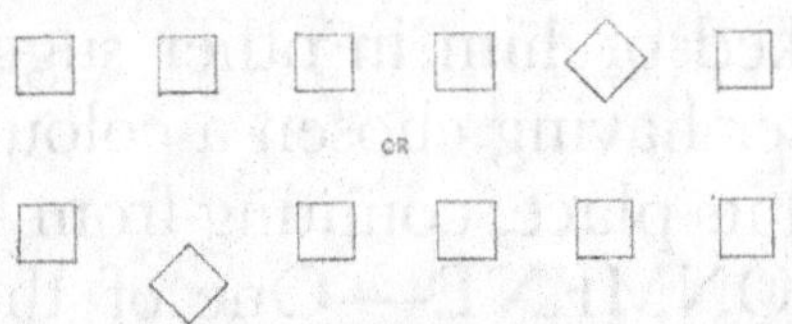

2. COLOURED COVER.—Instead of the usual black cover a coloured cover was used in these experiments. A square of the same colour as that of the cover was placed in the series of squares.

3. STRANGE SHAPE.—One of the coloured squares was here of some peculiar shape, of the form of a triangle, oblong rectangle, rhomboid, pentagon, star, etc., thus

□   △   □   □   □   □

OR

□   □   ⌂   □   □   □

4. COLOUR VERBALLY SUGGESTED.—One of the coloured squares was shown to the subject, who had to determine its colour. This was not an easy task, as the subject had to tell the constituents of the colour, and give the precise name of it. The subject usually kept the coloured square in his hand, and spoke about it for more than a minute. In ease he did not succeed, I told him the name of the colour. Then the square was replaced in the series, and the experiment proper began.

5. PLACE VERBALLY SUGGESTED.—The place of one of the coloured squares was suggested by calling out a number during the removal of the cover and the set of choice, as, for instance, "Three!" meaning the third in the row beginning from the left hand. In order that the subject should understand the number suggested and get used to this mode of counting, I asked of him in other suggestion experiments that, after having chosen a coloured square, he should also tell its place, counting from left to right.

6. ENVIRONMENT.—One of the six coloured squares was put on a larger square of differently coloured paper. A fringe environing the square was thus formed:

□   □   ▣   □   □

Special care was taken not to leave in the same place the square suggested, but to shift it with each subsequent experiment. The differently coloured squares suggested were each time put in different places, so that the subject should not form a habit of choosing from one place more than from another.

To counteract all expectation as to what the nature of the experiment was, the experiments were constantly changed as to the nature of the factor, and, to be the more sure of completely eliminating expectation, sham experiments were introduced. Instead of the usual coloured squares, the subject frequently found a row of black squares, looking like a funeral march. These black squares were often screened by a cover of gay colour.

Before I proceed to give a detailed account of the experiments, I think it would be well to give the precise meaning in which I here employ the terms of mediate and immediate suggestion and suggestibility.

By immediate suggestion I mean to indicate the full realization of the suggestion given to the subject—the fact of his taking the square suggested to him in a direct or indirect way.

By mediate suggestion I mean to indicate the fact of incomplete realization of the suggestion—the fact of taking a square next to the one suggested by the experiment—e.g.:

d, Immediate suggestion.
c or *e*, Mediate suggestion.
The results are as follows:

1. ABNORMAL POSITION.

Immediate suggestion - 47.85 Per cent.
Mediate suggestion - 5.37 "
Total suggestion - 53.22 "

2. COLOURED COVER.

Immediate suggestion - 38.16 Per cent.
Mediate suggestion - 5.83 "
Total suggestion - 43.99 "

3. STRANGE SHAPE

Immediate suggestion - 43 Per cent.
Mediate suggestion - 13 "
Total suggestion - 56 "

4. COLOUR VERBALLY SUGGESTED

Immediate suggestion - 28.89 Per cent.
Mediate suggestion - 4.44 "
Total suggestion - 33.33 "

5. PLACE VERBALLY SUGGESTED.

Immediate suggestion - 19.41 Per cent.
Mediate suggestion - 0.58 "
Total suggestion - 19.99 "

6. ENVIRONMENT.

Immediate suggestion - 30.44 Per cent.
Mediate suggestion - 22.22 "
Total suggestion - 52.66 "

Making now a table of the factors and arranging in the order suggestibility effected, we have the following:

TABLE OF IMMEDIATE SUGGESTIBILITY.

Abnormal position - 47.8 Per cent.
Strange shape - 43.0 "
Coloured cover - 38.1 "
Environment - 30.4 "
Colour verbally suggested - 28.8 "
Place verbally suggested - 19.4 "

Mediate suggestibility necessitates a re-arrangement of the factors:

TABLE OF MEDIATE SUGGESTIBILITY.

Environment - 22.2 Per cent.
Strange shape - 13.0 "
Coloured cover - 5.8 "
Abnormal position - 5.3 "
Colour verbally suggested - 4.4 "
Place verbally suggested - 0.5 Per "

A scrutiny of the table of immediate suggestibility shows that the factors of abnormal position and of abnormal or strange shape give the strongest suggestion. *A familiar thing in a strange abnormal position or shape produces the most effective suggestion.* Nothing speaks so much to the childish or popular mind as a caricature, monstrosity, a grotesque figure. A distorted picture of a familiar scene or person will at once attract the attention of the child, and powerfully affect its conduct in case the picture is intended to show the fate of bad children. The angelical happiness of saints, the pure, holy bliss of martyrs, the intolerable torments suffered by the wicked in hell, speak volumes to the vulgar religious mind. When Vladimir, the Russian Kniase (king), intended to abandon paganism and accept a monotheistic religion, missionaries came to him from the Jews, Mohammedans, and Christians. No argument could affect the barbarian. The cunning Greeks then showed him a picture representing the day of judgment. The righteous enjoy eternal bliss in the company of beautiful maiden-like angels, while the wicked, with distorted faces, writhe and wriggle in agonies of pain. The infidels are cooked in enormous kettles containing a hellish soup of hot, seething oil and bubbling sulphur and pitch. The sinners, the blasphemers, are mercilessly fried and roasted by horned, tailed, cloven-hoofed, grinning, hideous-looking devils. Vladimir was deeply affected by the picture of the Christian hell, and at once accepted the Greek faith. This Russian tradition may serve as a good illustration of the great power of suggestion possessed by the two factors of abnormal position and strange shape.

Turning now to the table of mediate suggestibility, we find that the factor of environment gives us as high a rate as 22.2 per cent, almost twice the rate of the mediate suggestibility possessed by the factor of strange shape, and more than five times the rate of the mediate suggestibility possessed by the factor colour verbally suggested. This can possibly be explained by the fact that one of the conditions of the environment factor was to put one of the squares on a differently coloured background. The fringed square looked somewhat prettier than its fellows, and it was this prettiness that enhanced the mediate suggestibility. *An adorned, beautiful object sheds glory on its homely neighbors and makes them more eligible.*

But however the case may be with the relative suggestibility of the particular factors studied, these last experiments on choice suggestion, together with the other suggestion experiments, establish the fact of normal suggestibility on a firm and unshakable basis. MAN IS A SUGGESTIBLE ANIMAL, *par excellence.*

---

1. Zeitschrift, Januar, 1894.
2. November and December, 1892.
3. Let me add here that the figures bring out rather the *relative* than the absolute suggestiveness of the factors studied.
4. As the squares were rather small in size they could with equal facility be reached with either hand and there was, therefore, no tendency to prefer the squares of one side more than those of the other side. Besides, control-experiments with black squares were made by me; and these experiments still further confirmed the view that this factor of preference was totally absent.

4

THE CONDITIONS OF NORMAL SUGGESTIBILITY

THE first and general condition of normal suggestibility is fixation of the attention.

In all my experiments the one indispensable condition was to fix the attention on some spot and then to prepare the subject for the acceptance of the suggestion. I asked the subject to look on some particular point chosen by me, the time of fixation usually varying from two to five seconds. In my experiments with letters and figures the attention of the subject was fixed on the white surface of the screen for about two seconds before the first character of the series appeared; then, again, between each figure or letter and the next following there was an interval of two or three seconds during which the subject had to look fixedly at the uniformly white screen. In my experiments with coloured squares, or on choice suggestion, the condition of fixation of attention was scrupulously observed; the subject had to fix his attention on a particular point for five seconds. The same condition was observed in my experiments on suggestion of movements and of acts. The fixation of attention, as I said, was usually not continued longer than five seconds. Thus, out of 4,487 experiments made on suggestion, only 500 experiments (those dealing with suggestion of movements) had a fixation time higher than five seconds.

Fixation of attention is one of the most important conditions of normal suggestibility——so much so that when this condition was absent the experiments were unsuccessful: the suggestion given invariably failed. The subject declared he was disturbed, mixed up, that he was not in the mood, that he could not make up his mind to "Write anything, to execute movements, or to choose squares.

2. The next condition of normal suggestibility is *distraction of the attention*. The subject had to fix his attention on some irrelevant point, spot, thing that had no connection with the material of the experiments, no resemblance to the objects employed for suggestion. Usually I asked my subjects to fix their attention on some minute dot, because a large spot or a big object might have interfered with the suggestion, on account of form, size, etc. The attention had to be diverted from the objects of the experiments. I found that when this condition of distraction of attention was absent the experiments, as a rule, failed. A. Binet, in his valuable article on Double Consciousness,[1] the results of which we will discuss later on, tells us that the suggestion of movements brought about in healthy, normal persons when in their waking condition required one "necessary condition: that attention should not be fixed on the hand and what is taking place there." Now Binet made his suggestion experiments on the hand movements of the subject; the

condition, then, he requires is that of distraction of the attention from the objects of the experiments.

3. In all the experiments I had to guard against variety of impressions. Slight noises coming from the adjoining rooms in the laboratory, a new man coming into the room where the, experiments were being carried on, a book dropping, an Italian playing on the street organ, and many other kindred impressions, were distinctly unfavourable to the experiments, and had to be avoided as much as possible. The subjects had to accustom themselves to the conditions and objects in the room, and any new impressions strongly interfered with the success of the suggestion. A fresh, new impression, however slight, proved always a disturbance. When the impression was a strong one, or when many impressions came together, the experiments were interrupted and the whole work came to a standstill. The experiments could be carried on only in a monotonous environment, otherwise they failed. Thus we find that *monotony* is an indispensable condition of normal suggestibility.

4. While fixing their attention the subjects had to keep as quiet as possible; for otherwise the subject became disturbed, his attention began to wander, and the suggestion failed. Before the experiments began the subjects were asked to make themselves as comfortable as possible, so that they should not have to change their position during the experiments. We find, then, that normal suggestibility requires as one of its conditions a *limitation of voluntary movements*.

5. *Limitation of the field of consciousness* may be also considered as one of the principal conditions of normal suggestibility. This condition, however, is in fact a result of the former ones—namely, fixation of attention, monotony, and limitation of voluntary

movements; for when these last conditions are present the field of consciousness is contracted, closed to any new incoming impressions, limited only to a certain set of sensations, fixed, riveted to only a certain point. Contraction of the field of consciousness may, however, be effected where the other conditions are absent. A *sudden, violent* impression may instantly effect an enormous shrinkage of the field of consciousness, and then the other conditions will naturally follow, or rather coexist; for consciousness will reverberate with this one violent sense impression and will thus attend to only the latter. There will also be monotony, since this one sudden and violent sense impression tolerates few neighbours and drives out fresh incomers. Voluntary movements will then certainly be limited, since the stream of consciousness is narrowed, and along with it its ideomotor side. The fact that limitation or contraction of the field of consciousness may occur by itself without having been preceded by the conditions mentioned above led me to consider it a separate condition of normal suggestibility.

6. The experiments, again, could not be carried on without the condition of inhibition. I asked the subject that, when he concentrated his attention and fixed a particular dot pointed out to him, he should try as much as it was in his power to banish all ideas—images that had no connection with the experiments in hand; that he should not even think of the experiments themselves; in short, that he should make his mind a *perfect blank*, and voluntarily *inhibit* ideas, associations that might arise before his mind's eye and claim attention. Of course, this condition was rather a hard task for the subject to comply with, still it was observed as far as it was possible. When this condition was neglected by the subject the experi-

ments invariably failed. *Inhibition*, then, is a necessary condition of normal suggestibility.

7. The very last condition, but at the same time the principal one, the most fundamental condition *sine qua non* experiments in normal suggestion, was *immediate execution*. The subject was told that as soon as he perceived the signal he should *immediately* write, act, or choose.

To make a synopsis of the conditions of normal suggestibility:

1. Fixation of attention.
2. Distraction of attention.
3. Monotony.
4. Limitation of voluntary movements.
5. Limitation of the field of consciousness.
6. Inhibition.
7. Immediate execution.

---

1. See also his book, Les alternations de la personnalité.

5

THE LAW OF NORMAL
SUGGESTIBILITY

WE must turn again to our experiments and give a close study to the results obtained. We take choice suggestion first. Now, out of the six factors studied, four belong to direct suggestion and two to indirect suggestion. The factors of abnormal position, strange shape, coloured cover, environment, are of one type, while the factors of colour verbally suggested and place verbally suggested are of the other opposite type of suggestion. Is there any difference in the rate of suggestibility of the two types of suggestion? Yes, and a very good one, too. For even a superficial glance at the two tables of immediate and mediate suggestibility, if the latter are only inspected from the standpoint of the two types of suggestion, will at once disclose this radical difference. The average immediate suggestibility of the four factors belonging to the first type—to indirect suggestion—amounts to 39.8 per cent, whereas the average rate of immediate suggestibility of the two last factors belonging to the second type—to direct suggestion—amounts only to 24.1 per cent.

And if we inspect the table of mediate suggestibility, we find again a similar difference; for the average mediate suggestibility of the first four factors belonging to the type of indirect suggestion gives a rate of 11.5 per cent.

Whereas the average rate of mediate suggestibility of the last two factors belonging to the type of direct suggestion amounts to only 2.1 percent.

The difference between the two types of suggestion becomes very striking indeed if we make a table of total suggestibility—that is, if we add together the mediate and immediate suggestibility of each factor. Making thus the table and arranging the factors in the order of their respective rates of total suggestibility, we have the following results:

Strange shape.. 56 Per cent

Abnormal position.............................. 53.2 "

Environment... 52.6 "

Coloured cover.. 43.9 "

Colour verbally suggested..............

33.3 "

Place verbally suggested...............

19.9 "

A mere glance at this table shows the great difference of the two types of suggestion; and this difference becomes yet more evident, still more striking, if we take the rate of the average total suggestibility of the first type of factors and compare it with that of the second. For the average total suggestibility of the first four factors amounts to as much as 51.4 per cent, while that of the last two amounts only to 26.6 per cent. The one rate is about twice the other. The conclusion is obvious, as it lies now before us clear and distinct in its outlines. *In the case of normal suggestibility indirect suggestion is far more effective than direct suggestion.*

If we examine closer the nature of the last two factors, colour verbally suggested and place verbally suggested, factors which we classed in the type of direct suggestion, we find that they are only relatively direct; for, after all, the subject was not explicitly and directly told to take that colour. What we really must say of them is, that they far more approach the type of direct suggestion than the other four factors do.

If now we inquire as to the rate of suggestibility when the factor is of the actual explicit type of direct suggestion, the answer is, naught. The experiments on suggestion of movements bring out clearly this answer. The suggestion employed there was that of the most direct and explicit kind, and, with the exception of Mr. S., the experiments proved a *total failure*. The subjects *ironically* complied with my command. The results were negative—zero. Direct suggestion is at the freezing point of normal suggestibility. It is only in proportion as a given factor becomes more indirect that it rises in the scale of suggestibility. In other words, the more indirect a factor is the higher is the rate of its suggestibility.

Should we like to have still further proofs we can easily get them; for a close scrutiny of the tables of immediate, mediate, and total suggestibility most clearly shows the truth of my position, namely, that *in the normal state a suggestion is more effective the more indirect it is, and in proportion as it becomes direct it loses its efficacy.* Abnormal position, strange shape, and environment are the most indirect, and they give the highest suggestibility (environment in mediate suggestibility gives a slightly higher rate because of the additional factor of attractiveness). Abnormal position and abnormal shape have about the same rate; for, on the whole, it makes no difference for man whether a familiar thing is put into an abnormal position or whether it appears in a strange garb: he is equally impressed and moved. As we come to the factor of coloured cover we find a slight decrease in the rate of suggestibility. For if we take the average immediate suggestibility of abnormal position and strange shape we have 45.4 per cent, while that of coloured cover is 38.1 per cent; the difference is 7.3 per cent; and we find a difference between the same factors in the case of total suggestibility, the difference being 10.6 per cent. Now the suggestion of coloured cover is somewhat more direct than that of abnormal position, or strange shape; for in spreading a coloured coyer over the squares, the subject, on seeing and fixing his attention on it, could not help suspecting that it was a square of the same colour that I wanted him to choose: opposition was aroused and the suggestion failed. Although I repeatedly baffled and disappointed the expectation of the subject by putting black squares under the coloured cover, or spreading one over a row of squares totally different in colour from that of the cover, still I could not completely dislodge the suspicion from the subject's mind; it was always lurking in the background of his consciousness.

Of the two factors, colour verbally suggested and place verbally suggested, the former is more indirect than the latter. In the one I merely showed a square to the subject and asked him to determine the colour, without hinting my intention (the subject very frequently being absorbingly interested in guessing the name); while in the other the number of the place of the suggested square was called out during the removal of the cover—the hint, therefore, was more direct. If now we look at the tables of immediate, mediate, and total suggestibility of the two factors we find a great difference in their rates of efficiency.

The immediate suggestibility of the factor colour verbally suggested is............

28.8 per cent

while that of place verbally suggested is...

19.4 "

the difference amounting to.........................

9.4 "

The mediate suggestibility of the factor colour verbally suggested is...........

4.4 "

while that of place verbally suggested is but...

0.5 "

the difference amounting to.......................

3.9 "

The total suggestibility of colour, etc., is...

33.3 "

while that of place, etc., is..........................

19.9 "

the difference being.......................................

13.4 "

If again we turn to our very first study with letters and figures, we find the results pointing to the same truth. The factors of frequency and last impression are far more indirect than those of coexistence and repetition, and we correspondingly find a great difference in their rates of suggestibility. Thus the average rate of frequency and of last impression is (63.3 + 42.6) ÷ 2 = 52.9 per cent; while the average rate of

68

suggestibility of repetition and of coexistence is (17.6 + 6.6) ÷ 2 = 12.1 per cent, the difference being 40.8 per cent.

The factor of last impression, again, is relatively more indirect than that of frequency, and correspondingly we find a difference in their rates of suggestibility.

The factor of last impression gives.....

63.3 per cent

while that of frequency gives.....................

42.6 "

the difference being...................................

20.7 "

The factor of repetition is relatively more indirect than that of coexistence, in the latter the suggestion being almost grossly obvious, and once more we find a corresponding difference in their rates of suggestibility.

Repetition gives....................................

17.6 per cent

while the factor of coexistence gives......

6.6 "

the difference being...................................

11"

Furthermore, the factor of last impression came with as high a rate as 63.3 per cent, but when the same factor of last impression enters into combination with that of coexistence, forming one factor of coexistence and last impression, the rate falls as low as 18.3 per cent, thus strongly contrasting the efficacy of direct with that of indirect suggestion.

What is the outcome of this whole discussion? Nothing less than the law of normal suggestibility—a law which we shall find later on of the utmost importance.

Normal suggestibility varies as direct suggestion, and inversely as direct suggestion.

6

THE CONDITIONS OF ABNORMAL SUGGESTIBILITY

THE great type of abnormal suggestibility is the hypnotic state; so much so that the Nancy school defines hypnosis as a state of heightened suggestibility. The conditions of abnormal suggestibility are, in fact, those of hypnosis. What are they?

1. The first and foremost is that of *fixation of the attention*. Thus Braid used to hypnotize his subjects by fixing their attention on some brilliant object or point. He considered a steady attention indispensable if hypnosis were to be attained; the subject must look steadily at the object, he must only think of the thing he was fixing, and must not allow his attention to be diverted from it. Of such permanent importance is fixation of attention that, according to Braid, if only this condition is observed one can hypnotize even in the dark. The ability to direct one's thoughts in any particular direction is very favourable to hypnosis. Those who can by no possibility fix their attention, who suffer from continual absence of mind, or those who are helplessly stupid and lacking the power of

concentration, are not hypnotizable. I find in my notes the case of an extremely stupid young boy of sixteen who, on account of lack of concentration of mind, is unable to solve the most elementary arithmetical problem. I foretold that he would be unhypnotizable (of course I did not tell that to him). Although I hypnotized in his presence three good subjects, he remained refractory. I tried all kinds of methods I could think of; the last one was that of Braid. For more than twenty minutes he fixed an object, his eyes being converged in the most orthodox fashion, inward and upward; tears were trickling down his cheeks, but he remained unaffected, and for the simple reason that his attention was not kept steady——it was roving and wandering all the while. All methods of hypnotization require fixation of attention as their indispensable condition. The adherents of the Salpêtrière school frequently hypnotize by fixing the subject's attention on the expectation of some sudden brilliant ray of light meant to induce the hypnotic state. The followers of the Nancy school fix the attention of the subject on the two fingers held before his eyes and on the sounds of suggestion given by the operator. "I hold two fingers," says Bernheim,[1] "before the patient's eyes and ask him to *concentrate* his attention on the idea of sleep." The efficacy of mesmeric passes is also due to the fixation of attention, for by those means the whole attention of the subject is directed to the particular place where the passes are made. "Let anyone," says Dr. Moll,[2] "allow his arm or his leg to be mesmerized by passes, and he will find that his whole attention is directed to this part of his body, and much more strongly than if his attention was concentrated on the limb in another manner."

"Die Hauptsache ist," Lehmann[3] tells us, "dass in der Hypnose die Aufmerksamkeit in einer bestimmten Richtung gebunden ist." This is not exactly true of the hypnotic state itself, but it holds true with regard to the induction of hypnosis. "Children under three and four and insane persons, especially idiots, are unusually hard to hypnotize," says Prof. James.[4] "This seems due to the impossibility of getting them to fix their attention continually on the idea of the coming trance." Prof. James seems to me to have hit the mark when he tells us that the concentration of attention on the coming trance induces hypnosis. In short, fixation of attention is an indispensable condition of hypnosis.

2. *Monotony of impressions* is another condition of the hypnotic state. If you want to hypnotize a subject, especially if it is for the first time, you must put him into a monotonous environment. You must prevent fresh, new impressions from reaching the sensorium of the subject. Whatever your mode of hypnotization may be, it must always be of the same kind. This might be effected by a strong stimulus acting for a moment or two, or, what is far more often the case, by a prolonged monotonous series of slight stimuli. Thus Binet[5] tells us that "slight and prolonged stimuli of the same nature" constitute one of the modes of producing the hypnotic state. Bernheim[6] expresses himself on this point more clearly: "Let us add," he says, "that in the majority of the cases the monotonous, wearying, and continuous impression of one of the senses produce a certain intellectual drowsiness, the prelude of sleep. The mind, entirely absorbed by a quiet, uniform, and incessant perception, becomes foreign to all other impressions; it is too feebly stimu-

lated, and allows itself to become dull." This condition of monotony is very clearly seen in the case of the Nancy method of hypnotization. The operator suggests in so many words the *same idea* of going to sleep: "Your eyelids are heavy; your eyes are tired; they begin to wink; you feel a sort of drowsiness; your arms and legs are motionless; sleep is coming; sleep ——." My mode of hypnotization consists in forming a monotonous environment; the light is lowered, and a profound silence reigns in the room; then gently and monotonously stroking the skin of the subject's forehead, and in a low, muffled, monotonous voice, as if rocking a baby to sleep, I go on repeating, "Sleep, sleep, sleep," etc., until the subject falls into the hypnotic state.

3. *Limitation of voluntary movements* is also one of the conditions of inducing hypnosis. The subject sits down on a chair in a comfortable position, and is asked to relax his muscles and make as few movements as possible——to keep as quiet as a mouse, This condition is, in fact, supplementary to that of fixation of attention, for many different movements strongly interfere with the steadiness of the attention. The attention changes, oscillates in different directions, and the induction of hypnosis is rendered impossible. Dr. Moll[7] says that "fascination is induced by limitation of voluntary movements." This is no doubt perfectly true, only Dr. Moll ought not to limit it to "fascination" alone, for limitation of voluntary movements is one of the principal conditions of inducing hypnosis in general.

4. *Limitation of the field of consciousness* must certainly be included among the conditions of inducing hypnosis. The consciousness of the subject must be

narrowed to one idea of sleep. "I endeavour," says Braid in his Neurypnology, "to rid the mind at once of all ideas *but one*." Wundt defines the very nature of hypnosis as limitation of the field of consciousness, and to a certain extent he is justified in his assertion, seeing that all the methods of hypnotization turn on it as on a pivot. Thus the method of Braid narrows the field of consciousness to a brilliant point, that of mesmerism to the passes, that of the Nancy school to the tips of the fingers held out before the subject, or to the one idea of expectation of sleep. To induce hypnosis we must in some way or other effect such a limitation.

We know that a strange emotion narrows down the field of consciousness. We often find that people under the emotion of intense excitement lose, so to say, their senses; their mind seems to be paralyzed, or rather, so to say, the one idea that produces the excitement banishes all other ideas, and a state of *monoideism*, or concentration of the consciousness, is thus effected. People are frequently run over by carriages, cars, or trains on account of the sudden great fright caused. The one idea of danger reverberates in the mind like a sudden powerful clap of thunder, confusing and stunning all other ideas; the mind is brought into a contracted cataleptic condition, and the field of consciousness is narrowed down to that one idea, to a single point. Now, we find that the hypnotic trance can also be induced by a strong and sudden stimulus acting on the sense organ. "Hypnotization," says Binet,[8] "can be produced by strong and sudden excitement of the senses." This mode of hypnotization may be successful with people of an intensely emotional nature or with hysterical subjects. A strong, sudden stimulus acts on them like a thunderclap, contracts their field of consciousness, and throws them into a hypnotic state. On the whole, we may say that limitation of the field of consciousness is one of the most important conditions of hypnotic trance.

5. The hypnotic trance, again, can not be induced without the condition of *inhibition*. The subject must inhibit all ideas, all images that come up before his mind. He must only think of the brilliant point, of the tips of the hypnotizer's fingers, of the passes, of the idea of going to sleep. "Look at me and think of nothing but sleep," tells Bernheim to his patients. "Make your mind a blank," is one of the conditions required by the hypnotizer of his subjects. Concentration of attention and limitation of the field of consciousness are, in fact, impossible without the presence of this condition of inhibition. The case of the boy mentioned above, who could not be hypnotized because his attention was roaming, because he was unable to concentrate his mind, was in reality due to the fact of lacking the power of inhibition. Inhibition, voluntary or involuntary, is an indispensable condition of hypnosis.

To make a synopsis of the conditions of hypnosis, or, what is the same, of abnormal suggestibility:

1. Fixation of attention.
2. Monotony.
3. Limitation of voluntary movements.
4. Limitation of the field of consciousness.
5. Inhibition.

---

1. Suggestive Therapeutics.

2. Hypnotism.
3. Die Hypnose.
4. Psychology, vol. ii.
5. Animal Magnetism.
6. Suggestive Therapeutics.
7. Hypnotism.
8. Animal Magnetism.

7

THE NATURE OF ABNORMAL SUGGESTIBILITY

FROM the condition of hypnosis we turn now to an inquiry into its nature. To do this I think it would be best to examine from a purely empirical standpoint the general states into which the hypnotic subject may fall.

Bernheim finds that there are not less than nine states or stages:

1. Drowsiness.
2. Drowsiness, with inability to open the eyes.
3. Suggestive catalepsy slightly present.
4. Suggestive catalepsy more pronounced.
5. Suggestive contractures fully induced.
6. Automatic obedience.
7. Loss of memory on waking. Hallucinations not possible.
8. Loss of memory. Slight possibility of producing hallucinations, but not post-hypnotically.
9. Loss of memory. Hypnotic and post-hypnotic hallucinations possible.

Dr. Liebault finds that there are only six of them:

1. Drowsiness.

2. Drowsiness. Suggestive catalepsy inducible.

3. Light sleep. Automatic movements possible.

4. Deep sleep. Phenomena rapport manifested.

5. Light somnambulism. Memory hazy on waking.

6. Deep somnambulism. Total amnesia. Phenomena of post-hypnotic suggestion possible.

Prof. August Forel reduces them to three:

1. Drowsiness.

2. Inability to open the eyes. Obedience to suggestion.

3. Somnambulism. Amnesia.

Dr. Lloyd-Tukey gives the following states:

1. Light sleep.

2. Profound sleep.

3. Somnambulism.

Max Dessoir reduces them to two:

1. Voluntary movements show changes.

2. Abnormalities in the functions of the sense organs are added.

Edmund Gurney, the most philosophical of all the writers and investigators on the subject of hypnotism, gives the following two states:

1. The alert state.

2. The deep state.

As a matter of fact, however, the subjects little respect all those quasi-scientific classifications of hypnotic states. Dr. Kingsbury is no doubt right in his remark that "patients vary as much in hypnosis as they do in their features." No doubt there are as many hypnotic states as there are persons; no doubt that it is utterly impossible to give cut-and-dried definitions for the infinite variety of hypnotic stages. Although all this is perfectly true, we still assert that there is a line of subdivision——a boundary line that separates one region of hypnotic phenomena from that of another. This boundary line is, in fact, implied in nearly all the classifications of hypnosis.

To find this boundary line, let us examine the state of mind of the subject when he is in a light hypnotic trance. The subject is in a passive condition. If during hypnotization he was sitting in a chair, there he will remain until roused, his limbs relaxed, his features placid, making as few movements as possible, occasionally changing his position if it becomes very uncomfortable. If his eyes are closed, he will continue to keep them in that condition. Try now to make a direct suggestion that might in the least interfere with what he considers as his voluntary life, with his freedom of action; challenge him, for instance, by raising his hand and telling him that he can not lower it, that he can not open his eyes; down goes the hand and up goes the eyelid, thus showing us that, passive as he appears to be, he does have control over his limbs. The controlling consciousness is there, only it is inactive, passive, and it requires a special external stimulus to set it going, to put it into activity. My friend Mr. L. told me once he wondered greatly at the passivity in which he was when in a state of hypnosis. He told me he firmly made up his mind that when hypnotized again he would start a conversation on different topics. A few minutes later I hypnotized him, but he remained as passive as usual. To start him into activity an impulse from without was first required. Mark now the peculiarity. The activity set going does not continue longer than the challenged act. I raise the subject's arm and challenge him to lower it; he does lower the arm, but keeps it down there in a passive condition. I tell the subject he is unable to walk, the challenge is accepted; he makes a step, very rarely two, showing me that he can walk, that he possesses full control over his legs, but remains passively in one place. He makes another step if you challenge him again. The controlling consciousness is in a *passive state*, and reasserts itself at every single challenge to act. The act done, and the controlling consciousness falls back into its form or state——the subject relapses into his passive condition. Hypnotization produces a deep cleft in the mind of the subject, a cleft by which the waking, controlling consciousness is separated from the great stream of conscious life.

Now when the cleft is not deep enough we have the different slight hypnotic states, but as the cleft becomes deeper and deeper the hypnosis grows more profound, and when the controlling consciousness is fully cut off from the rest of conscious life we have a state of fun hypnosis which is commonly called somnambulism, and in which there is complete amnesia on awakening. That is why we have tho strange accounts of hypnotic subjects, especially of those who are on the verge of somnambulism, that during hypnosis they were indifferent to the actions of their body——the latter acted by itself; that they were mere spectators of all the experiments performed on them, of all the strange actions, dramas, that transpired during the trance; that it seemed to them as if they themselves, their personality, retreated far, far away. "We have not to wonder that on the question "Where are you?" the subject sometimes gives the seemingly absurd reply of Krafft-Ebing's patient——"In your eye."

There are pathological cases on record which are

analogous to this state. The conscious controlling "I" seems to retreat far, far away from the world. Dr. Krishaber brings the case of a patient who gives the following account of himself: "I myself was immeasurably far away. I looked about me with terror and astonishment; the world was escaping from me. I remarked at the same time that my voice was extremely far away from me, that it sounded no longer as if mine. Constantly it seemed to me as if my legs did not belong to me. It was almost as bad with my arms. I appeared to myself to act automatically, by an impulsion foreign to myself. It was certainly another who had taken my form and assumed my functions. I hated, I despised this other; he was perfectly odious to me."

To return, however, to hypnosis. In the superficial stages, when the subject is not in a very deep trance, we frequently meet with curious phenomena of the following kind: I raise the hand of the subject and put it in some uncomfortable position and let it remain there; there it stays all the while. I challenge him to lower his hand. He does not answer. I repeat again the challenge. No reply. "Answer me: Why do not you lower the hand?" "I do not care to," comes the slow answer. I keep on challenging him for some seconds. At last the stimuli get summated, the controlling consciousness is stimulated, makes strenuous efforts, and the hand, shaking and in jerks, slowly descends. I tell the subject that he forgot his name, that he can by no means remember it. He keeps silent. " You forgot your name, you do not remember it," I assert firmly and positively. "Yes, I do," comes in a low voice the slow and tardy reply. "But you do not know your name." "Yes, I do." "No, you don't." "Yes, I do." And

so he wrangles with me for about three or five minutes, until at last he seems to brace himself up and
tells me his name. "But why did you not tell it to me
before?" "I really do not care to tell my name." The
cleft in the mind is here of some depth, and it requires a strong challenge, an intense stimulus, to set
the controlling consciousness into activity.

When the patient sinks into a deeper and deeper
hypnotic condition, when the hypnosis is so profound
as to verge on somnambulism, the waking, controlling
consciousness hangs, so to say, on a thread to the rest
of organic life; and when that thread, too, is cut off
by suggestion, or by some other means, the waking,
guiding consciousness loses all contact with the
stream of life.

We can easily state our theory in terms of physiological psychology. The nervous centres of man's nervous system, if classified as to function, may be
divided into inferior and superior. The inferior centres are characterized by reflex and automatic activity.
A stimulus excites the peripheral nerve endings of
some sense organ; at once a nervous current is set up
in the afferent nerves, This current in its turn stimu-
lates a plexus of central ganglia, the nervous energy
of which is set free and is propagated along the efferent nerves toward glands or muscles; secretions,
excretions, muscular contractions, or relaxations are
the final result, ingoing and outgoing nervous currents may be modified by the nervous centres; nervous currents may be intensified, decreased in energy,
or even entirely inhibited by mutual interaction, according to the law derived by Prof. Ziehen from the
general physiology of the nerves—namely: "If an excitation of definite intensity (m) take place in one cor-

tical element (b), and another excitation of a different intensity (n) take place at the same time in another cortical element (c), which is connected by a path of conduction with b, the two intensities of excitation may reciprocally modify each other." Although such a modification may frequently occur, still it remains true that the inferior centres are of a reflex nature. No sooner is the nervous energy of a lower centre set free than at once it tends to discharge itself into some kind of action, of movement. The physiological process of setting free the nervous energy in a central ganglion, or in a system of central ganglia, is accompanied in the simpler but more integrated, more organized centres by sentience, sensitiveness, sensibility,[1] and in the more complex but less integrated, less organized centres by consciousness, sensations, perceptions, images, and ideas.

Turning now to the superior or the highest nervous centres, we find that they possess the function of choice and will. A number of impressions, of sensations, of ideas reach those will-centres, and a sifting, a selecting, an inhibitory process at once begins. Some of the impressions are rejected, inhibited; others are permitted to work themselves out within certain limits, and others again are given full, free play. Psychologically, this process expresses itself in the *fiat* or the *neget*, in the "I will" or the "I will not." Everyone is well acquainted with the will-effort, especially when having to make some momentous resolution. These superior choice and will-centres, localized by Ferrier, Bianchi, and others in the frontal lobes, and by other writers in the upper layers of the cortex——these centres, on account of their selective and inhibitory function, may be characterized as inhibitory centres *par excellence*.

Now, parallel to the double system of nervous centres, the inferior and the superior, we also have a *double consciousness*, the inferior, the organic, the reflex consciousness, and the superior, the controlling, the choice, and will consciousness. The controlling consciousness may be characterized as the *guardian consciousness of the species*. And from an evolutionary teleological standpoint we can well see of what use this guardian consciousness is to the life of the species. The external world bombards, so to say, the living organism with innumerable stimuli; from all sides thousands of impressions come on, crowding upon the senses of the individual. Each impression has a motor tendency which, if not counteracted by other impressions, must fatally result in some action. It is not, however, of advantage to the organism always to act, and to act immediately on an stimuli reaching it; hence that organism will succeed in the struggle for life that possesses some inhibitory choice and will-centres. The choice and will-centres permit only a certain number of impressions to take effect; the rest are inhibited. Only those impressions that are advantageous to the life existence of the organism are allowed to take their course; the others are nipped in their bud. The guardian consciousness wards off as far as it is able all the harmful blows with which the environment incessantly assails the organic life of the individual.

Having all this in mind, we can now understand the nature of hypnosis. In the normal condition of man the superior and the inferior centres work in perfect harmony; the upper and the lower consciousness are for all practical purposes blended into a unity forming one conscious personality. In hypnosis the two systems of nervous centres are dissociated, the superior centres and the upper consciousness are inhibited, or, better, cut off, split off from the rest of the nervous system with its organic consciousness, which is thus laid bare, open to the influence of external stimuli or suggestions. Physiologically, hypnosis *is an inhibition of the inhibitory centres*, or, in other words, hypnosis is a *disaggregation of the superior from the inferior centres, necessarily followed, as is the removal of inhibition in general, by an increase of the ideo-motor and ideo-sensory reflex excitability*. Psychologically, *hypnosis is the split-off, disaggregated, organic, reflex consciousness pure and simple.*

This theory of hypnosis is, in fact, a generalization in which the views of the two schools, the Salpêtrière and the Nancy, are included. With the Nancy school, we agree that suggestion is all-powerful in hypnotic trance; the hypnotic trance is, in fact, a state of heightened suggestibility, or, rather of pure reflex consciousness; but with the Paris school we agree, that a changed physiological state is a prerequisite to hypnosis, and this modification consists in the disaggregation of the superior from the inferior centres, in the segregation of the controlling consciousness from the reflex consciousness. In hypnotic trance the upper inhibiting, resisting consciousness being absent, we have direct access to man's organic consciousness, and through it to organic life itself. Strong, persistent impressions or suggestions made on the reflex organic consciousness of the inferior centres may modify their functional disposition, induce trophic changes, and even change organic structures. But whatever the case may be with regard to psycho-therapeutics, this, it seems, may be fairly granted, that the process of hypnotization consists in the separation of the higher inhibitory cortical ganglion cells from the rest of the cerebro-spinal and sympathetic nervous systems. Hypnosis, we may say, is the more or less effected disaggregation of the controlling inhibitory centres from the rest of the nervous system; along with this disaggregation there goes a dissociation of the controlling guardian consciousness from the reflex organic consciousness. Dissociation is the secret of hypnosis, and amnesia is the ripe fruit.

The magnitude of this disaggregation greatly varies. If it is at its minimum, the hypnosis is light; if at its maximum, the hypnosis is deep, and is known as somnambulism.

From our standpoint of hypnosis we may say that there are only two great distinct classes of hypnotic states:

1. Incomplete dissociation of the waking, controlling consciousness.

2. Complete dissociation of the waking consciousness.

Stating the same somewhat differently, we may say that there are two states:

1. Incomplete hypnosis accompanied by a greater or lesser degree of memory.

2. Complete hypnosis with no memory.

In other words, hypnosis has two states:

1. The mnesic state.

2. The amnesic state.

Amnesia is the boundary line that separates two different hypnotic regions.

This view of the matter is, in fact, taken by Edmund Gourney; for he tells us that "we might without incorrectness describe the higher hypnotic phenomena as reflex action, in respect of the certainty with which particular movements follow on particular stimuli; but they are, and their peculiarity consists in their being, *conscious reflex action*."[2] "The heart of the problem [of hypnotism]" he says in another place, "lies not in CONSCIOUSNESS, but in WILL." In his paper on The Stages of Hypnotism,[3] E. Gourney distinguishes two states of hypnosis—the *alert* and the *deep* state. "The question then presents itself," he writes, "Is there any distinction of *kind* between the two states? I believe that there is such a distinction, and that the phenomena needed to establish it are to be found in the domain of *memory*." Gurney, however, thinks that not only is the *deep*, but the hypnotic state as a whole, that is, the alert one, too, is separated from the normal state by amnesia—a proposition which is not borne out by facts. On the whole, however, I may say that Gurney was on the right track; he cast a searching glance deep into the nature of hypnosis.

If we turn now to the classifications reviewed by us we find that they have a change of memory, amnesia, as their *fundamentum divisionis*. Max Dessoir's forms the only exception, but his classification sins against the truth of facts. For there are cases of subjects who fall into deep hypnosis and still there can be induced no abnormal changes in the sense organs. I myself have a somnambule, Mr. F., who can be led through a series of imaginary scenes and changes of personalities, but whose sense organs remain almost normal, perfectly free from suggestion; by no means can I make him *see* a picture on a blank paper, or feel the taste of sugar on eating salt, or take a glass of water for a glass of wine—phenomena which I easily induce in another somnambule, Mr. W. There are again other cases on record where the sense organs are deeply affected, but no abnormalities can be induced in the voluntary movements. Bernheim brings a few cases of this kind. *Amnesia is the only boundary line in hypnosis, and degeneration of consciousness is its source.*

Suggestion is at present the shibboleth of many a "scientific" psychologist. Suggestion is the magic key that opens all secrets and discloses all mysteries. Suggestion explains everything. To any question as to hypnosis asked of the suggestionist, he, like a parrot, has but one answer: "Suggestion"! Well may Binet say:[4]"It is insufficient to explain everything that takes place in hypnotized subjects by invoking the hackneyed term 'Suggestion!' And that suffices for all purposes; that explains everything, and, like the panacea of the ancients, it cures everything. As a matter of fact, theories of suggestion thus invoked amount to nothing less than makeshifts to save people the trouble of serious and delicate investigation." Suggestionists make of suggestion a kind of metaphysical absolute, a Spinozistic *causa sui*, for, according to this trance-philosophy, hypnosis is nothing but suggestion; and by what is it induced? Why, by suggestion! Suggestion is thus its own cause. Absurd as this trance-philosophy of suggestionism is, it is none the less the current view of many a "scientific" psychologist. Still the authorities on the subject do not always talk the suggestion jargon; in their more lucid states they use quite a different language. The pity only is that they do not grasp the full import and meaning of their own propositions; they do not see the far-reaching consequences of their own statements.

Dr. Moll, in his remarkable book on Hypnotism, sums up his theory of hypnosis thus: "We may, then, consider every hypnosis as a state in which the normal course of the ideas is *inhibited*. It matters not whether the ideas have to do with movements or with sense impressions. Their normal course is always inhibited. The idea of a movement called up in a subject in or out of hypnosis has a tendency to induce the movement. *But in waking life this idea is made ineffectual by the voluntary idea of the subject that he will prevent the suggested movement, the hypnotized subject can not do this.*[5] The same is the case with suggested paralysis. Sense delusions can be explained in a similar way. We tell the hypnotic subject, 'Here is a dog,' and he realizes it, and sees the dog. The limitation of the normal course of the ideas allows the idea of the dog to become a perception. The subject is unable to control the external ideas, or to put forward his own; the external ones dominate his consciousness. Psychologically speaking, what we mean by attention is the power of fixing certain ideas in the mind and of working with them. Consequently we may say that there is an alteration of attention in hypnosis. But attention may be either spontaneous or reflex. When by any act of will we choose one of several ideas and fix our attention upon it, this is spontaneous attention; but when one idea among several gets the upper hand through its intensity or for some other reason, and thus represses other ideas and draws exclusive attention upon itself, this is reflex attention. Now it is only spontaneous attention which is altered in hypnosis—i.e., the subject's ability voluntarily to prefer one idea to another is interfered with, while reflex attention is undisturbed, and it is through this last that a suggested idea, the choice of which has not, however, been left to the subject comes into prominence.

"Many investigators," continues Dr. Moll, "conceive hypnotism in this way. The works of Durand de Gros, Liébault, and more lately of Beard, Richet, Schneider, Wundt, and Bentivegni, are in the main direct to this point."

It is truly amusing to see how people concede the main substance to their opponents and still cling to the empty shell of their old creeds. Accepting inhibition of spontaneous attention as the source, as the nature of hypnosis, the psychologist of the suggestion school fully abandons his medical charm, his all-powerful magic suggestion. Inhibition of spontaneous attention, of voluntary control, leaving a residue of reflex attention, what is it, if not the full admission that the hypnotic state is a mental disaggregation, a dissociation of the controlling from the reflex consciousness?

Turning now to one of the leaders of the Nancy school, to the greatest popularizer of suggestionism——Prof. Bernheim——we find him to be still more explicit on this point. I humbly ask the reader's pardon for the lengthy quotation I am going to offer him. I find it will give additional confirmation to my view of the nature of hypnosis. In his book, "Suggestive Therapeutics," Bernheim gives us the following account of hypnosis, an account that practically amounts to a complete abandonment of his omnipotent deity——suggestion: "The one thing certain is that a *peculiar aptitude* for transforming the idea received into an act exists in hypnotized subjects who are susceptible to suggestion. In the normal consciousness every formulated idea is questioned by the mind. After being perceived by the cortical centres, the impression extends to the cells of the adjacent convolutions; their peculiar activity is excited; the diverse faculties generated by the gray substance of the brain come into play; the impression is elaborated, registered, and analyzed by means of a complex mental process which ends in its acceptation or neutralization; if there is cause, the mind vetoes it. In the hypnotized subject, on the contrary, the transformation of thought into action, sensation, movement, or vision is so quickly and so actively accomplished that the intellectual inhibition has not time to act. When the mind interposes, it is already an accomplished fact, which is often registered with surprise, and which is confirmed by the fact that it proves to be real, and no intervention can hamper it further. If I say to the hypnotized subject, 'Your hand remained closed,' the brain carries out the idea as soon as it is formulated; reflex is immediately transmitted from the cortitcal centre, where the idea induced by the auditory nerve is perceived, to the motor centre, corresponding to the central origin of the nerves subserving flexion of the hand; contracture occurs in flexion. There is then exaltation of the ideo-motor reflex excitability, which effects the unconscious (subconscious?) transformation of the thought into movement *unknown to the will*. The same thing occurs when I say to the hypnotized subject, 'You have tickling sensation in your nose.' The thought induced through hearing is reflected upon the centre of olfactory sensibility, where it awkens the sensitive memory image of the nasal itching as former impressions have created it and left it imprinted and latent. This memory sensation thus resuscitated may be intense enough to cause the reflex action of sneezing. There is also, then, exaltation of the ideo-sensorial reflex excitability, which effects the subconscious transformation of the thought into sensation, or into a sensory image. In the same way the visual, acoustic, and gustatory images succeed the suggested idea.

"Negative suggestions are more difficult to explain. If I say to the hypnotized subject, 'Your body is insensible, your eye is blind,' the impression transmitted by the auditory nerve to the centre of tactile or visual anæsthesia is that retinal vision exists, but the cerebral perception no longer exists. It seems as if it might be a reflex paralysis of a cortical centre which the suggested idea has produced in this case. The mechanism of suggestion in general may then be summed up in the following formula: *Increase of the reflex ideo-motor, ideo-sensorial excitability*. In the same way through the effect of some influence—strychnine, for example—the sensitive-motor excitability is increased in the spinal cord, so that the least impression at the periphery of a nerve is immediately transformed into contracture without the moderating influence of the brain being able to prevent this transformation. In the same way in hypnotization the ideo-reflex excitability is increased in the brain, so that any idea received is immediately transformed into an act, without the controlling portion of the brain, the higher centres, being able to prevent the transformation."

Thus we clearly see that when the suggestionist comes to discuss the nature of hypnosis, he abandons his position and admits that a split in the brain cutting off the higher controlling centres from the lower ones is at the basis of hypnosis. The very conditions of hypnosis proclaim this fact, for they are but keen psychical scalpels and have the power to effect a deep incision in the semi-fluid stream of consciousness. Fixation of attention, monotony, limitation of the field of consciousness, limitation of voluntary movements, inhibition—all of them are calculated to pare, to split off the controlling from the reflex consciousness. *The nature of hypnosis, of abnormal suggestibility, is a disaggregation of consciousness.*

1. See G. H. Lewes's Problems of Life and Mind, second series.
2. Mind. October, 1884. P. S. P. R., December, 1884. (Proceedings of the Society for Psychical Research)
3. Ibid., January, 1884. P. S. P. R., January, 1884.
4. On Double Consciousness.
5. The italics are mine.

8

THE LAW OF ABNORMAL
SUGGESTIBILITY

A CLOSE examination of the facts of hypnotic suggestion will readily yield us the law of abnormal suggestibility.

I hypnotize Mr. N., and tell him that on awakening, when he will hear me cough, he will go to the table, take the Bible, open it on the first page, and read aloud the first verse of the first chapter. He is then awakened. I cough. He rises, walks up to the table, but stops there and does not budge. I rehypnotize him. He tells me he did not want to carry out the suggestion. "But you must do it!" I insist. "You must go to the table, open the Bible on the first page, and read the first verse of the first chapter. You must do it! You can not help doing it!" He is then awakened, and this time the post-hypnotic suggestion is fully carried out.

I hypnotize Mr. L. "Rise!" I command. He rises. "Walk!" He walks. "You are unable to walk!" He makes a step or two, showing me that he can easily do it. "But it is impossible for you to walk; you can not walk; you are utterly unable to walk; you must not, and you can not walk; you lost all power of moving; no matter how you try, you find it impossible to take a step; you can not move; your legs; you have lost an control over them; they are stiff, rigid, and firmly fixed to the ground. Oh, no, you can not walk; it is a physical impossibility for you to walk." I go on in this way, pouring forth a torrent of suggestions; and this time my suggestion takes full effect. The subject tries hard to move; he can not do it, his legs are rigid, cataleptic.

I hypnotize Mr. J. F., a strong, powerful, healthy, burly fellow. "Rise!" I command. He rises. "Walk!" He walks. "You can not move!" I command again in a somewhat louder voice. The subject makes a step forward. "But you can not move!" I insist in a still louder voice than before, laying more stress on "can not." He makes a step hesitatingly and with great difficulty, like one dragging a heavy burden on his legs. "You can not move!" I call out in a louder and more commanding tone, putting still more emphasis on the suggestion "can not." The subject comes to a complete standstill. He is fully paralyzed; by no effort of will can he take a step forward.

We may put it down as a rule, that when the suggestion is not taken there is a far higher probability of bringing it into effect by repeating the suggestion over and over again in a louder key and in a more commanding voice. The rule of hypnotic suggestion is, *The more direct we make our suggestion the greater the chance of its success.*

If we examine the facts of suggestion in the deeper states of hypnosis we find that the same rule holds true. The hypnotizer must make himself perfectly understood by the subject, by the *reflex consciousness* of the patient.

I hypnotize Mr. L., make passes over his hand, and suggest that it is rigid, stiff. It becomes cataleptic. On a second occasion, when I make the passes, his hand becomes rigid; he knows from previous experiments what it is I want of him.[1]

The experiments of Braid, Heidenhein, etc., and the controversy between the Nancy and Salpêtrière school beautifully bing out this general rule of hypnosis. Thus Braid, in his Neurypnology, tells us of some phreno-hypnotic experiments he made with a subject. "This patient, he writes, "being pressed over the phrenologist's organ of time, always expressed a desire 'to write' a letter to her mother or her brother; over the organ of tune, 'to sing'; between this and wit, 'to be judicious'; the boundary between wit and causality, 'to be clever'; causality, 'to have knowledge,' and so on."[2]

Heidenhein found that in pressing certain regions of the subject's body certain abnormal phenomena appeared; that in pressing the neck echolalia resulted——the patient repeated everything that was said before him with the exactness of a phonograph; that the stimulation of the neck produced vocal sounds, as in Goltz's experiments. Silva, Binet, Féré, and Heidenhein believe that they can move single limbs of the somnambule by stimulating the parts of the head which correspond to the motor centres of the limbs concerned. Chalander even proposed to study the physiology of the brain in this way. Charcot, Dumontpallier, Berillon, Lepine, Strahl, Grützner, and Heidenhein regard hemihypnosis——that is, hypnosis of one side of the body——as a physiological condition induced by the closing of one eye or by friction of one half of the crown of the head. Binet and Féré claim that a magnet can effect a transfer of anæsthesia, etc., to the opposite side of the body.

Now such experiments invariably fail when made by other observers and on other subjects. Braid himself tells us:[3] "I also very soon ascertained that the same points of the cranium when thus excited did not excite the *same ideas or emotions* in the minds of different patients, which I considered ought to have been the case." He hastens, however, to add: "I have since discovered the cause of this—namely, *not having operated at the proper stage of the hypnotic condition.*" The italics are his own, although Braid meant in quite a different sense from that implied by me. You may press a hump on the head of a fresh subject, and press it as much and as long as you like, and nothing particular will result, or anything might follow. And the reason is, the subject does not know what to expect; he has no suspicion of what the experimenter wants him to do. Charcot and his school maintain that there are three states of what they name "le grande hypnotisme." These states are induced physiologically.

1. The lethargic state is induced by fixation upon an object, or by passing lightly upon the eyeball through the closed eyelids. In this stage suggestion is impossible, but we find in it anæsthesia, a certain muscular hyperexcitability; any muscle excited by pressure or light friction contracts; pressure upon the ulnar nerve provokes the ulnar attitude; and pressure upon the facial nerve is followed by distortion of the features of the corresponding side of the face.

2. A subject in the lethargic condition can be made to pass into the second or cataleptic state by raising his eyelids. If one eye only is opened the corresponding side of the body alone passes into the cataleptic condition, the other side remaining lethargic. Suggestions can be induced through the muscular

sense. If the subject's hand is put into a condition as if to give a kiss, his face assumes a smiling expression; if his hands are joined as in prayer, the face becomes grave and the subject kneels down. This condition of catalepsy can also be induced at once without having the subject pass through lethargy, and that is caused by some nervous shock produced by a brilliant point or a violent noise.

3. Lethargy and catalepsy can be transformed into somnambulism by light or repeated friction of the top of the subject's head. Anæsthesia, hyperacute sensibility, and susceptibility to all kinds of suggestion characterize this state.

Now when other observers came to verify these three states they invariably failed to reproduce them without the agency of suggestion. Wetterstrand never found them at all among 3,589 different persons. "I have been as little able," writes Dr. Moll, "as have many others, to observe the stages of Charcot in my experiments. I have, besides, often experimented on several hystero-epileptics, but have failed to observe the stages, in spite of Richet's opinion that everyone who experiments on such persons will obtain the same results as the school of Charcot did." Bernheim finds that these three stages can not be induced without suggestion. Continued suggestion alone has been able to produce them. Liébault, who hypnotized more than six thousand persons, never observed anything that should go to confirm the hypnotic stages as described by Charcot. "I have never been able," writes Bernheim,[4] "to determine without suggestion any phenomena by pressure exercised upon certain points of the cranium. For example, here is one of my somnambulistic cases. I press upon the different points of the cranium; no result. I say, 'Now I am going to touch that put of the cranium which corresponds to the movement of the left arm, and this arm will go into convulsions.' Having said this, I touch an arbitrary part of the head; immediately the left arm is convulsed. I state that I am going to induce aphasia by touching the region corresponding to speech. I touch any part of the head, and the subject no longer replies to my questions. Then I state that I shall touch the head in such a way that irritation of the centres of speech will result. The person then answers my questions in the following manner: "What is your name?" 'Marie, Marie, Marie.' 'How are you?' 'Well, well, well.' 'You have no pain?' 'None at all, none at all, none at all.' "

I myself made similar experiments on my subjects and with similar results. I pressed different regions of the head of my subject and nothing resulted. I then said, "I am going to press your shoulder and you will be unable to speak." I pressed it, and he could not speak. In my following séances, whenever I pressed that subject's shoulder he lost the power of speech.

I pressed the head of Mr. W. in different places and no result followed. I then said, "I will press the centre of speech and you will be unable to speak." I firmly pressed an arbitrary part of the head, and the subject was unable to speak. Without suggestion, by mere physiological means, we are unable to induce any particular changes in the hypnotic subject. The subject must know what we require of him.

It is not necessary to make suggestions to each subject separately. If a hypnotizable person is present at a séance, he takes the hint at once, and when he is hypnotized he manifests phenomena similar to the one he has witnessed. He knows exactly what the hypnotizer wants of him.

"Here is an experiment," writes Bernheim,[5] "which I made with M. Beaunis. We hypnotized a nurse in our service who was susceptible to somnambulism. She had never been present either as witness or as subject of the kind of experiment which I wanted to try on her. I put the upper left limb into the cataleptic condition in the horizontal position, the thumb and index fingers stretched out, the other fingers bent; the right arm remained relaxed. I applied the magnet to it for eight minutes. Nothing occurred. Then turning to M. Beaunis, I said: 'Now I am going to try an experiment. I shall apply the magnet to the right hand (on the unaffected hand), and in a minute you will see this arm lifted and take the exact attitude of the left one, while the latter relaxes and falls.' I placed the magnet just where it was at first, and in a minute the suggested transfer was realized with perfect precision. If, then, without saying anything more, I put the magnet back against the left hand at the end of a minute the transfer occurred in inverse order, and so on consecutively. Afterward I said, 'I shall change the direction of the magnet, and the transfer will take place from the arm to the leg.' At the end of a minute the arm fell and the leg was raised. I put the magnet against the leg without saying anything, and the transfer took place from the leg to the arm. If, without saying anything to the subject, I replace the magnet by a knife, a pencil, a bottle, a piece of paper, or use anything in its place, the same phenomenon occurs. The next day I repeated these experiments on another somnambulist who had been present the day before, and without saying anything to her, or to any of the persons present, *they succeeded marvellously; the idea of the transfer had been suggested to her mind by the circumstances of which she had been a witness.*"

In deep hypnosis, on account of the hyperæsthesia of the subject's senses, the slightest hint suffices. But here, too, the subject must be trained by previous experiments as to the interpretation of the hint. In short, we may fully assert that in hypnosis the subject must know what the hypnotizer wants of him, so that the more precise, exact, and frank the suggestion is, the surer will be its success. We may put it down as a rule for practitioners who intend to use hypnotism for therapeutic purposes, *In giving the suggestion to the patient, make your language plain, precise, and direct to the point.*

The following cases will show the necessity of observing this last rule:

Prof. W. James gave to one of his patients a posthypnotic suggestion to smoke only one pipe of tobacco a day. When the patient came again Prof. James asked him how many pipes he smoked a day? The answer was, "One only." On being hypnotized the patient confessed that he bought a pipe with a bowl of large dimensions, and that it was this one pipe he was smoking the whole day.

Mr. F. suffered from attacks of acute headache. On account of the violent pain he had to discontinue his work. He came to me to be cured by hypnotism. I have hypnotized him several times and greatly relieved his headache. He could continue his occupation without any inconvenience. At the eighth sitting he told me he had no more violent attacks, but was only suffering from occasional slight headaches. I suggested that he will have no more slight headaches. Next day he came to me complaining of a severe attack.

All the facts discussed in this chapter prove in the clearest way the truth that in hypnosis, in the state of abnormal suggestibility, the more direct a suggestion is the greater is the chance of its being realized, the stronger is its efficacy; and *vice-versa*, the more indirect a suggestion is the less is the chance of having it realized, the less is its efficacy. The law of abnormal suggestibility may be stated as follows:

Abnormal suggestibility varies as direct suggestion, and inversely as indirect suggestion.

<hr>

1. Sphygmographic or pulse tracings illustrate well this state of catalepsy.
2. I must add here that Braid, in his later investigations in hypnosis, became fully aware of the real source of the phenomena.
3. Neurypnology.
4. Suggestive Therapeutics.
5. Suggestive Therapeutics.

9

SUGGESTIBILITY AND THE WAKING CONSCIOUSNESS

I T is now high time to gather up the threads of our discussion and weave them into one organic, living whole; to bring the stray rays of light that reached us in the course of our research together into one focus, and illuminate the dark, mysterious regions we undertook to explore. To do this we must retrace our steps and inspect closer the conditions that admit one into that strange land of puzzles, wonders, and prodigies. A comparison of the conditions of normal and abnormal suggestibility will, I think, prove interesting and valuable, as it might give us a glimpse deep into the nature of suggestibility in general.

To facilitate this comparison, it would be best to make a table in which the conditions of normal and abnormal suggestibility should run parallel to each other.

TABLE OF CONDITIONS OF NORMAL AND ABNORMAL SUGGESTIBILITY

Normal Suggestibility

1. Fixation of attention
2. Distraction
3. Monotony
4. Limitation of voluntary movements
5. Limitation of the field of consciousness
6. Inhibition
7. Immediate execution

Abnormal Suggestibility

1. Fixation of attention
2. ——————————
3. Monotony
4. Limitation of voluntary movements
5. Limitation of the field of consciousness
6. Inhibition
7. ——————————

A glance at our last table will show at once that the conditions in both cases are essentially the same, with the only difference that in abnormal suggestibility two conditions are wanting—namely, distraction and immediate execution. This sameness of conditions clearly indicates that both normal and abnormal suggestibility flow from some one common source, that they are of like nature, and that they are due to similar causes. Now a previous study led us to the conclusion that the nature of abnormal suggestibility is a disaggregation of consciousness, a slit, a scar produced in the mind, a crack that may extend wider and deeper, ending at last in a total disjunction of the waking, guiding, controlling consciousness from the reflex consciousness, from the rest of the stream of life. Normal suggestibility is of like nature—it is a cleft in the mind; only here the cleft is not so deep, not so lasting as it is in hypnosis, or in the state of abnormal suggestibility; the split is here but momentary, evanescent, fleeting, disappearing at the very moment of its appearance.

This fleeting, evanescent character of the split gives the reason why suggestion in the normal state, why normal suggestibility requires immediate execution as one of its most indispensable conditions. We must take the opportunity of the momentary ebb of the controlling consciousness and hastily plant our suggestion in the soil of reflex consciousness. We must watch for this favourable moment; not let it slip by, otherwise the suggestion is a failure. Furthermore, we must be careful to keep in abeyance, for the moment, though, the ever-active, ever-restless waves of the controlling consciousness; we must find for them work in some other direction; we must direct, we must distract them. That is why normal suggestibility requires the additional conditions of distraction and of immediate execution. For in the normal state the waking, controlling consciousness is always on its guard, and when enticed, leaves its ground only a single step, and that only for but a moment. In normal suggestibility the psychical scar is faint; the lesion effected in the body of consciousness is superficial, transitory, fleeting. In abnormal suggestibility on the contrary, the slit is deep and lasting—it is a severe gash. In both cases, however, we have a removal, a dissociation of the waking from the subwaking, reflex consciousness, and suggestion being effected only through through the latter. *It is the subwaking, the reflex, not the waking, the con-*

trolling, consciousness that is suggestible. Suggestibility is the attribute, the very essence if the subwaking, reflex consciousness. That our suggestions should take root and bring forth fruit, that they should become fully realized, we must address them to the subwaking consciousness directly, and in order to do that a disaggregation of consciousness must be effected.

If we turn to the laws of normal and abnormal suggestibility, we find still further evidence in support of our view as to the nature of suggestibility and its relation to the subwaking, reflex consciousness. A mere comparison of the two laws reveals the truth of our position:

The Law of Abnormal Suggestibility
Abnormal suggestibility varies as direct suggestion, and inversely as indirect suggestion.

The Law of Normal Suggestibility
Normal suggestibility varies as indirect suggestion, and inversely as direct suggestion.

The two laws are the reverse of each other, thus clearly indicating the presence of a controlling, inhibitory conscious element in the one case, and its absence in the other. In the normal state we must guard against the inhibitory waking consciousness, and we must therefore make our suggestion as indirect as possible. In the abnormal state, on the contrary, no circumspection is needed: the controlling, inhibitory waking consciousness is more or less absent, the subwaking reflex consciousness is exposed to external stimuli, and our suggestions, therefore, are the more effective the more direct we make them. With full right may we now assert that suggestibility is a disaggregation of consciousness—a disaggregation in which the subwaking, reflex consciousness enters into direct communication with the external world.

The general law of suggestibility is now plainly obvious:

SUGGESTIBILITY VARIES AS THE AMOUNT OF DISAGGREGATION, AND INVERSELY AS THE UNIFICATION OF CONSCIOUSNESS.

THE SELF

1

THE SECONDARY SELF

THE law of suggestibility in general, and those of normal and abnormal suggestibility in particular, indicate a coexistence of two streams of consciousness, of two selves within the frame of the individual; the one, the waking consciousness, the waking self; the other, the subwaking consciousness, the subwaking self. But although the conditions and laws of suggestibility clearly point to a double self as constituting human individuality, still the proof, strong as it appears to me to be, is rather of an indirect nature. We must therefore look for facts that should directly and explicitly prove the same truth. We do not lack such facts. We turn first to those of hysteria.

If we put a pencil or scissors into the anæsthetic hand of the hysterical person without his seeing it, the insensible hand makes adaptive movements. The fingers seize the pencil and place it in a position as if the hand were going to write. Quite differently does the hand possess itself of the scissors: the hand gets hold of the instrument in the proper way, and seems ready for work, for cutting. Now all the while the subject is totally unconscious of what is happening there to his hand, since it is insensible, and he can not possibly see it, as his face is concealed by a screen. It is obvious that in order for such movements of adaptation to occur that there must be recognition of the object kept by the anæsthetic hand. But recognition requires a complex mental operation: it requires that the object should be perceived, should be remembered, and should be classed with objects of a certain kind and order. The very fact of the adaptation movements indicate the presence of some kind of embryonic will. Simple as these experiments are, they none the less strongly indicate the presence of a hidden agency that works through the anæsthetic hand; an agency that possesses perception, memory, judgment, and even will. Since these operations are essentially characteristics of consciousness, of a self, we must necessarily conclude that it is a conscious agency that acts through the insensible hand of the hysterical person. Since the activity of this intelligence, simple and elementary as it is, is unknown to the subject, it is quite clear that there is present within him a secondary consciousness standing in no connection with the primary stream of personal consciousness, and somehow coming in possession of the person's hand.

As we advance in our research and make the conditions more and more complicated, all doubt as to the presence of a conscious being, behind the veil of the subject's primary consciousness, completely disappears. "We put a pen," says Binet[1] "into the anæsthetic hand and we make it write a word; left to itself, the hand preserves its attitude, and at the expiration of a short space of time repeats the words often five or ten times. Having arrived at this fact, we again seize the anæsthetic hand and cause it to write some familiar word——for example, the patient's own name——but in so doing we intentionally commit an error in spelling.

In its turn the anæsthetic hand repeats the word, but, oddly enough, the hand betrays a momentary hesitation when it reaches the letter at which the error in orthography was committed. If a superfluous letter happens to have been added, sometimes the hand will hesitatingly rewrite the name along with the supplementary letter; again, it will retrace only a part of the letter in question; and again, finally, entirely suppress it." It is quite evident that we have here to deal with a conscious agent hesitating about mistakes and able to correct them; we can not possibly ascribe such activity to mere unconscious cerebration.

If again we take the anæsthetic hand and trace on the dorsal side of it a letter or a figure, the hand traces this figure or letter. Evidently the secondary consciousness is in full possession of these perceptions, although the primary consciousness of the subject is totally ignorant of them.

Furthermore, insensible as the anæsthetic hand is, since no pinching, pricking, burning, or faradization of it are perceived by the subject, still we can show that there exists a hidden sensibility in the hand; this can easily be proved by the æsthesiometer. If we prick the insensible hand with one of the points of a pair of compasses, the hand automatically traces a single point. Apply both points, and the automatic writing will trace two points, thus informing us of its degree of insensibility.

The amaurotic or hysterical eye gives us still stronger evidence of the existence of a secondary being perceiving things which lie outside the visual distance of the subject's waking consciousness. Hysterical subjects often complain of the loss of sight. As a matter of fact, when we come to test it we find that the subject does see what he claims not to see. This is detected by the so-called "box of Flees." This box is so skilfully arranged that the patient sees with his right eye the picture or the figure situated to the left, and with his left eye what is situated to the right. The hysterical person blind in the right eye, when put to such a test, declares that he sees the picture to the left side but not that to the right. He sees with the blind eye.

Amaurosis may also be tested in a somewhat different way. A pair of spectacles in which one glass is red and the other green is put on the patient's eye, and he is made to read six letters on a blank frame, alternately covered with red and green glass. When one eye is closed only three letters can be seen through the spectacles—namely, the ones corresponding in color to the spectacle glass through which the eye is looking; the other three can not be seen on account of the two complementary colors forming black. The patient, then, blind in one eye (say the right), ought to see only three letters when he has the spectacles on. When, however, put to this test the patient promptly reads the six letters. The right eye undoubtedly sees, only the image is retained by the secondary self, and a special arrangement of conditions is required to force that hidden self to surrender the image it stole.

To reveal the presence of this secondary self that perceives and knows facts hidden from the upper consciousness or primary self, I frequently employ the following simple but sure method, which may be characterized as the method of "guessing":

Impressions are made on the anæsthetic limb, and the subject who does not perceive any of the applied stimuli is asked just to make a "wild guess" as to the nature and number of the stimuli, if there were any. Now the interest is that nearly all the guesses are found to be correct. Dr. William A. White, of Binghamton State Hospital, finds that this method works well in his cases. "In the case of D. F.," Dr. White writes to me, "whose field of vision I sent you, I find by experiment, taking a hint from you, that, by introducing fingers between the limit of her field of vision (which is very contracted) and the limit of the normal field, she could guess each time and tell which finger was held up."

To bring out still more clearly and decisively the presence of a secondary consciousness that perceives the image which the hysterical person does not see, A. Binet performed the following experiment: "We place," he says,[2] "the hysterical subject before a scale of printed letters, and tentatively seek the maximum distance from the board at which the subject is able to read the largest letters. After having experimentally determined the maximum distance at which the subject can read the largest letters of the series, we invite him to read certain small letters that are placed below the former. Naturally enough, the subject is unable to do so; but if at this instant we slip a pencil into the anæsthetic hand, we are able by the agency of the hand to induce automatic writing, and this writing will reproduce precisely the letters which the subject is in vain trying to read. It is highly interesting to observe that during the very time the subject is repeatedly declaring that he does not see the letters, the anæsthetic hand, unknown to him, writes out the letters one after another. If, interrupting the experiments, we ask the subject to write of his own free will the letters of the printed series, he will not he able to do so: and when asked simply to draw what he sees, he will only produce a few zigzag marks that have no meaning." These experiments plainly prove that the secondary consciousness sees the letters or words, and directs the anæsthetic hand it possesses to write what it perceives.

Furthermore, if we remove the subject at too great a distance, so that the letters are altogether out of the range of vision of the secondary consciousness, the automatic writing begins to make errors—writing, for instance, "Lucien" instead of "Louise"; it tries to guess. Now if anything plainly shows the presence of a hidden intelligence, it is surely this guessing of which the subject himself is totally unconscious, for guessing is essentially a characteristic of consciousness. "An automaton," truly remarks Binet, "does not mistake; the secondary consciousness, on the contrary, is subject to errors because it is a consciousness, because it is a thing that reasons and combines thoughts." This last conclusion is still further proved by the following experiments: "There are patients," writes Binet[3] "(St. Am., for example), whose hand spontaneously finishes the word they are made to trace. Thus I cause the letter 'd' to be written; the hand continues and writes 'don.' I write 'pa,' and the hand continues and writes 'pavilion.' I write 'Sal,' and the hand writes 'Salpêtrière.'"

Here it is still more obvious that we are in the presence of a hidden agency that can take hints and develop them intelligently.

We saw above that distraction of attention is one of the indispensable conditions of suggestibility in the normal waking state. Now, M. Janet, in his experiments on hysterical persons, used chiefly this condition, or (as it may be called) "method of distraction," as a means for coming into direct oral communication with the secondary suggestible self. In hysterical persons it is easier to bring about the conditions of suggestibility, because, as a rule, they possess a contracted field of consciousness, and when engaged in one thing they are oblivious to all else. "When Lucie [the subject] talked directly with anyone," says M. Janet,[4] "she ceased to be able to hear any other person. You may stand behind her, call her by name, shout abuse in her ear, without making her turn round; or place yourself before her, show her objects, touch her, etc., without attracting her notice. When finally she becomes aware of you she thinks you have just come into the room again, and greets you accordingly." M. Janet availed himself of these already existent conditions of suggestibility, and began to give her suggestions while she was in the waking state. When the subject's attention was fully fixed on a conversation with a third party, M. Janet came up behind her, whispered in her car some simple commands, which she instantly obeyed. He made her reply by signs to his questions, and even made her answer in writing if a pencil were placed in her hands. The subject's primary consciousness was entirely ignorant of what was going on. In some cases the patient was made to pass through a series of awkward bodily positions without the least spark of knowledge on his side. The following is a very interesting and striking case:

P., a man of forty, was received at the hospital at Havre for delirium tremens. He improved and became quite rational during the daytime. The hospital doctor observed that the patient was highly suggestible, and invited M. Janet to experiment on him. "While the doctor was talking to the patient on some interesting subject," writes M. Janet,[5] "I placed myself behind P., and told him to raise his arm. On the first trial I had to touch his arm in order to provoke the desired act; afterward his unconscious obedience followed my order without difficulty. I made him walk, sit down, kneel—all without his knowing it. I even told him to lie down on his stomach, and he fell down at once, but his head still raised itself to answer at once the doctor's questions. The doctor asked him, 'In what position are you while I am talking to you?' 'Why, I am standing by my bed; I am not moving.'" The secondary self accepted motor suggestions of which the primary self was totally unaware.

As the orders thus whispered to the secondary, subwaking self become more complicated the latter rises to the surface, pushes the waking self into the background and carries out the suggested commands. "M. Binet had been kind enough," writes M. Janet,[6] "to show me one of the subjects on whom he was in the habit of studying acts rendered unconscious by anæsthesia, and I had asked his permission to produce on this subject the phenomenon of suggestion by distraction. Everything took place just as I expected. The subject (Hab.), fully awake, talked to M. Binet. Placing myself behind her, I caused her to move her hand unconsciously, to write a few words, to answer my questions by signs, etc. Suddenly Hab. ceased to speak to M. Binet, and, turning toward me, continued correctly by *the voice* the conversation she had begun with me by unconscious signs. On the other hand, she no longer spoke to M. Binet, and could no longer hear him speak; in a word, she had fallen into elective somnambulism (rapport). It was necessary to wake her up, and when awakened she had naturally forgotten everything. Now Hab. had no previous knowledge of me at all; it was not, therefore, my presence which had sent her to sleep. The sleep was in this case manifestly *the result of the development of unconscious actions*, which had invaded and finally effaced the normal consciousness. This explanation, indeed, is easily verified. My subject, Madame. B——, remains wide awake in my neighbourhood so long as I do not provoke unconscious phenomena, but when the unconscious phenomena become too numerous and too complicated she goes to sleep." We have here clear and direct proof as to the presence of a conscious agency lying buried below the upper stratum of personal life, and also as to the identity of this hidden, mysterious self with the hypnotic self. *The self of normal and that of abnormal suggestibility are one and the same.*

Turning now to hypnosis, we find that the classical experiments of P. Janet and Gourney on deferred or post-hypnotic suggestion furnish clear, valid, and direct evidence of the reality of a secondary consciousness, of an intelligent, subwaking, hypnotic self concealed behind the curtain of personal consciousness.

"When Lucie was in a state of genuine somnambulism," writes P. Janet, "I said to her, in the tone used for giving suggestions, 'When I clap my hand twelve times you will go to sleep again.' Then I talked to her of other things, and five or six minutes later I woke her completely. The forgetfulness of all that had happened during the hypnotic state, and of my suggestion in particular, was complete. I was assured of this forgetfulness, which was an important thing here, first, by the preceding state of sleep, which was genuine somnambulism with all its characteristic symptoms; by the agreement of all those who have been engaged upon these questions, and who have all proved the forgetfulness of similar suggestions after waking; and, finally, by the results of all the preceding experiments made upon this subject, in which I have always found this unconsciousness. Other people surrounded Lucie and talked to her about different things; and then, drawing back a few steps, I struck my hand five blows at rather long intervals and rather faintly, noticing at the same time that the subject paid no attention to me, but still talked on briskly. I came nearer and said to her, 'Did you hear what I just did?' 'What did you do?' said she, 'I was not paying attention.' 'This' (I clapped my hands). 'You just clapped your hands.' 'How many times?' 'Once.' I drew back and continued to clap more faintly every now and then. Lucie, whose attention was distracted, no longer listened to me, and seemed to have completely forgotten my existence. When I had clapped six times more in this way, which with the preceding ones made twelve, Lucie stopped talking immediately, closed her eyes, and fell back asleep. 'Why do you go to sleep?' I said to her. 'I do not know anything about it; it came upon me at once,' she said.

"The somnambulist must have counted, for I endeavoured to make the blows just alike, and the twelfth could not be distinguished from the preceding ones. She must have heard them and counted them, but without knowing it; therefore, unconsciously (subconsciously). The experiment was easy to repeat, and I repeated it in many ways. In this way Lucie counted unconsciously (subconsciously) up to forty-three, the blows being sometimes regular and sometimes irregular, with never a mistake in the result. The most striking of these experiments was this: I gave the order, 'At the third blow you will raise your hands, at the fifth you will lower them, at the sixth you will look foolish, at the ninth you will walk about the room, and at the sixteenth you will go to sleep in an easy-chair.' She remembered nothing at all of this on waking, but all these actions were performed in the order desired, although during the whole time Lucie replied to questions that were put to her, and was not aware that she counted the noises, that she looked foolish, or that she walked about.

"After repeating the experiment I cast about for some means of varying it, in order to obtain very simple unconscious judgments. The experiment was always arranged in the same way. Suggestions were made during a well-established hypnotic sleep, then the subject was thoroughly wakened, and the signals and the actions took place in the waking state. 'When I repeat the same letter in succession you will become rigid.' After she awoke I whispered the letters, 'a,' 'c,' 'd,' 'e,' 'a,' 'a.' Lucie became motionless and perfectly rigid. That shows an unconscious judgment of resemblance. I may also cite some examples of judgments of difference: 'You will go to sleep when I pronounce an uneven number,' or 'Your hands will revolve

121

around each other when I pronounce a woman's name.' The result is the same; as long as I whisper even numbers or names of men nothing happens, but the suggestion is carried out when I give the proper signal. Lucie has therefore listened unconsciously (subconsciously), compared, and appreciated the differences.

"I next tried to complicate the experiment in order to see to what lengths this faculty of an unconscious (subconscious) judgment would go. 'When the sum of the number which I shall pronounce amounts to ten you will throw kisses.' The same precautions were taken. She was awakened, forgetfulness established, and while she was chatting with other people who disturbed her as much as possible, I whispered, at quite a distance from her, 'Two, three, one, four,' and she made the movement. Then I tried more complicated numbers and other operations. 'When the numbers that I shall pronounce two by two, subtracted from one another, leave six, you will make a certain gesture'——or multiplication, and even very simple divisions. The whole thing was carried out with almost no errors, except when the calculation became too complicated and could not be done in her head. There was no new faculty there, only the usual processes were operating unconsciously (subconsciously).

"It seems to me that these experiments are quite directly connected with the problem of the intelligent performance of suggestion that appears to be forgotten. The facts mentioned are perfectly accurate. Somnambulists are able to count the days and hours that intervene between the present time and the performance of a suggestion, although they have no memory whatever of the suggestion itself. Outside of their consciousness there is a memory that persists, an attention always on the alert, and a judgment perfectly capable of counting the days, as is shown by its being able to make these multiplications and divisions."

The experiments of E. Gourney confirm the same truth—that behind the primary upper consciousness a secondary lower consciousness is present.

"P-ll," writes E. Gourney, "was told on March 26th that on the one hundred and twenty-third day from then he was to put a blank sheet of paper in an envelope and send it to a friend of mine whose name and residence he knew, but whom he had never seen. The subject was not referred to again till April 18th, when he was hypnotized and asked if he remembered anything in connection with this gentleman. He at once repeated the order, and said, 'This is the twenty-third day—a hundred more.'

"S. (hypnotizer). How do you know? Have you noted each day?

"P——ll. No; it seemed natural.

"S. Have you thought of it often?

"P——ll. It generally strikes me early in the morning. Something tells me, 'You count.'

"S. Does that happen every day?

"P——ll. No, not every day—perhaps more likely every other day. It goes from my mind. I never think of it during the day. I only know it has to be done.

"He was questioned again on April 20th, and at once said, 'That is going on all right—twenty-five days'; and on April 22nd, when in the trance, he spontaneously recalled the subject and added

'Twenty-seven days.' After he was awakened (April 18th), I asked him if he knew the gentleman in question or had been thinking about him. He was clearly surprised at the question." The hypnotic self knew he had to do something, knew the particular act and the precise day when he had to perform it; watched the flow of time, counted the days and all that was going on, without the least intimation to the consciousness of the waking personal self.

E. Gourney then conceived the happy idea of further tapping the intelligence and knowledge of this subwaking hypnotic self by means of automatic writing.

"I showed P——ll," says E. Gourney,[7] "a planchette ——he had never seen or touched one before——and got him to write his name with it. He was then hypnotized, and told that it had been as dark as night in London on the previous day, and that he would Le able to write what he had heard. He was awakened, and as usual was offered a sovereign to say what it was he had been told, and as usual without impunity to my purse. He was then placed with his hand on the planchette, a large screen being held in the front of his face, so that it was impossible for him to see the paper or instrument. In less than a minute the writing began. The words were, 'It was a dark day in London.'

"When asked what he had written, he did not know. He was given a post-hypnotic suggestion to poke the fire in six minutes, and that he should inform us how the time was going, without any direction as to writing. He wrote soon after waking, 'P——ll, will you poke the fire in six minutes?'"

To prove decisively the intelligence of the secondary, sub waking, hypnotic self, Gourney gave the entranced subject arithmetical problems to solve, and immediately had him awakened. When put to the planchette the subject gave the solution of the problem, without being conscious as to what he was doing. It was the hypnotic self who made the calculation, who solved the arithmetical problem.

W——s was told to add together 5, 6, 8, 9, and had just time to say "5," when he was awakened in the fraction of a second with the words on his lips. The planchette immediately produced "28."

P——ll was told during trance to add all the digits from 1 to 9; the first result was 39, the second 45 (right). Rehypnotized, and asked by S. what he had been writing, he said, "You told me to add the figures from 1 to 9 = 45." "Did you write it?" "Yes, I wrote it down."

W——s was hypnotized and told that in six minutes he "as to blow a candle out, and that he would be required at the same time before this to write the number of minutes that had passed and the number that had still to elapse. He was awakened, laughed and talked as usual, and, of course, knew nothing of the order. In about three and a half minutes (he was taken by surprise, so to say) he was set down to the planchette, which wrote, "Four and a half-one more." About a minute passed, and W——s was rehypnotized, but just as his eyes were beginning to close, he raised himself and blew out the candle, saying, "It is beginning to smell." Hypnotized and questioned, he remembered all that he had done; and when it was pointed out to him that four and a half and one do not make six, he explained the discrepancy by saying, "It took half a minute for you to tell me; I reckoned from the end of your telling me."

S——t was told in the trance that he was to look

out of the window seven minutes after waking, and that he was to write how the time was going. He was then awakened. This was 7:34⅓ P. M. I set him to the planchette, and the writing began at 7:34½ I did not watch the process, but when I stood holding the screen in front of his eyes I was so close to his hand that I could not help becoming aware that the writing was being produced at distinct intervals. I remarked that he was going by fits and starts, and seemed to have to pause to get up steam. Immediately on the conclusion of the writing at 7:40 he got up and drew aside the blind, and looked out. Examining the paper, I found "25, 34, 43, 52, 61, 7."

Clearly he had aimed at recording at each moment when he began the number that had passed and the number that remained. The subwaking, suggestible, hypnotic being seems to he not a physiological automaton, but a self, possessing consciousness, memory, and even a rudimentary intelligence.

Sphygmographic tracings of the radial artery seem to point to the same conclusion. Thus in the normal state, on the application of agreeable stimuli, such as perfumes, the curves become broader, the pulse slower, indicating a muscular relaxation of the heart; while on the other hand, if disagreeable or painful stimuli are applied, such as pricking, faradic or galvanic currents, ammonia, acetic acid, formaline, etc., the pulse becomes rapid, the "Rückstoss elevation," or the dicrotic wave, becomes accentuated, and even rises in height (in cases where the dicrotic wave is absent it reappears under pain), the heart beats increase, indicating a more frequent muscular contraction.

If now the subject is hypnotized and made anæsthetic and analgesic, and agreeable and disagreeable stimuli are applied, although the subject feels no pain whatever, still the characteristics of the pain and pleasure curves are strangely marked, indicating the presence of a diffused subconscious feeling.

Records of respiration and of the radial artery, or what is called pneumographic and sphygmographic tracings, bring out clearly the real nature of the subconscious.

This is done in the following way: A simultaneous pneumographic and sphygmographic record is first taken of the subject while he is in his normal waking state. A second record is then taken, with the only difference that disagreeable and painful stimuli, such as faradic current or odours of ammonia or acetic acid, are introduced. The tracings will at once show the painful sensations of the subject. The curves will suddenly rise, revealing the violent reactions to the unwelcome stimuli.

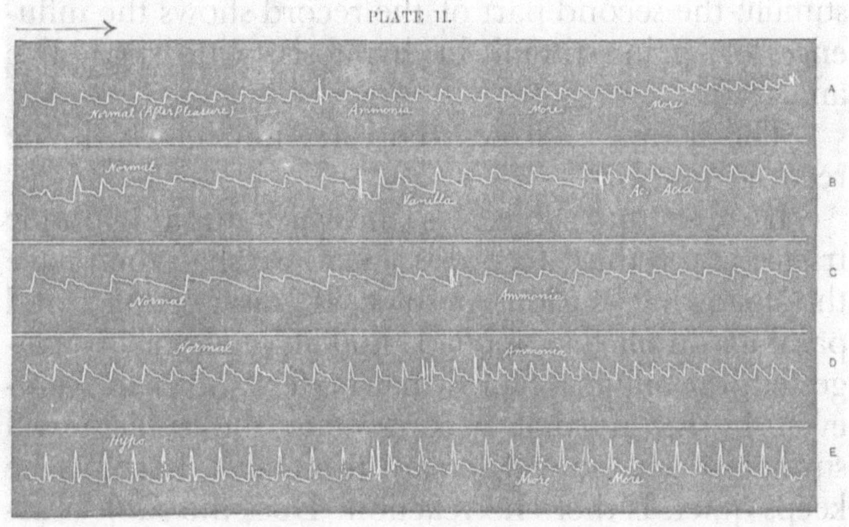

PLATE II. *A*, *B*, *C* and *D* are sphygmographic or pulse tracings in the fully waking normal state. The first part of each tracing in *A*, *C* and *D* shows the normal pulse of the subject; the rest is under the influence of pain stimuli such as ammonia or acetic acid. *B*, in the first part of the record is normal, with no stimulus; the second part of the record shows the influence of the pleasant stimulus of vanilla; the third part of *B* shows the effect of acetic acid.

Tracings *B* and *C* are of the same subject whose characteristic normal (rather abnormal) pulse was that of C normal. Under the influence of pleasant stimuli (*B*, "vanilla") the abnormal (normal to this subject) characteristics of this pulse became more manifest. Under the influence of painful stimuli (acetic acid, ammonia, etc.) the abnormal characteristic (normal pulse of this subject) disappeared, and the pulse became a typical normal pulse.

Tracing *E*, in the first part of the record, shows the pulse in hypnosis, but with no application of any stimuli; the second part of the record shows the influence of pain stimuli in hypnosis with suggestive analgesis.

The arrow indicates the direction in which the record runs.

If now the subject is thrown into a hypnotic trance and a third record is taken, we shall then have the following curious results: If disagreeable and painful stimuli are applied, and if analgesia is suggested, the subject claims that he feels no pain whatever. In his normal waking state the subject will strongly react, he will scream from pain, but now he keeps quiet. Is there no reaction? Does the subject actually feel no pain? Far from being the case. If we look at the pneumographic tracings we find the waves

128

uniformly deep and broad, the respiration is hard and laboured; a similar change we find in the tracings of the radial artery. The pain feeling is there, only it is not concentrated; it is diffused. The upper consciousness does not feel the pain, but the subconsciousness does. The painful or uneasy feeling is diffused all over the organic consciousness of the secondary self.

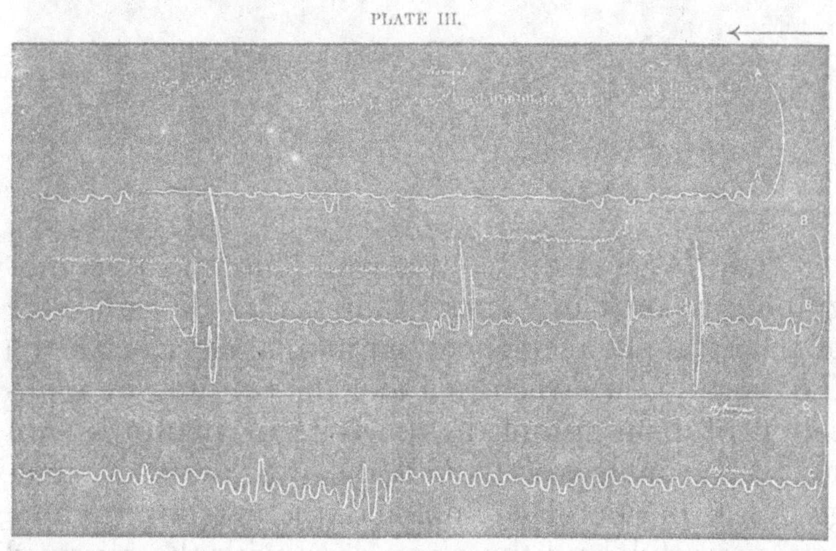

Plate III. *A A* are sphygmographic and pneumographic tracings of the subject in the normal state. *B B* are tracings of normal state with pain stimuli, and the reaction of the subject is shown in the abruptly ascending waves. *C C* are tracings of the subject in the state of hypnosis, with suggested analgesia or loss of pain sensibility, and under the uninterrupted application of pain stimuli (acetic acid, ammonia, electricity, pricking, etc.)

The upper tracing of each couplet is sphymographic; the lower is pneumographic.)

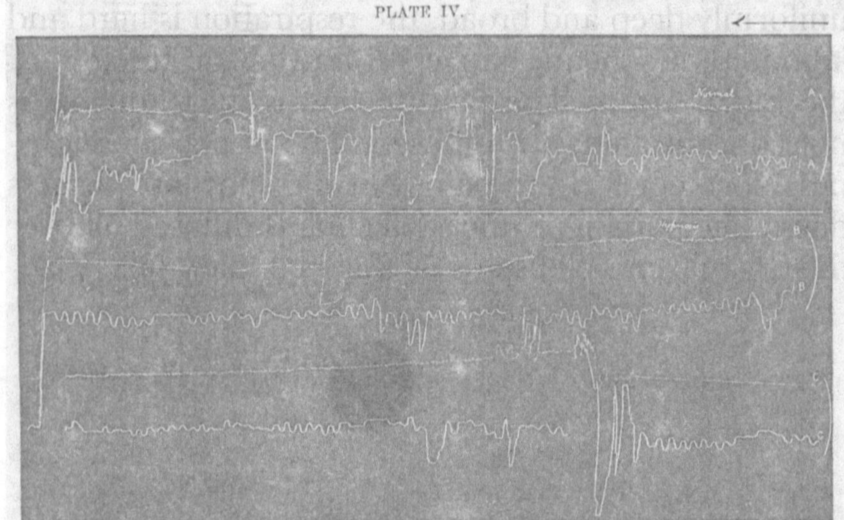

Plate IV. *A A* are sphygmographic and pneumographic records in normal state under the influence of pain stimuli (acetic acid, ammonia, electricity, etc.) *B B* and *C C* are tracings under the continuous application of pain stimuli in the state of hypnosis with suggestive analgesia. In *C C* the suggestion of analgesia was in one place annulled, the reaction became very powerful, and the curve rose; with the renewed suggestion of analgesia the reaction disappeared and the curve immediately fell.

The upper tracing of each couplet is sphymographic; the lower is pneumographic.)

1. Binet, On Double Consciousness. *Vide* Binet, Sur les alternations de la Conscience, Revue Philosophique, v, 27, 1884.
2. Binet, On Double Consciousness; also, Revue Philosophique, v, 27.
3. Binet, On Double Consciousness; also, Revue Philosophique, v, 27.
4. Pierre Janet, L'Automatisme Psychologique.
5. Ibid.

6. Ibid.
7. E. Gourney. Post-hypnotic States, Pr. S. P. R, April, 1887. (Proceedings of the Society for Psychical Research)

2

THE SUBCONSCIOUS SELF AND UNCONSCIOUS CEREBRATION

THE facts of post-hypnotic negative hallucinations or of systematized anæsthesia still further reveal the presence of a subconscious self below the upper waking consciousness. The following interesting experiments made by Bernheim and M. Liegeois, and quoted by Binet in his remarkable book, The Alternations of Personality, may serve as good illustrations:

"Elise B., eighteen years old, a servant, suffering from sciatica. She was a respectable young girl, steady, of average intelligence, and, with the exception of her sciatica, presenting no neuropathic manifestations, symptoms, nor hereditary tendencies.

"It was very easy, after her first sitting, to bring on somnambulism coupled with a state in which she was sensitive to hallucinations both hypnotic and post-hypnotic, and to amnesia on awaking. I easily developed negative hallucinations with her. During her sleep I said to her, 'When you wake you will no longer see me: I shall have gone.' When she awoke she looked about for me, and did not seem to see me. I talked to her in vain, shouted in her ear, stuck a pin in her skin, her nostrils, under the nails, and thrust the point of the pin in the mucous membrane of the eye. She did not move a muscle. As far as she was concerned, I had ceased to exist, and all the acoustic, visual, tactile, and other impressions emanating from myself did not make the slightest impression upon her; she ignored them all. As soon, however, as another person, unknown to her, touched her with the pin, she perceived it quickly, and drew back the member that had been pricked.

"I may add, in passing, that this experiment is not equally successful with all somnambulists. Many patients do not realize negative sensorial suggestions, and others only partially. Some, for example, when I declare that they shall not see me on awaking, do not see me, indeed, but they do hear my voice and feel my touch. Some are astonished to hear me and feel the pricks without seeing me, others do not attempt to understand it, and, finally, others believe that the voice and the sensation come from another person who is present. Sometimes the negative hallucination is made complete for *all their sensations* when the suggestion is given in this way: 'When you wake, if I touch you and prick you you will not feel it; if I speak to you you will not hear me. Moreover, you will not see me: I shall have gone.' Some subjects' sensations are quite neutralized after this detailed suggestion; with others, only the visual sensation is neutralized, all the other negative sensorial suggestions remaining ill effectual.

"The somnambulist of whom I speak realized everything to perfection. Logical in her delusive conception, she apparently did not perceive me with any of her senses. It was useless to tell her that I was there and that I was talking to her. She was convinced that they were simply making fun at her expense. I gazed at her obstinately, and said: 'You see me well enough, but you act as if you did not see me. You are a humbug; you are playing a part.' She did not stir, and continued to talk to other people. I added with a confident manner: However, I know all about it. You can not deceive me. It is only two years since you had a child, and you made away with it. Is that true? I have been told so.' She did not move; her face remained peaceful. Wishing to see, on account of its medico-legal bearing, whether a serious offence might committed under cover of a negative hallucination, I roughly raised her dress and skirt. Although naturally very modest, she allowed this without a blush. I pinched the calf of her leg and thigh. She made absolutely no sign whatever. I am convinced that she might have been assaulted in this state without the slightest resistance.

"That established, I asked the head of the clinic to put her to sleep again and suggest to her that I should again be there when she awoke. This she realized. She saw me again, and remembered nothing that had happened in the interval. I said to her: 'You have just seen me. I talked with you.' She was astonished, and said, 'Why, no, you were not there.' 'I was there, and I did talk with you. Ask these gentlemen if I didn't.' 'I saw these gentlemen very well. M. P. tried to persuade me that you were there. But that was only a joke. You were not there.' 'Very well,' I said, 'but you remember everything that happened while I was not there—all that I said and did to you.' 'But how could you say and do anything to me when you were not there?' I insisted. Speaking seriously, and looking her in the face, I laid stress on every word: 'It is true, I was not there, but you remember just the same.' I put my hand on her forehead and declared, 'You remember everything, absolutely everything. There——speak out: what did I say to you?' After a moment's concentrated thought, she blushed, and said, 'Oh, no, it is impossible; I must have dreamed it.' 'Very well; what did I say to you in this dream?' She was ashamed, and did not want to say. I insisted. At last she said, 'You said that I had had a child.' 'And what did I do to you?' 'You pricked me with a pin.' 'And then?' After a few minutes she said, 'Oh, no, I would not have allowed you to do it; it is a dream.' 'What did you dream?' 'That you exposed me,' etc.

"In this way I was able to call up the memory of all that had been said and done by me while she supposed that she did not see me. Therefore, in reality she both saw and heard me, notwithstanding her apparent obtuseness——she neither saw nor heard me. She saw me with her bodily (subconscious) eyes, but she did not see me with the eyes of the mind (upper consciousness). She was smitten with blindness, deafness, and psychical anæsthesia as far as I was concerned. All sensorial impressions emanating from me were distinctly perceived, but remained unconscious for her (upper consciousness).

"Similar experiments were performed by M. Liegeois. 'I no longer existed,' writes M. Liegeois, 'as far as Madame M. was concerned, to whom M. Liébault had, at my request, suggested that when she woke she would no longer see or hear me. I spoke to her: she did not reply. I stood before her: she did not see me. I pricked her with a pin: she felt no pain. She was asked where I was: she said she did not know——that I had undoubtedly gone, etc.

"I then conceived the idea of making some suggestions in loud tones to this person, for whom I had seemed to become an entire stranger; and, what was very singular, she obeyed these suggestions.

"I told her to rise: she rose. To sit down: she seated herself. To make her hands revolve round one another: she did so. I suggested a toothache to her, and she had a toothache; sneezing, and she sneezed. I said that she was cold, and she shivered; that she ought to go to the stove——in which there was no fire——and there she went; until I told her that she was warm, and then she was all right. During all this time she was, as far as all the assistants were concerned, as fully awake as they were. When questioned by them, she replied that I was absent, she did not know why; perhaps I would soon come back, etc. Questioned by me with the use of the first personal pronoun, all my questions remained unanswered. She only realized the ideas I expressed impersonally, if I may use such an expression, and as if she drew from her own thought. It is her unconscious (subconscious) ego that causes her to act, and the conscious ego has not the slightest idea of the impulse that she receives from without.

"The experiment seemed to me sufficiently interesting to bear repeating on another subject, Camille S., and here is a concise resume of the proofs and verifications secured some days later from this girl:

"Camille S, is eighteen years old, and a very good somnambulist. M. Liébault and I have known her for nearly four years. We have often put her to sleep. We always found her to be perfectly sincere, and we came to have entire confidence in her. This statement is necessary, as we shall see, to give weight to the singular results obtained which confirmed absolutely the first observation made on Madame M.

"M. Liébault put Camille to sleep, and at my request suggested to her that she would no longer see or hear me; then he left me to experiment in my own way. When she awoke the subject was in communication with everybody, except that I no longer existed for her. Yet, as I am about to show, that is not quite accurate. It was as if there were two personalities within her—one that saw me when the other did not see me, and that heard me when the other paid no attention to what I was saying.

"In the first place, I assured myself of the state of her sensibility. And it was very curious that this existed for all the assistants, but did not exist for anything emanating from me. If anyone else pricked her she quickly drew her arm back. If I pricked her she did not feel it. I stuck pins in her that remained hanging from her arms and cheek. She complained of no sensation, not feeling them at all. This fact of anæsthesia, not real, but in a measure personal, is certainly very singular. It is quite new, if I am not mistaken. In the same way, if I held a bottle of ammonia under her nose she did not push it away, but she turned away from it when it was presented to her by a strange hand.

"While she was in this condition, neither seeing nor hearing me—apparently, at least—almost all the suggestions are carried out that may he made in the waking state. I sum them up in the order in which they follow, from my notes taken at the time, June 14th, 1888.

"I need not repeat that if I speak directly to Camille S.—if I ask her, for example, how she is, how long it is since she stopped growing, etc.—her countenance remains impassive. She neither sees nor hears me——at least she is not conscious of so doing.

"I then proceed, as I said above, impersonally, talking not in my own name, but as if an internal voice of her own was speaking, and expressing such ideas as the subject would be likely to get from her own private thought. Then somnambulistic automatism shows itself in this new and unexpected guise as complete as any of the other forms already known.

"I said aloud,' Camille is thirsty; she is going to the kitchen for a glass of water, that she will bring back and set on this table.' She did not seem to have heard me, and yet in a few minutes she acted as I had said, and carried out the suggestion with that brisk and impetuous manner which has already been frequently noticed in somnambulists. She was asked why she brought the glass that she put on the table. She did not know what was meant. She had not moved. There was no glass there.

"I said, 'Camille sees the glass, but there is no water in it, as they are trying to make her believe; it is wine, and very good wine, too; she is going to drink it, and it will do her good.' She promptly performed the order thus given to her, then immediately forgot all about it.

"I made her say some words in succession that were scarcely proper. 'Devil take it!' 'Confound it!' 'Con——' and she repeated all that I suggested to her, but instantly losing the memory of what she had just said.

"A certain M. F., astonished at this, upbraided her for using these unseemly expressions. She said: 'I did not say those vulgar words. 'What do you take me for ? You are dreaming; you must have gone mad.'

"She saw me without seeing me, as this shows. I

said, 'Camille is going to sit on M. L.'s knee.' She immediately jumped violently on my knee, and, on being questioned, declared that she had not moved from the bench where she was seated a moment before.

"M. Liébault spoke to me. As she neither saw nor heard me consciously, she was astonished, and then began a conversation with him in which I placed the part of a prompter who dwelt in her own brain. I suggested all the following words to her, and she uttered them, thinking that she was expressing her own thought:

"'M. Liébault, aren't you talking to the wall? I must put you to sleep to cure you. We will change rôles, etc.

"'M. F., how is your bronchitis?'

"M. F. asked her how and why she said all this. She replied, after I had whispered to her: 'How do you think it comes to me? Just as it comes to every one. How do your own thoughts come?' and she continued to enlarge upon the theme given her by me.

"She seemed to be in a perfectly normal state, and held her own with all the assistants with great presence of mind. Only in the midst of her conversation she inserted the phrases that I created in her mind, unconsciously making them her own.

"Thus, while she was arguing with M. F., whom she told that she would take to Mareville,[1] her interlocutor having objected, 'I am not insane,' she replied: 'All insane people say that they are not insane. You say that you are not insane, therefore you must be insane.' She was very proud of her syllogism, and never suspected that she had just got it from me.

"Wishing to make sure, once more, that she saw me without being conscious of it, I said: 'Camille is

going to take a bottle of cologne out of M. L.'s vest
pocket; she will uncork it and enjoy its delightful
odour.' She rose, came directly to me, looked first in
the left, then in the right pocket; took out a bottle of
ammonia, uncorked it, and inhaled it with pleasure. I
was obliged to take it away from her. Then, still under
the influence of suggestion, she took off my right.
shoe. M. F. said to her: 'What are you doing there?
You are taking off one of M. L.'s shoes!' She was offended. 'What are you talking about? M. L. is not
here, so it is not possible for me to take off his shoe.
You are still more insane than you were just now!'
And when M. F. raised both arms while he was
talking to me, Camille cried: 'Absolutely, I must take
you to Mareville. It is too bad! Poor M. F.!' He did not
seem to be cast down by her remark. 'But what shoe is
that that you are holding? What is it?' I came to my
subject's assistance, and said: 'It is a shoe that Camille
must try on; she was not able to do it this morning at
home, because the shoemaker did not keep his ap-
pointment. He was drunk, and he has only just
brought it. She is going to try it on right here.'

"All that was accepted, repeated exactly, and
promptly performed as if by spontaneous inspiration.
For propriety's sake she turned toward the wall to try
on my shoe. She found it a little large, and returned it
to me, because I said she ought to return it to me.

"Finally, at my suggestion, she took the glass back
to the kitchen. When she returned, questioned by M.
F., she declared that she had not left the room, that
she had not drunk anything, and that she had not had
a glass in her hands. It was of no use to show her the
wet ring that the bottom of the glass had left on the
table. She did not see any ring; there was none; they
were trying to fool her. And then, in order to prove

what she said, she passed her hand over the table several times, making the leaves fly on which I took my notes, and which shared in my privilege of being invisible, without seeing them. If there had been an inkstand there, it too would undoubtedly have been thrown to the floor.

"In order to bring this series of tests to an end, I said aloud: 'Camille, you are going to see and hear me. I will open your eyes. You are now all right.' I was three metres from her, but the suggestion operated. Camille passed without any apparent transition stage from the state of negative hallucination into which M. Liébault had thrown her into the normal state, which in her case was, as usual, accompanied by complete amnesia. She had no idea of all that had just happened——the numerous experiments, varied in every conceivable way, the hallucinations, the words, the actions in which she played the principal part——all this was forgotten; it was all, as far as she was concerned, as if it had not been."

I can not do better than to bring M Liegeois's own interpretation of his experiments, an interpretation with which I fully agree:

"During the negative hallucinations," says M. Liegeois, "the subject sees what he does not seem to see, and hears what he does not seem to hear. Two personalities (selves) exist within him——an unconscious (subconscious) ego that sees and hears, and a conscious ego that does not see nor hear." And I may add that not only do the two egos exist within the state of negative hallucination, but also within the normal state.

The facts of hypnotic memory alone strongly indicate the intelligent nature of the subconscious. Can the theory of unconscious cerebration[2] explain, for instance, the fact of suggested amnesia during hypnosis? I hypnotize Mr. V. F., and make him pass through many lively scenes and actions. I give him hypnotic and post-hypnotic suggestions. The subject is wakened and hypnotized time and again. At last he is put into a hypnotic state, and is suggested that on awaking he shall not remember anything of what had happened in the state of hypnosis. The subject, on emerging from his trance, remembers nothing of what he has passed through. I then put my hand on llis forehead and tell him in a commanding voice, "You remember now everything!" As if touched by the wand of a magician, the suppressed memories become endowed with life and movement and invade the consciousness of the subject. Everything is now clearly remembered, and the subject is able to relate the tale of his adventures without the omission of the least incident. So detailed is the account that one can not help wondering at the extraordinary memory displayed by the subject. How is the theory of unconscious cerebration to account for this strange fact? Prof. Ziehen, in his Physiological Psychology, tells us that "it is still a matter of doubt whether, despite their complicateness, all the facts of the hypnotized individual are not motions accomplished without any concomitant psychical processes," and that "even the recollection of the hypnotic psychical processes do not necessarily argue in favor of their existence during hypnotic trance." This extreme view is certainly wrong; for the subject during hypnosis not only acts, moves, but he also speaks, answers questions intelligently, reasons, discusses; and if such an individual may still be regarded as a mere machine, on the same grounds we may as wen consider any rational man as a mere unconscious automaton.[3]

The advocates of unconscious cerebration must admit at least this much, that hypnosis is a conscious state. Now, on the theory of unconscious cerebration it is truly inconceivable how psychical states can be suppressed, the accompanying unconscious physiological processes alone being left, and all that done by a mere word of the experimenter. The restoration of memory is still more incomprehensible than even the suggested amnesia. A command by the experimenter, "Now you can remember!" brings into consciousness a flood of ideas and images. It is not that the experimenter gives the subject a clew which starts trains of particular images and idcas, but the mere general, abstract suggestion, "You can remember!" is sufficient to restore memories which to all appearances have completely vanished from the mind of the subject. Are the unconscious physiological nervous modifications so intelligent as to understand suggestions and follow them? Does unconscious cerebration understand the command of the experimenter, and does it oblige him to become conscious? On closer examination, we find the term unconscious cerebration to be of so loose a nature that under its head are often recorded facts that clearly indicate the working of an intelligence. Thus Mr. Charles M. Child brings the following fact as a specimen of unconscious cerebration:[4]

"I had earnestly been trying," a gentleman writes to Mr. Child, "to make a trial balance, and at last left off working, the summary of the *Dr.* and *Cr.* sides of the account showing a difference of £2 10s., the Dr. side being so much smaller. The error I had not found on Saturday night when I left the counting-house. On this same Saturday night I retired feeling nervous, and angry with myself. Some time in the night I dreamed thus: I was seated at my desk in the countinghouse and in a good light; everything was orderly and natural, the ledger lying before me. I was looking over the balance of the accounts and comparing them with the sums in the trial-balance sheet. Soon I came to a debit balance of £2 10s. I looked at it, called myself sundry names, spoke to myself in a deprecating manner of my own eyes, and at last put the £2 10s. to its proper side of the trial-balance sheet and went home. I arose at the usual Sunday time, dressed carefully, breakfasted, went to call on some . . . friends to go to church. Suddenly the dream flashed on my memory. I went for the keys, opened the office, also the safe, got the ledger, and turned to the folio my dream had indicated. There was the account whose balance was the sum wanted which I had omitted to put in the balance sheet, where it was put now, and my year's posting proved correct."

The adherents of unconscious cerebration tacitly include under this term not only unconscious physiological processes, or nerve modifications, but also psychical states. Keeping clearly in mind the real meaning of unconscious cerebration as referring to physiological processes or nerve modifications with no psychical accompaniment, the difficulties of unconscious cerebration to account for the phenomena of hypnotic memory become truly insurmountable. For if the physiological processes subsumed under the category of unconscious cerebration are completely lacking any psychical element whatever, how can a general abstract negative phrase suppress particular psychical states, and how can a similar positive phrase bring the forgotten memories hack to consciousness? It is simply incomprehensible.

Furthermore, while the subject is in a hypnotic condition we can suggest to him that on awaking he shall not remember anything, but that when put to the automatic recorder he shall be able to write everything that has taken place in the state of hypnosis. The subject is then awakened; he remembers nothing at all of what he had passed through while in the state of hypnotic trance. As soon, however, as he is put to the automatic recorder the hand gives a full, rational account of all the events. If now you ask the subject what it is he has written, he stares at you in confusion; he knows nothing at all of the writing. How shall we account for this fact on the theory of unconscious cerebration? Can unconscious physiological processes write rational discourses? It is simply wonderful, incomprehensible.

These, however, are not the only difficulties which the theory of unconscious cerebration has to encounter. Take the following experiment: I gave Mr. V. F. the suggestion that on awaking he should put my coat, on three times, take it off, and put it on again; that he should do it when he should hear a signal which should be a knock; amnesia was suggested, and also the possibility of writing the suggestion. The subject was then roused from his trance. There was not the slightest recollection of what had been suggested, but when he was put to the automatic recorder the hand at once proceeded to write in full everything. In the middle of the writing, "When a signal will be given. . ." I stopped the subject's hand and asked him what he was writing about. "I do not know," he answered. "How is it," I asked again, "you write, and you do not know what you write?" "I do not know; I think it was something about a coat." "What was it you were writing about a coat?" "I do not know; maybe about the make of a coat." Then when the signal came he rose and put on the coat three times.

To take another experiment of the same kind: I give the subject the suggestion that he should bow to the gas whenever the door should be opened; again amnesia is suggested, with the possibility of writing. The subject is stopped when he finished his account. "What was it you wrote?" I ask. The subject looks surprised. I repeat my question. "I do not know; I think something about a door?" "What was it about a door?" "I do not know." I have made many similar experiments, and all of them with the same results. It is evident that the writing is not an unconscious automatic process, for the subject possesses a general knowledge of what he has written, or even of what he is going to write. Now, on the theory of unconscious cerebration this general knowledge ought to be entirely lacking, since the physiological processes of the suppressed memory have no psychical accompaniment. It would not do to say that the subject knows each word as he writes it, but becomes unconscious of it, forgets it, as soon as it is written down; because the subject is able to tell the central idea——that is, he has a general knowledge of it; and, what is more, he is able to tell us this general central idea even before he finishes the writing——in fact, he can do it when stopped in the middle of the phrase. On the theory of secondary consciousness, however, the experiments could not possibly give other results. The secondary consciousness understands the suggestions given by the experimenter, accepts them, obeys the commands, keeps the suppressed memories, and sends up a general knowledge of them to the upper consciousness,[5] and, if commanded, communicates the suppressed particular suggestions in all their details.

The advocates of unconscious cerebration assume too much: they assume that normal memory, or recollection in the normal state, can be fully accounted for by unconscious physiological processes, and the only thing required is to apply this theory to the phenomena of hypnotic memory. It would be well to examine this theory and see how strong its claims are in the case of normal memory.

Many a modern psycho-physiologist no doubt smiles at the crude, ancient psycho-physiological theory of perception. Images or copies of objects emanate from objects, get deposited in the mind; hence perception, cognition, memory. The modern psycho-physiological speculations, however—the speculations of Maudsley, Carpenter, Ziehen, Ribot, etc.—are no less crude. Thus Ziehen, for instance, conceives that each sensation deposits a copy of itself—an image, an idea—in some one of the memory ganglion cells, and memory consists in the reproduction of this copy—the hen lays an egg from which another hen may come out. Maudsley expresses the same thing in slightly different terms; instead of "deposits of images in memory ganglion cells," he uses" modifications of nerve elements." "It may be supposed," says Maudsley, "that the first activity did leave behind it, when it subsided, some after-effect, some modification of the nerve element, whereby the nerve circuit was disposed to fall again readily into the same action, such disposition (unconscious) appearing in consciousness as recognition or memory." Ribot and many other psychologists, with slight variations in minor points, follow the same beaten track. All of them agree that it is the nerve modifications produced by the physiological processes of sensations, emotions, etc., that constitute the basis, nay, the very essence, of memory itself. It does not require a close examination to find the deficiencies of this theory. A mere modification left behind as a trace can not possibly explain memory, recollection, the fact of referring a particular bit of experience to an experience felt before. The retention of a trace or of a nervous modification, and the reproduction of that trace or modification, can not in the least account for the fact that a series of sensations, ideas, images, emotions, felt at different times, should become combined, brought into a unity, felt like being similar, like being one and the same, like being repetitions, copies of one original experience. It is not retention or reproduction, but it is the recognition element that constitutes the essence of memory. The rose of to-day reminds me of the rose seen yesterday, of the same rose seen the day before yesterday. Now, the image of the rose may be retained, may even be reproduced, but if it is not recognised as having happened in my past, there can he no recollection; in short, without recognition there is no memory. As Prof. James strongly puts it, "the gutter is worn deeper by each successive shower, but not for that reason brought into contact with previous showers." Does the theory of unconscious physiological processes, of material brain traces, of nerve modifications—does this theory take into account this element of recognition? Can the theory of unconscious cerebration offer the faintest suggestion as to how that element of recognition is brought about? What is that something added to the unconscious physiological trace or nerve modification that effects a conscious recognition?

Furthermore, first impressions can be localized in the past, but so can also each subsequent revival. How shall we explain, on the theory of unconscious physiological nerve registration, that the original, the primitive sense experience, as well as each subsequent revival, can be referred to as distinct psychical facts? For if the structural nerve elements are slightly modified with every revival, how shall we account for this psychical distinction of the original sense experience as well as of the modified revivals? The remembered experience leaves its own individual trace, then a trace of its being a copy of a former original impression, and also a trace of its being a member in a series of similar traces, each trace being both a copy of one another and a copy of the original impression. How this is done is a mystery.

The difficulties of the unconscious registration theory increase still more if we consider that the account of memory as usually given by psychologists is rather inadequate. Memory is the recurrence or reproduction in consciousness of a former experience. We saw a certain object yesterday, and to-day, when we happen to think of that object, we say that the image or idea is the reproduction and recognition in memory of the previous perception. This, however, is but a partial account of what actually takes place in the process of recollection. Psychologically speaking, when we remember something we have not a reproduction of some past experience, but an actual present experience with the quality of *pastness* about it. I remember the rose I saw and smelled the day before; what I have here is simply a present experience in the moment content of consciousness, and this experience is projected into the past of my subjective time. The image of the rose I have now turns out to be a rose of yesterday, and the yesterday itself is a part in the content of the present moment consciousness; in other words, my present experience is projected into my present subjective yesterday. The present image is the primary fact, and the projection of it into the past is but a secondary effect; but, then, the process is reversed——the present experience is regarded as secondary, and the secondary as primary. Subjectively considered, *memory is the reproduction of the present into the past*. It is only if regarded from an objective standpoint that memory becomes the reproduction of the past into the present. In short, in memory there is a douhle process going on: the projection of the subjective present into the subjective past, and then, again, the projection of the objective past into the objective present. This process may be graphically represented as follows:

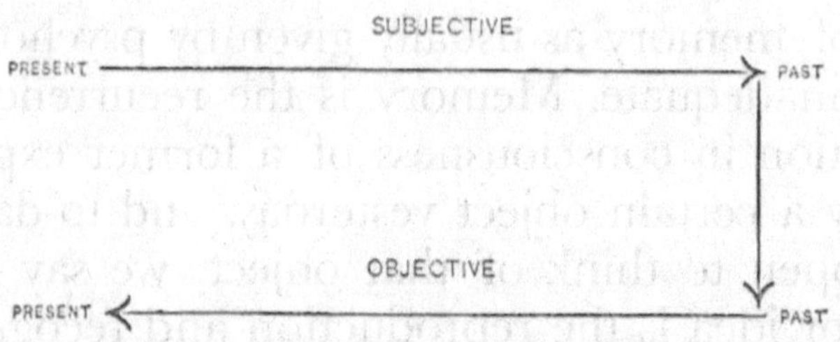

Does the physiological registration theory account for this double process? It certainly does not. If now the theory of unconscious physiological traces or nerve modifications is found inadequate to explain the most elementary act of conscious memory, can we rely upon it, when offered to us in the garb of unconscious cerebration, to account for such complex psychical phenomena as hypnotic memory?

Unconscious cerebration failing, we must fall back on the psychical interpretation of hypnosis in general, and of hypnotic memory in particular. *The subconsciousness is not an unconscious physiological automaton; it is a secondary consciousness, a secondary self.*

1. Lunatic asylum near Nancy.
2. On unconscious cerebration, see Carpenter's Mental Physiology; Ireland, The Blot upon the Brain; Laycock, Unconscious Cerebration, Journal of Mental Science, January and April, 1876; Pierce and Podmore, Subliminal Self or Unconscious Cerebration, Proc. Soc. for Psych. Res., vii, 1875.
3. Besides, post-hypnotic amnesia is rarely spontaneous; as a rule, it is induced by suggestion.
4. Unconscious Cerebration, American Journal of Psychology, November, 1892.
5. I am rather disposed to think that the answer in these cases is given not by the upper but by the lower consciousness of the subject.

3

THE DOUBLE SELF

IN the last chapter we came to the conclusion that the subconsciousness is not a mere unconscious physiological automatism, but a consciousness, a self in possession of memory, and even intelligence. Experiments and observations, however, go further to prove that this hidden intelligence may be of still higher organization; it may possess even some degree of self-consciousness, which may grow and develop. By means of the so-called method of distraction Prof. Janet entered into direct communication with the secondary self of his subject, Louise.

" Do you hear me ?" asked Prof. Janet.[1]

"*Ans*. No.

"J. But, in order to answer, one must hear." *Ans*. Certainly.

"J. Then how do you manage?

"*Ans*. I do not know.

"J. There must be somebody who hears me.

" *Ans*. Yes.

"J. Who is it ?

" *Ans.* Not Louise.

"J. Oh, some one else. Shall we call her Blanche?"

"*Ans.* Yes, Blanche.

"J. Well, then, Blanche, do you hear me?"

"*Ans.* Yes."

This name, however, had soon to be given up, as it happened to have very disagreeable associations in Louise's mind; and when Louise was shown the paper with the name Blanche, which she had unconsciously written, she was angry and wanted to tear it up. Another name had to be chosen.

"J. What name will you have?

"*Ans.* No name.

"J. You must; it will be more convenient.

"*Ans.* Well, then, Adrienne."

Now it proved that Adrienne knew of things of which Louise was entirely ignorant. Louise's special terror, which recurred in wild exclamation in her hysterical fits, was somehow connected with hidden men. She could not, however, recollect the incident. But Adrienne, when questioned, was able to describe all the details.

Louise was thrown into catalepsy; then M. Janet clinched her left hand (she began at once to strike out), put a pencil in her right hand, and said, "Adrienne, what are you doing?" The left hand continued to strike and the face to bear the look of rage, while the right hand wrote, "I am furious!" "With whom?" "With F." "Why ?" "I do not know, but I am very angry." M. Janet then unclinched the subject's left hand and put it gently to her lips. It began to blow kisses," and the face smiled. "Adrienne, are you still angry?" "No, that is over." "And now?" "Oh, I am happy." "And Louise?" "She knows nothing; she is asleep."

This case is extremely interesting as indicating at

first the lack of self-consciousness in the hypnotic sub-waking self, but acquiring it in the course of communication with the external world. Under favourable conditions the subwaking self wakes from the deep trance in which it is immersed, raises its head, becomes completely conscious, and rises at times even to the plane of personality.

When Leonie B. (a subject of M. Janet) is hypnotized her personal character undergoes a radical change. She assumes a different name, that of Leontine. Now Leontine (that is Leonie hypnotized) was told by Prof. Janet that after the trance was over and Leonie had resumed her ordinary life she, Leontine, was to take off her apron and then to tie it on again. Leonie was then awakened and conducted by Prof. Janet to the door, talking with her usual respectful gravity. Meantime her hands untied the apron and took it off. Prof. Janet called Leonie's attention to the loosened apron. "Why, my apron is coming off!" Leonie exclaimed, and with full consciousness (waking consciousness) she tied the apron on again. She then continued the talk. At Leontine's prompting the hands once more began their work, and the apron was taken off again, and again replaced, this time without Leonie's attention having been directed to the matter at all. Only then Leontine was fully satisfied and became quiet. Next day Prof. Richet hypnotized Leonie again, and presently Leontine as usual emerged. "Well," she said, "I did what you told me yesterday. How stupid the other one looked while I took off her apron! Why did you tell her that the apron was falling off? I was obliged to begin the job all over again."

Once this secondary self attains self-consciousness and gets crystallized into a new and independent personality, it now and then rises to the surface and assumes control over the current of life. he secondary personality may blame, dislike, ridicule, the primary personality. Thus Leontine calls Leonie "that stupid woman." Sometimes the secondary personality may treat the primary with great animosity, and may even threaten to destroy it. Prof. Janet received from Madame B. a very curious letter. "On the first page," he says,[2] "was a short note, written in a serious and respectful style. She was unwell, she said——worse on some days than on others——and she signed her true name, Madame B. But over the page began another in a quite different style. 'My deal' sir,' thus the letter ran, 'I must tell you that B. really makes me suffer much; she can not sleep; she spits blood; she hurts me; I am going to demolish her; she bores me; I am ill also. This is from your devoted Leontine.' "

Dr. Osgood Mason reports the following interesting case:[3] "Alma Z. has been under my observation during the past ten years. In childhood she was remarkable for her intelligence and unusual endowments. Up to her eighteenth year she was in robust health, excelling all her companions not only in intellectual attainments but also in physical culture, being expert in gymnastic exercises, skating, and athletic sports generally. At that time, owing to overwork in school, . . .peculiar psychical conditions made their appearance. Instead of the educated, thoughtful, dignified, womanly personality, worn with illness and pain, there appeared a bright, sprightly child personality, with a limited vocabulary, ungrammatical and peculiar dialect, decidedly Indian in character, but, as used by her, most fascinating and amusing. The intellect was bright and shrewd, her manner lively and good-natured, and her intuitions were remarkably correct and quick; but, strangest of all, she was free from pain, could take food, and had comparatively a good degree of strength. She called herself 'Twoey,' and the normal or usual personality she always referred to as 'No. 1.' She possessed none of the acquired knowledge of the primary personality, but was bright and greatly interested in matters going on about her in family affairs, and everything which pertained to the comfort and well-being of No. 1.

"The new personality would usually remain only a few hours, but, occasionally, her stay was prolonged to several days; and then the normal self——the No. 1 of 'Twoey'——returned with all her intelligence, patience, and womanly qualities, but also with the weakness and suffering which characterized her illness.

"No.1 and No.2 were apparently in every respect separate and distinct personalities. Each had her own distinct consciousness and distinct train of thought and memories.

"When No.1 was absent and 'Twoey' took her place, on resuming her consciousness she commenced at the place where her own personality had been interrupted and resumed her ordinary life exactly at that point. To No. 1 the existence of any second personality was entirely unknown by any conscious experience, and the time which 'Twoey' occupied was to her a blank. If 'Twoey' appeared at noon on Tuesday and remained until Thursday night, when she disappeared and No. 1 resumed her own consciousness and life, she would commence at Tuesday noon where that consciousness was interrupted. The intervening time to her was a blank. No. 2, however, while having her own distinct life, knew also the life of No. 1, but as a distinct personality, entirely separate from herself. No. 1 also came to know' Twoey' by the description given by others, and by the change in her own personal belongings and affairs which she saw had been effected during her absence. The two personalities became great friends. No. 2 admired No. 1 for her superior knowledge, her patience in suffering, and the lovely qualifies which she recognised, and she willingly took her place in order to give her rest, and, as it seemed, the possibility of living at all. No. 1 also became fond of Twoey on account of the loving care which she bestowed upon her and her affairs, and for the witty sayings and sprightly and pertinent conversations which were reported to her, and which she greatly enjoyed.

"'Twoey' seemed to have the power of going and coming at will. She often left communications to No. 1, mostly written (for she became able to write in her peculiar dialect—very difficult to decipher), telling her what had been done in her absence, where she would find certain things, or advising her when she deemed it necessary; and her advice was always sound and to the point.

"Under an entire change in medical treatment—change of scene and air and the use of animal magnetism and hypnotism—health and normal conditions were restored, and Twoey's visits became only occasional, under circumstances of extreme fatigue or mental excitement, when they were welcome to the patient and enjoyed by her friends. Two years later the patient married, and became a most admirable wife and intelligent and efficient mistress of the household.

"Later on, however, the No. 2 condition or personality began to return with greater frequency, but at length one night 'Twoey' announced that she would soon take her departure, but that another visitor would come to take her place. Presently an alarming attack of syncope occurred, lasting several hours; and when consciousness did at last return, it was represented by a third personality, entirely new and entirely distinct, both from the primary self and also from the 'Twoey' with whom we were so well acquainted. The new personality at once announced itself as 'The Boy,' and that it had come in the place of 'Twoey' for the special aid of No. 1; and for several weeks, whenever this third personality was present, all its behaviour was entirely consistent with that announcement.

"Gradually, however, she became accustomed and reconciled to her new role and new surroundings, and adapted herself with most astonishing grace to the duties of wife, mother, and mistress of the house, though always when closely questioned she persisted seriously in her original declaration that she was 'The Boy.' The personality was of much more broad and serious type than that of the frolicsome 'Twoey,' and while entirely separate in consciousness and personality from No. 1, she was much nearer to her in general outline of character. The acquired book knowledge of No. 1——the Latin, mathematics, and philosophy acquired at school——were entirely wanting in the new personality; the extensive knowledge of general literature——the whole poems of Tennyson, Browning, and Scott which No. 1 could repeat by heart, also her perfect familiarity with the most beautiful and poetic portions of the Bible——all these were entirely lacking in this personality. In a general knowledge of affairs, however, in the news of the day from all over the world, and in current literature, she at once became thoroughly interested and thoroughly intelligent, and the judgment was keen and sound.

She took the greatest delight in every kind of amusement—the theater and literary and musical entertainments—and her criticisms of performances and of books were independent, acute, and reliable. At the same time her household affairs and her interest in them and all subjects pertaining to the family were conspicuous.

"Of the preceding personalities she was fully cognizant, and had great admiration and affection for them both. She would listen to no disparaging remarks concerning 'Twoey,' and her admiration for No. 1 was unbounded. Neither 'Twoey' nor No. 3 ever seemed anxious to continue and prolong their visits, but, on the contrary, were always desirous that No. 1 should regain her health sufficiently to get on without them; and they referred with much feeling to the causes which prevented it.

"The peculiar and interesting incidents which diversified these different states of consciousness would fill a volume. No. 1, when in her condition of greatest weakness, would occasionally astonish her listeners by announcing to them some event which they bad kept profoundly secret from her. For instance: 'You need not be so quiet about it; I have seen it all. Mrs. C. died the day before yesterday. She is to be buried tomorrow'; or, 'There has been a death over in such and such a street. 'Who is it that died?' Twoey's sagacity, amounting almost to prediction, was often noticed, and many a time the neglect to be guided by her premonitions was deeply regretted. 'The Boy,' or No. 3, frequently exhibited peculiar perceptive powers. At times the sense of hearing would be entirely lost, so that the most violent noises close to her ears and when perfectly unexpected failed to startle or disturb her in the slightest degree, although usually she was easily startled by even a slight, sudden, or unexpected noise. Under these circumstances she had a peculiar faculty of perceiving what was said by watching the lips of the speaker, though ordinarily neither she nor the primitive self had any such faculty.

"In this condition she had often carried on conversations with entire strangers, and entertained guests at table without having it once suspected that all the while she could not hear a sound of any sort. I have myself seen her sit and attend to the reading of a new book simply by watching the lips of the reader, taking in every word and sentiment, and laughing heartily at the funny passages, when I am perfectly sure she could not have heard a pistol shot from her head.

"When the No. 3 personality had persisted for a considerable period—weeks, for instance, at a time, as it has sometimes done—the temporary return of No. 1 under the influence of some soothing condition or pleasing sentiment or emotion has been beautiful to witness. I saw this transformation once while sitting with her in a box at the Metropolitan Opera House. Beethoven's concerto in C Major was on the programme; in the midst of the performance I saw the expression of her countenance change; a clear, calm, softened look came into the face as she fell; back in her chair and listened to the music with the most intense enjoyment. I spoke a few words to her at the close of the number, and she replied in the soft and musical tones peculiar to her own normal condition, and I recognised without the slightest doubt the presence of No. 1. A few minutes later her eyes closed; presently she drew two or three short, quick respirations; again her countenance changed, and No. 3 was back again. She turned to me and said, 'So No. 1

came to hear her favourite concerto?' I replied, 'Yes; how did you know it?', Oh, I was here and listened to it too.' 'Where were you?' I asked. 'I sat on the front of the box. I saw you speaking to her. How greatly she enjoyed the music!' and then she went on listening to the music and commenting upon the programme in the usual discriminating manner of No. 3."

In this interesting case, communicated by Dr. Osgood Mason, we find a weakening by disease of the upper controlling personality, the subconscious self gained mastery, rose to the plane of conscious individuality and became a person, a "Twoey." The" Twoey" personality, however, seemed to have been unstable, and a new personality, that of "The Boy," emerged. Both "Twoey" and "The Boy" were but two different expressions, two different particular, individualized manifestations of the same underlying reality—the subconsciousness. It was from the depth of the subconscious self that those bubble personalities rose to the surface of conscious life.

As a rule, the stream of sub waking consciousness is broader than that of waking consciousness, so that the submerged subwaking self knows the life of the upper, primary, waking self, but the latter does not know the former. There are, however, cases on record that show that the two streams may flow in two separate channels, that the two selves may be totally ignorant of each other. The subwaking self, in attaining self-consciousness, personality, may become so much individualized as to lead a perfectly independent life from that of the waking self. And when the lower new person rises to the surface and assumes control of the current of life, he shows no signs of having once known the old master, the old person. An interesting case of this kind is given by Prof. W. James in his Psychology, and fully described by Mr. Hodgson in the Proceedings of the Society for Psychical Research for the year 1891. I quote from Prof. W. James's book:[4]

"On January 17, 1887, Rev. Ansel Bourne, of Greene, R. I., an itinerant preacher, drew five hundred and fifty-one dollars from a bank in Providence with which to pay for a certain lot of land in Greene, paid certain bills, and got into a Pawtucket horse car. This is the last incident which he remembers. He did not f return home that day: He was published in the papers as missing, and, foul play being suspected, the police sought in vain his whereabouts. On the morning of March 14th, however, at Norristown, Pa., a man calling himself A. J. Brown, who had rented a small shop six weeks previously, stocked it with stationery, confectionery, fruit, and small articles, and carried on this quaint trade without seeming to anyone unnatural or eccentric, woke up in a fright and called in the people of the house to tell him where he was. He said that his name was Ansel Bourne, that he was entirely ignorant of Norristown, that he knew nothing of shopkeeping, and that the last thing he remembered—it seemed only yesterday was drawing money from the bank in Providence. He would not believe that two months had elapsed. The people of the house thought him insane. Soon his nephew came and took him home. He had such a horror of the candy store that he refused to set foot in it again.

"The first two weeks of the period remained unaccounted for, as he had no memory, after he had resumed his normal personality, of any part of the time, and no one who knew him seems to have seen him after he left home. The remarkable part of the change is, of course, the peculiar occupation which the so-called Brown indulged in. Mr. Bourne has never in his life had the slightest contact with trade. Brown was described by the neighbours as taciturn, orderly in his habits, and in no way queer. He went to Philadelphia several times; replenished his stock; cooked for himself in the back shop, where he also slept; went regularly to church; and once at a. prayer-meeting made what was considered by the hearers a good address, in the course of which he related an incident he had witnessed in his natural state of Bourne.

"This was all that was known of the case up to June 1, 1890, when I induced Mr. Bourne to submit to hypnotism, so as to see whether in the hypnotic trance his Brown memory (Brown self-consciousness) would not come back. It did so with surprising readiness—so much so, indeed, that it *proved quite impossible to wake him while in hypnosis remember any of the facts of his normal life.* He had heard of Ansel Bourne, 'but did not know as he had ever met the man.' When confronted with Mrs. Bourne, he said that he had never seen the woman before. On the other hand, he told us of his peregrinations during the last fortnight, and gave all sorts of details during the Norristown episode. . . . I had hoped by suggestion to run the two personalities into one, and make the memories continuous, but *no artifice would avail to accomplish this, and Mr. Bourne's skull to-day still covers two distinct personal selves.*"

---

1. L'Automatisme psychologique, 129.
2. P. Janet, L' Antomatisme psychologique.
3. The Journal of Nervous and Mental Diseases, September, 1893.
4. W. James, Psychology, vol. i.

4

THE INTERRELATION OF
THE TWO SELVES

THE phenomena of abnormal states reviewed by us clearly reveal the presence of a subwaking self below the threshold of the waking self-consciousness. Turning now to a different class of phenomena, we find still further confirmation of the same truth. There is a great class of phenomena in which the subwaking self is brought to the light of day, but so as not to suppress the primary self. The two streams of consciousness run parallel to each other, the two selves coexist. The primary personality enters into direct intercourse with the risen lower, subwaking self. The phenomena I mean here are those of automatic writing.

Usually, as the automatic writer begins his practice on the planchette, the pencil brings out but mere scrawls and scratches; but as the practice continues, letters, figures, words, phrases, and even whole discourses, flow from under the automatic pencil. It takes some time before there occurs a cleavage between the subwaking self and the waking personality.

Gradually the subwaking self rouses itself from its trance, begins to bring out latent memories, starts to lisp, attempts to think coherently, gathers more intelligence and reason, attains even some degree of self-consciousness, gives itself a name, becomes at times eloquent, pouring forth fiat discourses on metaphysics and religion.

To induce the first stages of automatic writing the same conditions are requisite as those of normal suggestibility. The subject starting his first lesson in automatic writing must strongly *concentrate* his attention on some letter, figure, or word; he must *distract* his attention from what is going on in his hand; he must be in a *monotonous* environment; he must not be disturbed by a variety of incoming sense impressions; he must keep quiet, thus *limiting his voluntary movements*; *his field of consciousness must be contracted*; no other ideas but the requisite ones should be present in the mind; and if other ideas and images do enter his mind, they' must be *inhibited*. These conditions, as we know, are favourable to dissociation, disaggregation of consciousness. In the phenomena of automatic writing we have a disaggregation of consciousness——the secondary subwaking consciousness is severed from the primary, waking self-consciousness. Both selves coexist; one does not interfere with the freedom of the other. Once the cleavage is accomplished the further observance of the conditions is, of course, superfluous——the phenomena of automatic writing manifest themselves freely, the subwaking self cheerfully discourses on all sorts of subjects whenever it is in the mood, and as long as it continues its independent life.

There are, of course, different stages of cleavage. The incipient stage of automatic writing is described by Mr. P. Myers in the Proceedings of the Society for

Psychical Research.[1] The account is given by Mr. H. Arthur Smith: "I think I have observed that when my hand was on it [on the planchette], the wrist being grasped by the other hand, a word on which I concentrated my attention was written without any conscious volitional effort. I am doubtful as to this, as it is a difficult thing to be sure of the absence of volition, but such is my decided impression." The cleavage here between the two selves was faint, shadowy; nothing further occurred.

Then, again, we have the case (given by Mr. F. Myers in the Proceedings of the Society for Psychical Research, November, 1884) of Mr. A., who can write words by mere attention (fixation), without any muscular effort whatever. He fixes his mind on a word, and his hand writes it with an involuntary spasm, while he is studiously avoiding all intentional impulse.

A case of a more advanced stage of automatic writing is given in the Psychological Review for July, 1895. The subject knows beforehand what the hand is going to write, and he is not quite sure from whom the writing proceeds, whether from himself or from some "other." The cleavage is incomplete, partial.

The highest stage of cleavage, when the subwaking self gathers round its being masses of intelligence and discourses on philosophical and religious questions, may be well illustrated by a very interesting and very instructive case of automatic writing given by Prof. W. James in his Psychology:

"Some of it [automatic writing]," writes Mr. Sidney Dean to Prof. W. James, "is in hieroglyph or strange compounded arbitrary characters, each series possessing a seeming unity in general design or character, followed by what purports to be a translation or rendering into mother English. I never attempted the seemingly impossible feat of copying the characters. They were cut with the precision of a graver's tool, and generally with a single rapid stroke of the pencil. . . . When the work is in progress I am in the normal condition, and seemingly two minds, intelligences, persons, are practically engaged. The writing is in my own hand, but the dictation not of *my own mind and will*, but that of another, upon subjects of which I can have no knowledge, and hardly a theory; and I myself consciously criticise the thought, fact, mode of expressing it, etc., while the hand is recording the subject-matter, and even the words impressed to be written. . . .

"Sentences are commenced without knowledge of mine as to their subject or ending.

"There is in progress now at uncertain times, not subject to my will, a series of twenty-four chapters upon the scientific features of life, moral, spiritual, eternal. Seven have already been written in the manner indicated. These were preceded by twenty-four chapters relating generally to the life beyond material death, its characteristics, etc. Each chapter is signed by the name of some person who has lived on earth, some with whom I have been personally acquainted, others known in history. . . . I know nothing of the alleged authorship of any chapter until it is completed and the name impressed and appended. I am interested not only in the reputed authorship—of which I have nothing corroborative—in the philosophy, thought, of which I was in ignorance until these chapters appeared. It is an intelligent ego that writes, or else the influence assumes individuality, which practically makes the influence a personality. It is not myself; of that I am conscious at every step of the process."

When the cleavage of the two selves from each other occurs, and the subwaking self begins to express himself and gets into possession of some organ which was before under the control of the waking personality, this organ becomes anæsthetic. The upper waking self does not get any more the peripheral sense impressions coming from that organ. It is now the subwaking self who possesses himself of these sense impressions and becomes conscious of them. The secondary self may extend its range of activity in its intercourse with the external world; it may go on enriching itself with the spoils got by plundering the waking self. Amaurosis, hysterical anæsthesia, and analgesia are facts in point. Anæsthesia is found not only in hysteria, but also in such cases in which the cleavage is but transitory, and the possession of the organ into which the subwaking self comes is but momentary. Such anæsthesia is, of course, fugitive, and lasts only as long as the organ is possessed or possessed by the subwaking self. Prof. W. James beautifully demonstrated this truth in the case of automatic writing:[2]

"William L. Smith, student at the Massachusetts Institute of Technology, aged twenty-one, perfectly healthy and exceptionally intelligent, ...sat with Hodgson and myself, January 24, 1889, with his right hand extended on the instrument [planchette], and his face averted and buried in the hollow of his left arm, which lay along the table. Care was taken not to suggest to him the aim of the inquiry (i. e., to test for anæsthesia induced in healthy subjects by the mere act of automatic writing).

"The planchette began by illegible scrawling. After ten minutes I pricked the back of the right hand several times with a pin; no indication of feeling. Two pricks on the left hand were followed by withdrawal, and the question, 'What did you do that for?' to which I replied, 'To find whether you were going to sleep.' The first legible words which were written after this were, 'You hurt me.' . . . After some more or less illegible writing I pricked the right wrist and fingers several times again quite severely, with no sign of re-action on S.'s part. After an interval, however, the pencil wrote, 'Don't you prick me any more.' S. then said, 'My right hand is pretty well asleep.' I tested the two hands immediately by pinching and pricking, but found no difference between them, both apparently normal. S. then said that what he meant by 'asleep' was the feeling of 'pins and needles' which an insen-sible limb has when 'waking up.'

"The last written sentence was then deciphered aloud. S. laughed, having become conscious only of the pricks on his left hand, and said, 'It is working those two pin pricks for all they are worth.' I then asked,

"'What have I been excited about to-day?"

"'May be correct, do not know, possibly sleeping.'

"'What do you mean by sleeping?'

"'I do not know. You ↓ (the subject's right hand made this figure evidently to indicate pricking) me 19, and think I'll write for you.'"

We find here local anæsthesia induced in the hand possessed or obsessed temporarily by the subpersonal self. And when, on a later day, the pencil was placed in the left hand instead of the right, the left hand took up the memories of the right hand's previous pains. No wonder the memory was the same, for it was the same subwaking self possessed or obsessed of dif-ferent organs. The last experiment may be regarded as an *experimentum crusis* of the significant truth that what the subwaking self obsesses of that the waking self is deprived. The latter may, however, be informed of the particular experience by reading the automatic writing, or by gazing into a crystal. Once the cleavage occurred, we may say that, as a rule, *the growth, the development of the individualized subwaking self is in inverse ratio to that of the waking consciousness.*

---

1. November, 1884.
2. Proceedings of the American Society for Psychological Research, vol. i.

5

SUBCONSCIOUS SENSE-PERCEPTION IN THE WAKING STATE

THUS far we have dealt with such uncanny abnormal states as hysteria, hypnosis, automatism. We saw in them the manifestation of the split-off secondary self, and we also hinted at the relation the latter bears to the waking self.

Is there any direct evidence of the presence of the subwaking self in the normal state of perfectly healthy individuals? Yes, there is, and very strong evidence, too. Once more I turn to hypnosis, but this time not as showing the cleavage that occurs in that state, but rather as pointing out the *plane* of cleavage, the presence of a subwaking self when the individual *is in his normal state*.

The subwaking hypnotic self surpasses the waking self in its sensitiveness; its range of sensibility extends farther than that of the upper personality. The senses of touch, pressure, and temperature are much more delicate in the hypnotic condition. The æsthesiometer showed in Mr. J. F., one of my subjects, when in normal state, the sensibility of the skin on the forehead to be eighteen millimetres, while the same in hypnosis (slight degree) was but fourteen millimetres. The sensibility of Mr. A. F. in normal state was fourteen millimetres, while in hypnosis (falls into the deepest state) it was eight millimetres. Mr. D. W. showed a sensibility in the normal state fourteen millimetres, but when in hypnosis (falls into the deepest state) it was eight millimetres.

"It is quite certain," writes Braid,[1] "that some patients can tell the shape of what is held an inch and a half from the skin on the back of the neck, crown of the head, arm, or hand, or other parts of the body, the extremely exalted sensibility of the skin enabling them to discern the shape of the object so presented from its tendency to emit or absorb caloric. . . . A patient could feel and obey the motion of a glass funnel passed through the air at a distance of fifteen feet."

The entranced subject is able to walk freely about the room with bandaged eyes or in absolute darkness without striking against anything, because, as Moll, Braid, Poirault, and Drjevetzky point out, he recognises objects by the resistance of the air and by the alteration of temperature.

We find in the hypnotic subject hyperæsthesia, of vision, of hearing, and of smell.

One can not help being struck by the great acuteness of the sense of healing in hypnotic trance. To give an example. While Mr. W. was in a state of hypnosis Mr. G. whispered in my ear, "Six o'clock." I scarcely could hear the whisper. I then turned to Mr. W. and asked him whether he heard what Mr. G. said. "Yes," he answered, "Mr. G. said 'Six o'clock.'"

To prove visual hyperæsthesia in my subject, A. F., I gave him a book to read while he was in hypnotic trance and his eyes were closed. "Read!" I commanded. "I can not," he answered. " Yes, you can; you must read. Try!" He began to read. So miraculous seemed this experiment that one of the gentlemen present exclaimed, "Now I believe in hypnotism." The fact, however, really was that Mr. A. F. raised his eyelids, but so slightly, so imperceptibly, that no one of the people present could notice it, and even I myself am not quite sure I saw it clearly; I only suspected it was so. However the case might have been, it was altogether impossible for anyone in his normal state to read under similar conditions of closure of the eyelids.

An extraordinary example of visual hyperæsthesia is brought by Bergson, whose subject could read the image of a page reflected in the experimenter's cornea. The same subject could discriminate with the naked eye details in a microscopic preparation. "The ordinary test of visual hyperacuteness[2] in hypnotism," writes Prof. W. James, "is the favourite trick of giving a subject the hallucination of a picture on a blank sheet of cardboard and then mixing the latter with a lot of similar sheets. The subject will always find the picture on the original sheet again and recognise infallibly if it has been turned over or upside down, although the bystanders have to resort to artifice to identify it again. The subject notes peculiarities on the card too small for waking observation to detect." The experiment may be made in a far simpler manner: A blank sheet of cardboard is given to the subject, and instead of giving him a hallucination, a thing not very easy to do with many subjects, as they often do not realize the suggested hallucination, the subject is simply asked to take good notice of the card. The card is then mixed with other similar sheets. The subject in variably picks out the sheet shown to him. I have repeatedly made these experiments on my subjects.

The same holds true in the case of smell. There is an exaltation of this sense in hypnosis. Braid's subject restored articles to the rightful owners, finding the latter out by mere smell. "They [the subjects]," writes Braid,[3] "began sniffing, and traced out the parties robbed and restored it [the article] to them. On being asked, 'How do you know the person?' the answer was, 'I smell them [or him].' Every time the experiment was tried the result was the same and the answer the same."

Carpenter, in his Mental Physiology, tells of a youth who in hypnosis could find out by the sense of smell the owner of a glove which was placed in his hand from among a party of more than sixty persons, scenting at each of them, one after the other, until he came to the right individual. In another case the owner of a ring was unhesitatingly found from among a company of twelve, the ring having been withdrawn before the somnambule was introduced."

In short, the range of sensibility of the hypnotic subwaking consciousness is wider than that of the waking self.

Now, if this subpersonal, subwaking hypnotic self is present in the normal state, we ought to find that sensory impressions, which on account of their faintness or indistinctness did not reach the waking self, were still perceived by the subwaking self. With this view in hand I made the following experiment:

I placed Mr. L. and Mr. P. at such a distance that they could not hear my whisper. Although Mr. L. is an intimate friend of mine, on whose honesty I can fully rely, still, for the sake of having the experiment carried out in a rigorous fashion, I placed near him

Mr. P., whose ear was far more acute than that of Mr. L., in order to testify that nothing could be heard at such a distance. I then whispered in the ear of Mr. G. the following words: "The Subliminal Consciousness, by Mr. Myers." I repeated this phrase five times in succession in the same whisper, asking each time of Mr. L. and Mr. P. whether they had heard anything. The reply was "No; nothing." They strained their ears, but could not perceive any words except an indistinct whisper. I then hypnotized Mr. L., who fell into a slight hypnosis (Mr. P. could not be hypnotized; it was the first seance in which he took part), and asked him to tell what he bad heard. "I did not hear anything." "Try hard, and you will be able to tell," I commanded him. " I heard only a certain rhythm in your whisper, and that was all." "Well, then, guess! "I can not." "But you must!" "I think you said, My——" "What more? Go on!" I urged him. "I think you said 'consciousness.'" "Go on!" "I think you said 'sub.'"

"Several friends," writes Max Dessoir, "were in my room, one of whom, Mr. W., was reading to himself, while the rest of us were talking with one another. Some one happening to mention the name of Mr. X., in whom Mr. W. is much interested, Mr. W. raised his head and asked, 'What was that about Mr. X.?' He knew nothing he told us about our previous conversation; he had only heard the familiar name, as often happens. I then hypnotized him, with his consent, and when he was pretty deeply entranced I asked him again as to the conversation. To our great astonishment, he now repeated to us the substance of our whole conversation during the time that he was reading to himself."

Similar experiments I performed on A. Fingold. The subject, when in the state of hypnosis, gave me details of a conversation which he could not have possibly overheard *consciously*, and of which be knew nothing at all in his previous waking state.

The sub waking self, not being occupied with the work that engaged the attention of the upper consciousness, was on the alert, and listened to the conversation, which escaped the fixed and distracted attention of the waking personality.

It is clear, then, that the subwaking hypnotic self is present in the normal state and call hear and guess that of which the waking self has no inkling.

---

1. Braid, Neurypnology.
2. James, Psychology, vol. ii.
3. Braid, Neurypnology.

6

THE SUBCONSCIOUS SELF
AND HALLUCINATIONS

URNING now to the interesting phenomena of crystal-gazing we meet with facts of like nature proving the same truth.

"I find in the crystal," writes a crystal-gazer,[1] "a bit of dark wall covered with jessamine, and I ask my-self, Where have I walked to-day? I have no recollection of such a sight——not a common one in the London streets; but to-morrow I repeat my walk of this morning, with a careful regard for the creeper-covered walls. To-morrow solves the mystery. I find the very spot, and the sight brings with it the further recollection that at the moment we passed the spot I was engaged in absorbing conversation with my companion, and my voluntary attention was preoccupied.

"On March 9 I saw in the crystal a rocky coast, a rough sea, an expanse of sand in the foreground. As I watched, the picture was nearly effaced by that of a mouse. . . .Two days later I was reading a volume of poetry which I remembered having cut open, talking the while, certainly not consciously reading. As I turned over the leaves a couple of lines struck me:

Only the sea intoning,
Only the wainscot mouse."

The same automatic writer looked in the crystal and saw a newspaper announcement. It reported the death of a lady at one time a very frequent visitor in my circle and very intimate with some of my nearest friends; an announcement, therefore, which, had I consciously seen it, would have interested me considerably. I related my vision at breakfast, quoting name, date, place, and an allusion to 'a long period of suffering' borne by the deceased lady, and added that I was sure that I had not heard any report of her illness, or even for some months any mention of her likely to suggest such an hallucination. I was, however, aware that I had the day before taken the first sheet of the Times, but was interrupted before I had consciously read any announcement of death. Mrs. H. Sidgwick immediately sought for the paper, when we discovered the paragraph almost exactly as I had seen it."

In his article, Some Experiments in Crystal Vision, Prof. James II. Hyslop, of Columbia College,[2] reports the case of Mrs. D., "who used to have a visual hallucination (in the crystal) of a bright-blue sky overhead, a garden with a high-walled fence, and a peculiar chain pump in the garden situated at the back of a house. She attached no significance to it, but took it for one of the many automatisms in her experience which were without assignable meaning to her. But two summers ago she had gone west, to her old home in D., Ohio, and made the acquaintance of a lady whom she had never known before, and by chance was invited to take tea with her one evening. She went, and after tea remarked that she would like to have a drink of water. The lady of the house remarked: 'All right; let us go out into the garden and get a fresh drink from the well.' They went, and, behold, there was the identical blue sky, high fence, and chain pump which she had so often seen in her vision! After going home in the evening Mrs. D. told her mother of her experience, remarking how strange it was. Her mother replied that when Mrs. D. was a little girl about two or three years old she used to visit this house very frequently with her mother."

Prof. James relates the case of a Cambridge lady who happened to misplace a valuable set of silver knives. She searched everywhere, but could not discover its whereabouts. Having heard of crystal-gazing, the lady thought she might as well try it. She procured a crystal and looked into it for a few minutes. Something appeared at the bottom of the crystal; gradually the image took the shape of a box with straight objects lying in it diagonally. The image had the following shape:

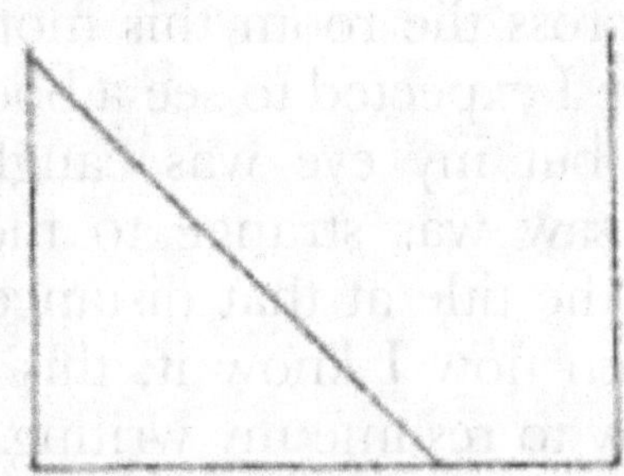

Presently she found herself taking a chair, mounting it, and reaching out her hand for a top closet. There was the realization of her visual hallucination——here was the box, and inside it the set of knives placed *diagonally*.

"I saw in the crystal," writes another crystal-gazer,[3] "a young girl, an intimate friend, waving to me from her carriage. I observed that her hair, which had hung down her back when I last saw her, was now put up in young-lady fashion. Most certainly I had not consciously seen even the carriage. Next day I called on my friend, was reproached by her for not observing her as she passed, and perceived that she had altered her hair in the way which the crystal had shown.

"I was writing at an open window and became aware that an elderly relative inside the room had said something to me; but the noise of the street prevented my asking what had been said. My ink began to run low, and I took up the inkstand to tip it. Looking into the ink I saw a white florist's parcel as though reflected on its surface. Going into another room, I there found the parcel in question, of which I had had no knowledge. I returned carrying it, and was greeted with the remark: 'I told you half an hour ago to attend to those flowers; they will all be dead.'

"I looked across the room this morning to a distant table, where I expected to see a book I wanted. It was not there, but my eye was caught by another book, which I saw was strange to me. I tried, but could not read the title at that distance (I have since proved that, even now I know it, this is impossible), and turned away to resume my writing. On my blank paper, as in a crystal scene, I read 'The Valley of Lilies,' which I found to be the title of the book. I have no recollection of ever seeing the book before."

The phenomena of shell-hearing belong to the same class of facts with those of crystal-gazing. The shell often reports to its listener facts and conversations that have escaped the latter's attention. "The shell," writes a shell-hearer, "is more likely after a dinner party to repeat the conversation of my neighbour on the right than that of my lawful interlocutor on the left."[4]

Now all these facts of crystal-gazing and shell-hearing clearly reveal the presence of a secondary, submerged, hyperæsthetic consciousness that sees, hears, and perceives what lies outside the range of perception of the primary personal self.

---

1. Proceedings of the Society for Psychical Research, May, 1889.
2. Proceedings of the Society for Psychical Research, December, 1896.
3. Myers, The Subliminal Self, Proceedings of the Society for Psychical Research, vol. viii.
4. Myers, The Subliminal Consciousness, Proceedings of the Society for Psychical Research, vol. viii.

7

THE SUBWAKING SELF AND
THE NORMAL INDIVIDUAL

THE subwaking self gets manifested in automatic writing, crystal-gazing, and hypnosis, but these phenomena do not occur in everyone. To prove, therefore, fully our proposition that the secondary self is part and parcel of our normal state, we must .make experiments on perfectly healthy and normal subjects who never dealt in crystal-gazing, shell-hearing, automatic writing, nor were they ever put into the state of hypnosis. I made three thousand laboratory experiments, eight hundred of which I made on myself and two thousand two hundred on fifty subjects, and the results gave direct and conclusive proof of the presence of the subwaking, subpersonal, hyperæsthetic self in our normal state. Since the results of my experiments tell us of the subwaking consciousness something more than its mere bare presence, I reserve the account of them for the next chapter, where the discussion of them will be more appropriate. Meanwhile the experiments of Binet will fully suffice for our present purpose. Binet set himself the task to find out "whether the phenomena of the duplication of consciousness are to be met with in healthy, non-hysterical individuals," or, in other words, whether there can be detected the presence of another self in perfectly healthy and normal subjects. He conducted the experiments in the following way:

"I requested my subjects," says Binet,[1] "to whom, of course, no explanation was given of what was going to be done, to seat themselves before a table and leave their right hands to me, while I gave them something interesting to read. One of the experiments it appeared to me easiest to effect was that of the repetition of passive movements. A pencil being placed in the hand of the subject, who was attentively reading a journal, I made the hand trace a uniform movement, choosing that which it executes with most facility—for example, shadings, or curls, or little dots. Having communicated these movements for some minutes, I left the hand to itself quite gently; the hand continued the movement a little. After three or four experiments the repetition of the movement became more perfect, and with Mlle.g. at the fourth sitting the repetition was so distinct that the hand traced as many as eighty curls without stopping." Furthermore, there was a rudimentary memory of the movements imparted. "When the hand had been successfully habituated to repeating a certain kind of movement—for example, curls—it was to this kind of movement that it had a tendency to return. If it was made to trace the figure a hundred times and was afterward left to itself, the stroke of the figure became rapidly modified, and turned into a curl." This subwaking self, like a child, learned to use the hand and to write, and showed that it remembered what it once learned, and that it was easier for it to perform the acts once acquired.

"When any kind of movement had been well repeated it could be reproduced without solicitation every time a pen was put in the subject's hand and she fixed her attention on reading. But if the subject thought attentively of her hand the movement stopped.

"With a slight pressure I was able to make the hand go obediently in all directions, carrying the pen with it. This is not a simple mechanical compulsion, for a very feeble and very short contact is sufficient to bring a very long movement of the hand. The phenomena, I believe, can be approximated to a rudimentary suggestion by the sense of touch. Nothing is more curious than to see the hand of a person who is awake and thinks she is in full possession of herself implicitly obey the experimenter's orders."

Thus we find that by distracting the attention of the waking self we may gain access to the subwaking self of the normal individual and teach it to use the bodily organs which we place at its disposal to express itself. It can not attain, however, to any degree of efficiency, because the disaggregation effected is but slight and transitory——the controlling consciousness is wide awake. Meanwhile, during the time the secondary self takes its exercises in writing slight anæsthesia supervenes. Pain is not as well perceived, the æsthesiometer shows diminished sensibility.

Furthermore, Binet finds that "the more the subject is distracted (by reading, mental calculation, etc.) the more irregular become the voluntary movements of the hand, and if the distraction is very intense these movements may cease completely. On the contrary, the more distracted the subject is, the more *reg-*

ular and considerable become the automatic movements of the hand. The contrast is striking." Here once more we strike upon the truth, and this time in the case of perfectly normal people, that the growth and expansion of the subwaking consciousness is in inverse ratio to that of the waking self-consciousness.

However the case may be with this last proposition, one central truth remains firm, valid, unshaken, and that is the presence of a subpersonal self in normal life.

The results of laboratory experiments on perfectly healthy people in their normal waking state, the phenomena of hypnosis, of automatic writing, of crystalgazing, and of shell-hearing—all go to form a strong, irrefragable chain of evidence in support of the truth that behind the primary self a secondary consciousness lies hidden.

---

1. A. Binet, On Double Consciousness. *Vide* Binet, On Double Consciousness in Health, Mind, vol. xv.

8

THE INTERCOMMUNICATION OF THE TWO SELVES

THE two selves in normal man are so co-ordinated that they blend into one. For all practical purposes a unity, the conscious individual is still a duality. The self-conscious personality, although apparently blended with the subwaking self, is still not of the latter. The life of the waking self-consciousness flows within the larger life of the subwaking self like a warm equatorial current within the cold bosom of the ocean. The swiftly coursing current and the deep ocean seem to form one body, but they really do not. The one is the bed in which the other circulates. The two do not mingle their waters; and still, separate and different as the two are, they nevertheless intercommunicate. The warmth of the Gulf Stream is conducted to the ocean, and the agitation of the ocean is transmitted to the Gulf Stream. So is it with the two selves. Apparently one, they are, in fact, two——the warm stream of waking self-consciousness does not mingle its intelligence with that of the subwaking self. But though flowing apart, they still intercommunicate. Messages come from the one to the other; and since the range of sensibility—life—is wider and deeper in the case of the subwaking self, the messages, as a rule, come not from the waking to the subwaking, but, on the contrary, from the sub waking or secondary to the waking or primary self. The two streams of consciousness and their intercommunication may be represented thus:

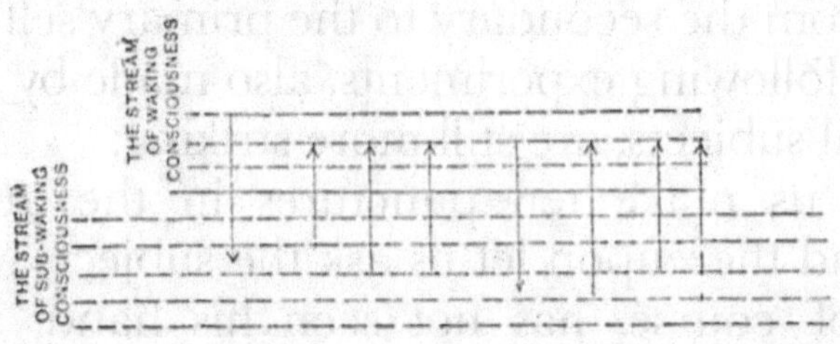

We find such messages in the case of hysteria. Ask the hysterical patient to think of a number, and if he holds a pen or a pencil in the anæsthetic hand he will write down the number, or if he has a dynamometer in his hand he will press distinctly as many times as there are units in the number, not being aware of what he is doing. In these cases the message is transmitted from the primary to the secondary self.

"L., an hysterical patient totally anæsthetic," says Binet,[1] "gazed fixedly at a blue cross; the position and arrangement of the cross by simultaneous contrast caused the production of a yellow colour about the cross. During this time the right hand, into which, without the patient's knowledge, a pen had been slipped, did not cease to write, 'Blue, yellow, blue, yellow, etc.'" Here once more we have the message transmitted from the primary to the secondary self.

On the other hand, "let us seize the anæsthetic hand," says Binet, " and let us cause it to trace behind a screen the word 'Paris.' We know that this word will be repeated several times. Then, upon addressing ourselves to the principal subject (that is, to the waking self-consciousness) we will ask him to write the word 'London.' The subject, entirely ignorant of what has just taken place, eagerly seizes the pen with the intention to carry out our wish, but to his utter astonishment the indocile pen, instead of writing 'London,' writes 'Paris.' "Here we have a motor message transmitted from the secondary to the primary self.

The following experiments, also made by Binet on hysterical subjects, are still more striking:

"Let us make ten punctures in the anæsthetic hand, and thereupon let us ask the subject, who, as a matter of course, has not seen his hand, which is hidden behind a screen, to think of some number and to name it; frequently the subject will answer that he is thinking of the number ten. In the same manner let us put a key, a coin, a needle, a watch, into the anæsthetic hand, and let us ask the subject to think of any object whatsoever; it will very often happen that the subject is thinking of the precise object that has been put into his insensible hand."

If we turn to hypnosis, we find again the frequent occurrence of such messages.

I hypnotized Mr. A. F., and told him two stories; then I suggested to him that when he wakes up he shall remember nothing at all of what I had told him——that is, the memory shall remain only in possession of the subwaking self. I then awakened him. My friends who were present at the *séance* asked him if he knew what I told him. He was surprised at the question; he could not remember anything. A few minutes later I went up to him, put my hand on his brow, and said: "You can remember now everything that passed during hypnosis. Try hard; you can!" He thought some time, and at once, as if he received sudden information, told us the two stories in detail. Another time I made him pass through a' series of actions, again giving the suggestion of oblivion, and again with the same results. He thought he slept deeply for about half an hour. As soon as I put my hand to his forehead the subwaking self sent at once a despatch of the detained information to the waking consciousness. Once I made Mr. A. F. pass through a series of scenes and different complicated events of life. The suggestion of oblivion was again enforced. When he was awakened he remarked that he slept very long——for about an hour and a half; he could not remember anything. I put my hand to his brow, gave the suggestion of recollection, and the hypnotic self at once sent up the intelligence.

Now, if the hyperæsthetic, subwaking self and the waking self-consciousness, their interrelations and intercommunications, subsist also in normal life, as they most certainly do in the states of hypnosis, automatic writing, and crystal-gazing——if they subsist, I say, also in the life of every man, we ought to find it out by experiments. We ought to find that sensory impressions that lie outside the range of sensibility of the waking self, but within the range of the subwaking self, that such sensory impressions will still be transmitted to the primary self. The guesses of the subject must rise far above the dead level of chance——probability. And such is actually the case.

The first set of experiments I made on myself. My right eye is amblyopic; it sees very imperfectly; for it, things are enshrouded in a mist. When the left eye is closed and a book is opened before me I am unable to tell letter from figure; I see only dots, rows of them, all indistinct, hazy, oscillating, appearing and disappearing from my field of vision. When a single letter or figure is presented to my right eye, I see only a black dot, as a kernel surrounded by a film of mist.

I asked Mr. B. to make twenty-five slips and write down on each slip four characters—letters, figures, or both—in different combinations, but so that in all the twenty-five slips the number of letters should equal the number of figures. When a slip was presented to my right eye, the other being closed, I had to guess which of the characters was letter and which was figure. When the first series of twenty-five was ended the slips were shuffled, and a second series began. Later on, the same slips were used for two more series. I made two groups of experiments with two series in each group. Each series consisted of a hundred experiments, so that there were four hundred experiments in all.

In this class of experiments, named Class A, the results are as follows:

In the first series of the first group, out of one hundred characters sixty-eight were correctly guessed. Since there were only two guesses—letter or figure—fifty per cent must be subtracted, as so much might have been due to mere chance (we shall find, however, from our other experiments that the percentage subtracted is too high); eighteen per cent thus remains in favour of messages coming from the secondary self—in other words, eighteen per cent is left in favour of secondary sight.

In the second series of the first group, out of one hundred characters seventy-two were guessed aright; here again we must subtract fifty per cent which might have been due to chance; thus twenty-two per cent remains in favour of secondary sight.

In the first series of the second group, seventy characters were guessed out of one hundred shown; subtracting fifty, we have twenty per cent in favour of secondary sight.

In the second series of the second group, out of one hundred characters shown seventy-six were guessed rightly; subtracting fifty, we have twenty-six per cent in favour of secondary sight.

Out of four hundred experiments made, the general character was guessed two hundred and eighty-six times, which gives 11.5 per cent; subtracting fifty per cent, we have 21.5 per cent in favour of secondary sight.

Figures often speak more eloquently, more convincingly, than volumes. The results of the correct answers as to the general nature of the character due to secondary sight arc far below the actual one, for in subtracting fifty per cent we subtracted too much, as our experiments will show farther on; still they were so striking that I communicated them to Prof. James, and he was kind enough to encourage me in my work, and advised me to pursue the inquiry further in the same direction.

The experiments were now somewhat modified. Five different letters, and as many different figures, were chosen. The letters were A, B, E, N, T; the figures, 2, 4, 5, 7, 9. Each capital or figure was written on a separate card. I knew the characters, and had to guess none but these. I had not to name merely letter or figure, thus having only two guesses, as the case was in the experiments of Class A, but I had to name one of the ten characters shown; in short, I had always to give the particular name. Now here each guess could either be general, or both particular and general, or fail altogether. When I took letter as letter, or figure as figure, but gave the wrong name—for instance, I took 5 for 7, or E for N—I guessed rightly the general nature only of the character shown. When I gave the correct name, I guessed, of course, both the particular and the general nature. When, however, I mistook a letter for a figure or a figure for a letter, I failed, and failed completely. As the series of ten was finished the cards were shuffled and a new series was started. But few experiments were made at a time, as I had to keep my left eye closed, and looked only with my right eye, which soon became extremely fatigued.

These experiments, named Class B, give the following results:

Out of four hundred experiments made, the general character was guessed correctly two hundred and seventy-three times, of which the particular character was guessed correctly one hundred and eighty-eight times.

The remarkable success of these last experiments led me to try the same on people with normal vision. The experiments were carried on in the following way: Ten cards were taken; on each one was put down in faint outlines a small capital or figure, the number of figures being equal to that of the letters, so that there were five cards with a different letter on each, and again five cards with a different figure on each. The subject in these experiments was put at such a distance that the character was outside his range of vision; he saw nothing but a mere dot, blurred, and often disappearing altogether. The subject was told that there were ten cards in the pack, that the number of letter cards was equal to that of the figure cards, but he was not told thc particular names of the characters. Each time a card was shown the subject had to give some particular name of character he took that dot to be. "They are all alike, mere blurred dots," complained the subjects. "No matter," I answered; "just give any letter or figure that rises in your mind on seeing that dot."

The number of subjects was eight. I worked with each separately, giving five rounds to each subject, making the number of experiments fifty, and four hundred in all.

In this class of experiments, named Class C, the results are as follows:

Out of four hundred experiments two hundred and fifty-five correct guesses were as to general character, of which ninety-two were also correct as to the particular character.

In the last experiments of Class C the characters were written in print; still I could not succeed to have the letters well formed: the characters were not made of exactly the same thickness and size. I therefore made other sets of experiments, and this time with twenty quite different subjects. I took ten cards and pasted on them letters and numerals of the same size. Each card had a different letter or figure of the following size: **K**

The number of figure cards being equal to that of letter cards (five figure cards and five letter cards), I told the subject that I had a series of ten cards, a letter or a numeral on each, and that the number of figure cards equalled that of the letter cards, but I did not tell him the particular names of the characters.

I worked with each subject separately, making only two series with ten experiments in each. The subject was placed at such a distance from the card that the character shown was far out of his range of vision. He saw nothing but a dim, blurred spot or dot.

The subject had to name some character which that particular dot shown might possibly be. "It is nothing but mere guess," commented the subjects.

At the end of the first series the cards were shuffled and the second series was given. Each subject Raw the same card but twice. The number of the subjects being twenty, all the first series form a group of two hundred experiments, and so do the second series.

The results in Class D are as follows:

In the first group, out of two hundred characters, one hundred and thirty were guessed as to their general character, of which the particular gave forty-nine.

In the second group, out of two hundred, one hundred and forty were of a general character, of which the particular was fifty-four.

I then made with the same number of subjects another set of experiments that should correspond to Class B, made on myself——namely, to tell the subjects the particular characters used, which were:

Letters. . . . . B, Z, K, U, H.
Figures. . . . . 2, 4, 5, 7, 9.

The characters were all of the same size, printed, and the letters were all capitals. The subject had to name only one of these characters. Only two series of ten each were made with each subject, thus giving two groups of two hundred experiments each.

The results in Class E are as follows :

In the first group, out of two hundred characters, one hundred and forty were guessed correctly as to their general character, of which sixty-eight were correct particular guesses.

In the second group, out of two hundred, one hundred and fifty-one were guessed correctly as to the general character, of which seventy-one were particular guesses.

As I remarked above, the subjects often complained that they could not see anything at all; that even the black, blurred, dim spot often disappeared from their field of vision; that it was mere "guessing"; that they might as well shut their eyes and guess. How surprised were they when, after the experiments were over, I showed the how many characters they guessed correctly in a general way, and how many times they gave the full name of the particular character shown!

Now all these experiments tend to prove the presence within us of a secondary subwaking self that perceives things which the primary waking self is unable to get at. The experiments indicate the interrelation of the two selves. They show that messages are sent up by the secondary to the primary self.

Furthermore, the results seem to show that, in case the particular message fails, some *abstract general account* of it still reaches the upper consciousness. An inhibited particular idea still reaches the primary self as an abstract idea. *An abstract general idea in the consciousness of the waking self has a particular idea as its basis in the subwaking self.*

The great contention of nominalism and conceptualism over the nature of abstract general ideas thus may find here its solution. The conceptualists are no doubt right in asserting that a general abstract idea may exist in consciousness apart from the particular idea or perception perceived, but they do not say that this consciousness is that of the waking self. The nominalists, again, are right in asserting that a general abstract idea or concept has a particular idea or percept as its basis; but they do not add that this percept may be totally absent from the waking consciousness and only present in the subwaking consciousness. *No general abstract idea without some particular percept as basis.*

To return, however, to my work in hand. While the above-mentioned experiments on secondary sight were under way another set of experiments was carried out by me, the purpose of which was to tap directly the suggestibility of the secondary self, and to find out the influence the subconscious has on the primary consciousness.

The mechanism of the experiments was as follows:

On slips of paper I made a series of complicated drawings. Each slip had a different pattern. The subject had to look at the pattern of the drawing for ten seconds, and then the slip was withdrawn and he had to reproduce the drawing from memory—a task extremely difficult. It took him about fifteen seconds and more before he could make anything bearing the slightest resemblance to the drawing shown. When he finished the drawing an elongated cardboard with eight digits pasted in a row was shown to him and the subject had to choose whichever digit he pleased. Now, on the margin of each slip was written a digit contained in the number of digits on the cardboard from which the subject had to choose. The subject, not having the slightest suspicion of the real purpose of the experiment, being *perfectly sure* that the whole matter was concerning imitation of the drawings, and being assured by me that the choosing of the digits on the cardboard was nothing but a device "*to break up the attention*" in passing from one drawing to another, and being besides intensely absorbed in the contemplation and reproduction of the drawing, which was extremely complicated——the subject, I say, wholly disregarded the figure on the margin——he did not even notice it. I so fully succeeded in allaying all suspicions and distracting the attention of the subjects that when Prof. James interrogated one of them, an intelligent man, he was amazed at the latter's complete ignorance as to what was actually going on.

The purpose of these experiments, as I slid, was to address myself directly to the subwaking consciousness, and to see whether it sent up suggestion-messages to the primary consciousness, which by the very mechanism of the experiments was thrown off its guard. In the previous suggestion-experiments, in spite of all precautions taken, the subject was more or less conscious of what was going on. I could not completely banish all suspicions, and success, therefore, could only be assured by the many conditions favourable to normal suggestibility, and especially that of *immediate execution*, so that no time was given to the upper self to inhibit the carrying out of the suggestion. In the present experiments, on the other hand, the suggestion was addressed *directly* (of course, as far as this was possible in the normal waking state) to the subwaking self. The upper primary self, being completely absorbed with the drawing, did not notice the figure, or, if he did, he soon learned to disregard it, because he thought it insignificant, and because it would only distract his attention. But although the figure was not noticed and fully disregarded (a fact I was careful to find out from the subjects in an indirect way), it still impressed the sense organ, reached the secondary self, which took it as a suggestion, sending it up as a message to the primary self or personality and influencing the latter's choice.

This choice suggestion is strikingly analogous to post-hypnotic suggestion. I hypnotized, for example, Mr. J. F., and told him that ten minutes after awakening he will put out the gas. He was awakened, and ten minutes later he put out the gas. On my asking him why he did it, he answered he did not know why, but somehow the idea came into his mind, and he enacted it and did put out the gas. The post-hypnotic suggestion rises up from the depths of the secondary self as a fixed, insistent idea. A similar state of mind it was of interest to find in the case of the subjects in the present experiment; under consideration. The suggestion given was to be carried out only after the imitation of the drawing—that is, some fifteen, twenty, or twenty-five seconds later. Now, when the suggestion was eight, and the subjects chose eight, they very often told me that they did not know why, but that number came at once into their mind on being presented with the cardboard of figures. We have not to wonder at it, for the same psychical elements are here at work as in the state of post-hypnosis. In hypnosis the suggestion is taken up by the secondary, subwaking, suggestible self, and then afterward this suggestion breaks through the stream of the waking consciousness, coming up as an insistent idea; so here, too, in these choice experiments the suggestion was impressed on the sub waking self *directly and firmly*, and this suggestion was then sent up to the waking consciousness. And just as we find in the case of post-hypnotic suggestion, that not always and not all suggestions given during hypnosis are successful in being carried out, so here, too, in our experiments, the suggestions——messages from the subconscious regions——were not always taken by the upper consciousness of the subject. We cannot possibly expect invariably success in a state when the waking self is in full swing and possesses all the power of inhibition. Still the success was remarkable.

Before giving the results let me say a few words as to the classification of the experiments. When I started my first experiments of this kind a suspicion crept into my mind that it might be fully possible that in case a suggestion given did not succeed it might still succeed *partially* as mediate suggestion, by arousing some association which will be obeyed. For instance, in giving 6 as a suggestion, 6 itself might not be chosen, but some number that succeeds or precedes it, such as 5 or 7, or possibly a numeral next to the suggested one in place, say 1 or 2, for I arranged my figures on the cardboard in such a way as to break up the natural succession of the digits. I was therefore careful to make two separate classes for these two kinds of association suggestions—namely, *suggestion by locality and suggestion by numbers*, which we may term as locality and number suggestions. The results of my experiments showed me the mediate suggestion was here of but little importance.

I made one thousand experiments and operated with twenty subjects, of which sixteen were fresh ones, not having taken part in any of my other experiments.

The figures on the cardboard were arranged thus:

$$2\ 6\ 4\ 7\ 1\ 5\ 3\ 8$$

In suggesting number 6 the subject could have taken by number suggestion—that is, either 5 or 7; or by locality suggestion—that is, either 4 or 2.

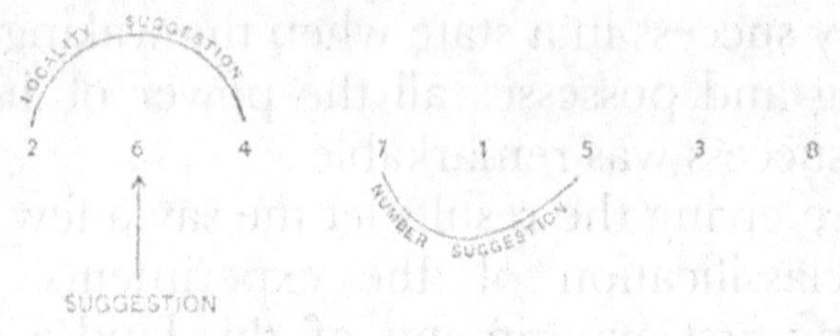

The results are as follows:

Immediate suggestion. 32.1
Mediate suggestion: locality. 6.2,
       number. 3.3

How shall we explain the fact that in our experiments the percentage of correct guesses is far above the one due to chance alone? Two theories are on the field to account for this fact: one is the well-known unconscious cerebration, and the other is my own point of view, or what I may call the psycho-physiological theory.

On the theory of unconscious cerebration, each figure shown outside the range of vision made an impression on the retina. This impression was transmitted to the sensorium, to the central ganglia of the brain, the occipital lobes, exciting there physiological processes that are not strong enough to rise above the threshold of consciousness. In short, each figure stimulated the peripheral sense organ, giving rise to a central but unconscious physiological process. Now, according to the theory of unconscious cerebration, it was this unconscious physiological proce8s that helped the subject to form correct guesses.

The psycho-physiological theory, while agreeing with the theory of unconscious cerebration as to the physiological account, makes a step further. Each figure certainly made an impression on the peripheral sense organ and induced central physiological processes, but these processes had their psychical accompaniments. Far from being mere mechanical, unconscious work, these physiological processes were accompanied by consciousness; only this consciousness was present not to the upper, but to the lower subconscious self.

If we analyze the theory of unconscious cerebration we find it deficient in giving a full account of the matter. No doubt each figure started some central physiological process, but a physiological process without any psychical accompaniment can not possibly serve as a clew to the psychical process of correct guessing; for as long as a material process remains material, it is from a psychical standpoint as well as nonexistent——that is, it can not possibly be taken cognizance of by an already existing consciousness, but, by hypothesis itself, it does not and it can not give rise to a consciousness. It is only in so far as physiological processes have psychical accompaniments that they can serve at all as a clew for correct guessing. In short, the percentage of correct guesses in our experiments can not be accounted for on the theory of unconscious cerebration; there must therefore have been *conscious perception*.

Furthermore, to have a correct *general* idea of a scarcely perceptible dot as being letter or figure, there must evidently be some perception of the *particular* traits of the dot; there must be a subconscious perception of the particular letter or figure.

Moreover, to be still more sure that subconscious perception is a *vera causa* in correct guessing, I made the following experiments:

On five cards were put five proper names, one

name on each card. The cards were then shown to the subjects, who were put at such a distance that they could see only some faint dots. The subject was told that there were five cards, and that on each card there was some proper name—the name of a river, of a city, of a bird, of a man, and of a woman—but he was not told the proper name itself. Now each time a card was shown the subject had to guess which is city, river, bird, man, or woman. The number of subjects was ten. The total number of experiments made was five hundred.

Of these five hundred experiments, three hundred and six were wrong guesses and one hundred and ninety-four were correct guesses. Since there were five names to guess, one fifth, or twenty percent, of the total number of guesses might have been due to chance—that is, one hundred guesses may be put down to chance, but there still remains a residuum of ninety-four guesses, or 18.8 per cent of the total number of experiments.

This residuum must be explained by something other than chance. Now, on the theory of unconscious cerebration the fact of this residuum is almost incomprehensible. How can one guess correctly what one does not see—that it looks like man, river, or city—unless one actually perceives the proper name shown?

On the psycho-physiological or on the subconscious perception theory we can fully see the reason or this residuum. The names were actually perceived. The lower, secondary self, or the subconsciousness, perceived the proper names, but only some of them could be communicated to the upper consciousness.

The facts and experiments discussed above seem to point, by mere force of cumulative evidence, to the presence within us of a secondary, reflex, subwaking consciousness—the highway of suggestion—and also to the interrelation and communication that subsist between the two selves.

---

1. A. Binet, On Double Consciousness.

presence within us of a secondary, reflex, subwaking
consciousness.—The highway of suggestion—and
also to the interrelation and communication that subsist between the two selves.

9

THE SUBCONSCIOUS SELF
IN THE WAKING STATE

THE results of our experiments prove the
secondary self to be the highway of suggestion.
Suggestibility is the very essence of the subwaking
self; and since this is also the essential characteristic
of the hypnotic self, we may therefore conclude that
the subwaking self of the normal individual is identical with the hypnotic self. We arrived already at this
conclusion in a former chapter, when we were discussing The Double Self; and now, having started
from quite a different point, we once more come to
the same truth. The proof therefore seems to be complete. Still, in order to elucidate thoroughly the subject under investigation, I bring here one more proof
as to the identity of the normal subconsciousness and
the hypnotic self.

An acquaintance of mine, Mr. W., a highly suggestible young man, came to visit me. For the sake of
amusement, without expecting any definite result, I
tried upon him the following experiment: I took an
umbrella, put it on the ground, and asked him to pass

it. He did it easily. "Well," I said, "but this is not the way I want you to go about it." I put myself opposite him. "I will count slowly, one, two, three, four, and each time you make a step." I counted; he passed the umbrella. "Now, once more!" I counted with great solemnity, with great emphasis, and laid particular stress on number four. He passed the umbrella, but, it seemed to me, with some hesitation and difficulty. Without giving him time to rest, I exclaimed, "And now, once more!" I counted slower than before, with greater emphasis and laid still more stress on four, and while pronouncing it I stretched out my arm and made my hand as rigid as possible. To my great surprise, and to that of those present, Mr. W. could not pass the charmed umbrella. His legs became rigid, and his feet were as if fastened to the ground. He was suspected of simulation. The gentlemen who witnessed the experiment could not conceive how a strong, sane young man, in the full possession of his consciousness, should not be able to pass such an innocent object as an umbrella. Mr. W. really could not accomplish this ordinary feat, which a child of two can easily do; he tried hard; his face became red and bathed in perspiration on account of the muscular strain, but all his efforts were futile. "No," he exclaimed at last in great dismay, "I can not do it! "

Later on, in the presence of two Boston High School instructors, I repeated again the same experiment on Mr. W., and with the same result. Mr. W. exerted himself to the utmost, but all his efforts were in vain; he could not pass the charmed line. By this time he became accustomed to this strange phenomenon, and he sat down with a smile, acknowledging that he could nut step over the umbrella.

I then tried on Mr. W. another experiment. Pronounce "Boston."——"Boston," and he said it easily enough. "And now again." I stretched out my hand and made it perfectly rigid. "P-p-p-p-oston!" he ejaculated with great difficulty. "Again." I made my hand still stiffer, and pointed it almost directly in his face. No sound. "Don't look at me," he said at last, "and I'll be able to say it."

"Well, then," I said, "try the following sentence: 'Peter Piper picked a peck of pickled peppers.' " He began to say it, but when he came to "peck of" I raised my hand and stiffened it. "P-p-p-e-cc-k" came from his lips; he began to stammer and could not continue.

"Well, then," I said, "let me see if you are able to pronounce your name." He pronounced it. "Try again." I stiffened my hand, and again the same re-sult——he was unable to pronounce his own name.

"Is it possible," asked Mr. W. of me, "that if you meet me on the street you could make me of a sudden dumb and paralytic?" I gave him an evasive answer.

"Try now to write 'Boston,'" I requested Mr. W. He did it, and wrote with great ease." Again." I stiff-ened my hand, loudly and authoritatively suggesting a like rigidity of his hand. His hand grew more and more rigid; "Boston" became more and more broken; the hand went in jerks and jumps, breaking at last the point of the pencil.

"And now let me see whether you are able to write your name." Again the same result. He could not write his own name.

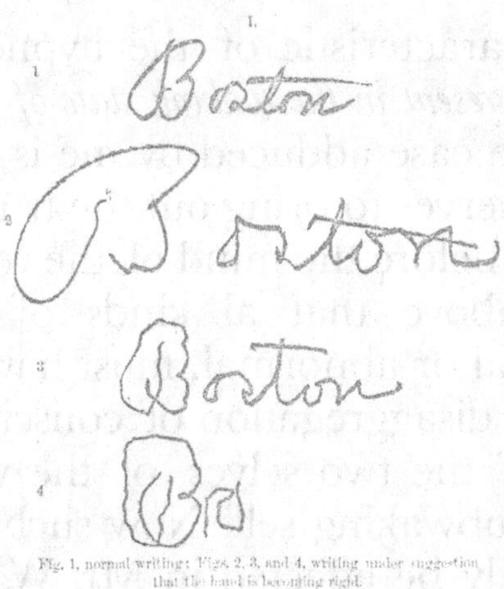

Fig. 1, normal writing; Figs 2, 3, and 4, writing under suggestion that the hand is becoming rigid.

Fig. 1, normal signature; Figs. 2, 3, 4, and 5, signature under suggestion of the hand being rigid.

Afterward I hypnotized Mr. W., and found he fell into the very last stage of somnambulism.

Now these last experiments, together with others of the kind adduced by Bernheim, Delboeuf, etc., and mentioned by me in a previous chapter, certainly do give strong evidence of the presence of the hypnotic self in the normal waking state. We have here a young man who in his normal waking condition takes suggestions characteristic of the hypnotic state. *The hypnotic self is present in the waking state of man as the sub-waking self.* The case adduced by me is certainly rare, unique, but it serves to bring out the truth of our contention clearly before the mind of the reader.

We saw above that al kinds of suggestibility, whether normal or abnormal, must have as their pre-requisite some disaggregation of consciousness, a dis-aggregation of the two selves, of the waking and of the hypnotic subwaking self. Now such a disaggregation could easily be effected in Mr. W., and this was proved by the fact of his subsequent falling into the deepest somnambulic condition on being hypnotized. For, as we have shown above, *the difference between normal and abnormal suggestibility is only a difference of degree of disaggregation.* In the hypnotic state this disaggregation is comparatively more complete, far more permanent, than in that of normal suggestibility. In the normal state, even when the subject is highly suggestible, the disaggregation is transitory, fleeting; it occurs only during the time of the suggestion, and the equilibrium is restored on the suggestion being over; but this is not the case in the state of abnormal suggestibility. In the waking state, however suggestible the individual may be—that is, however easy it is to dissociate momentarily the one self from the other—still the waking self does not lose its hold on the subwaking self; the waking self can still control; his authority, although somewhat impaired, has nevertheless power and commands obedience. This is beautifully shown by the experiments I made on Mr. W. the day after.

Next day Mr. W. came to me again. Again I tried on him the same experiments so successfully carried out the day before, but this time the results were quite different.

I put the umbrella on the ground and asked him to step over it. He did it without the slightest inconvenience. I counted slowly, stiffened my hand, but of no avail. He stepped over the umbrella, although occasionally with some slight difficulty.

"Just try to write your name,' I said. He wrote it. "Again." He wrote it once more. I asked him to write slowly; meanwhile I raised my hand, stiffened it, kept it before his very eyes. The results were now extremely interesting. His hand became cataleptic; he could not manage it. *In a loud voice he began to give suggestions to himself.* "I *am able* to write my name; I *can* write my name; I will and shall write it; yes, I can; I can write my name;" etc. Each time as he caught sight of my raised hand and listened to the torrent of suggestions I poured forth his hand became slightly cataleptic and the letters became broken, but each time as he repeated his suggestions the hand went on writing, The waking self of Mr. W. and I were contending for the possession of Mr. W.'s secondary self; and Mr. W. succeeded at last in gaining full control over his secondary self. My suggestions were completely disregarded.

Fig. 1, normal; Figs. 2-8, subject could not continue; he caught sight of me and his hand became rigid; Fig. 8, the pencil breaks on account of the great strain; Figs. 9 and 10, the subject regained full control over his hand.

These last experiments and observations bring out clearly the fact that the hypnotic consciousness is present in the waking state as the subconscious self.

10

THE PROBLEM OF PERSONALITY

IT is certainly of great interest to know whether the subconscious revealed behind the upper consciousness is a personality or not. To answer this question we must first turn to the problem of personality. "What is personality? Omitting the metaphysical hypotheses of the soul and of the transcendental ego, we find on the field of empirical psychology two contending theories of personality: the one is the association theory of the English and of the Herbartians, the other is the "wave theory" of Prof. James.

The personal self is regarded by the associationists as a train of ideas of which memory declares the first to be continuously connected with the last. The successive associated ideas run, as it were, into a single point. Memory and personality are identified. Personality is considered as a series of independent ideas so closely associated as to form in memory one conscious series. "The phenomena of self[1] and that of memory," says J. S. Mill, "are merely two sides of the same fact. . . . My memory of having ascended Skiddaw on a given day and my consciousness of being the same person who ascended Skiddaw on that day are two modes of stating the same fact. . . . I am aware of a long and uninterrupted succession of past feelings, going back as far as memory reaches, and terminating with the sensations I have at the present moment, all of which are connected by an inexplicable tie. . . . This succession of feelings which I call my memory of the past is that by which I distinguish myself (personality)." Mill's identification of memory and personality is rather unfortunate, for brutes have memory[2] but it is certainly questionable whether they have personality. "We shall, however, soon see that not only Mill, but psychologists who seem to take the opposite view, fall into the same fallacy of identifying personality with memory. In another place J. S. Mill expresses himself clearer as to his meaning of personality: "If we speak of the mind as a series of feelings, we arc obliged to complete the statement by calling it a series of feelings which is aware of itself as past and future." Mill, however, clearly sees the difficulty of his position——namely, "the paradox that something which, *ex hypothesi*, is but a series of feelings can be aware of itself as a series." He endeavours to extricate himself from this difficulty by saying "that we are here face to face with that final inexplicability at which, as Sir W. Hamilton observes, 'we inevitably arrive when we reach ultimate facts.'"

Now Prof. James takes Mill to task, and points out that Mill himself, when "speaking of what may rightly be demanded of a theorist, says: 'He is not entitled to frame a theory from one class of phenomena, extend to another class which it does not fit, and excuse himself by saying that if we can not make it fit it is because ultimate facts are inexplicable.'" The class of phenomena which the associationist school takes to frame its theory of the ego are feelings unaware of each other. The class of phenomena the ego presents are feelings of which the latter are intensely aware of those that went before. The two classes do not "fit," and no exercise of ingenuity can ever make them fit. No *shuffling* of unaware feelings can make them aware. In another place Prof. James says: "This inexplicable tie which connects the feelings, this 'something in common' by which they are linked and which is not the passing feelings themselves, but something 'permanent' of which we can 'affirm nothing' save its attributes and phenomena, what is it but the metaphysical substance come again to life?"

Prof. James's criticism of associationism is certainly just and acute, and one can not help agreeing with him. But now, what is Prof. James's own theory of personality? The passing thought, according to Prof. James, is the thinker. Each passing wave of consciousness, each passing thought, is aware of all that has preceded in consciousness; each pulse of thought as it dies away transmits its title of ownership of its mental content to the succeeding thought. To put it in his own words:

"Each thought out of a multitude of other thoughts of which it may think is able to distinguish those which belong to its own ego from those which do not. The former have a warmth and intimacy about them of which the latter are completely devoid. . . "Each pulse of cognitive consciousness, each thought, dies away and is replaced by another. The other, among the things it knows, knows its own predecessor, and finding it 'warm,' greets it, saying, 'Thou art mine and part of the same self with me.' Each later thought, knowing and including thus the thoughts which went before, is the final receptacle, and, appropriating them, is the final owner of all they contain and own. Each thought is thus born an owner, and dies owned, transmitting whatever it realizes as itself to its own later proprietor. As Kant says, it is as if elastic balls were to have not only motion but knowledge of it, and a first ball were to transmit both its motion and its consciousness to a second, which took both up into its consciousness and passed them to a third, until the last ball held all that the other balls had held, and realized it as its own. It is this trick which the nascent thought has of immediately taking up the expiring thought and adopting it which is the foundation of the appropriation of most of the remoter constituents of the self. Who owns the last self owns the self before the last, for what possesses the possessor possesses the possessed. . . . A thing," Prof. James goes on to say, "can not appropriate itself——it *is* itself; and still less can it disown itself. There must be an agent of the appropriating and disowning; but that agent we have already named. It is the thought to whom the various 'constituents' are known. That thought is a vehicle of choice as well as of cognition, and among the choices it makes are those appropriations or repudiations of its own. But the thought never is an object in its own hands. It. . . is the hook from which the chain of past selves dangles, planted firmly in the present. . . . Anon the hook itself will drop into the past with all it carries and then be treated as an object and appropriated by a new thought in the new present, which will serve as a living hook in its turn.

"To illustrate by diagram, let A, B, and C stand for three successive thoughts, each with its object inside of it. If B's object be A and C's object be B, then A, B, and C would stand for three pulses in a consciousness of personal identity."

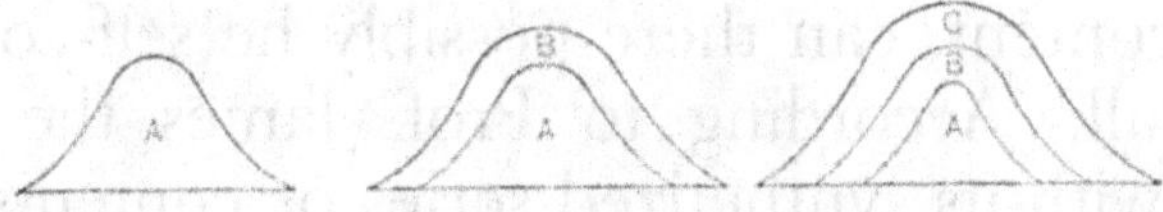

Like the associationists, Prof. James looks for personality in the function of memory; like them, he regards personality as a series, with the only difference that he postulates a synthesis of that series in each passing thought. Each thought has the title to the content of previous thoughts, but this momentary thought does not know itself. The thought can only be known when dead, when it has become a content of a succeeding wave of consciousness. In short, Prof. James seems to think that personality is a synthesis of a series, and that this synthesis is not conscious of itself. We see at once that although Prof. James attacks so valiantly and justly the association theory, he himself falls into an error no less flagrant——he omits from his account of personality the fact of self-consciousness.

Mill, in starting with a disconnected series of sensations and ideas, could not see how that series could possibly become synthetized and conscious of itself as such, as a series, and he was compelled to fall back in that refuge of ignorance, the unknowable, placing this synthetic conscious activity into a noumenal world, but he at least clearly saw that personality requires selfconsciousness. Prof. James, however, while accounting for the synthetic side of the "pure ego," totally omits the self-conscious side of personality. He even emphasizes this lack of self-consciousness in the passing thought, the present personal thinker. "All appropriations," he says, "*may* be made to it, *by* a thought not at the moment immediately cognised by itself." If, then, the passing thought can be known only as content, can there possibly he self-consciousness at all? According to Prof. James the passing thought with its synthetized series or contents can be known only as object, but then the consciousness of an object is not self-consciousness. Where, then, does the fact of self-consciousness come in? Self-consciousness can not be in the mere object-consciousness, for in it the object occupies the whole field of mental vision, and, besides, the object content is but the material, the inheritance of former dead owners. Self-consciousness, again, is not present in the passing thought, for the passing thought, according to Prof. James, "can not own itself"; nor can self-consciousness be in the succeeding thought, for then the pre dons thought has already perished, and it is now. another thought that is conscious of the thought gone——a state that can in no wise be self-consciousness; it is rather other-consciousness. How, then, is self-consciousness possible? Prof. James attempts to escape from the difficulties by making the thoughts feel "warm," but surely "animal warmth" advances us very little toward a clear comprehension of the "pure ego." A warm thought, whatever it may mean to Prof. James, is as much an object as a cold thought.

The fact is that Prof. James, in asserting that the present passing thought or the present moment of consciousness lacks knowledge of itself, seems to have forgotten his own distinction of the two kinds of knowledge——knowledge about and knowledge of acquaintance. The blind man who knows the theory and laws of light has knowledge about, but he sadly lacks the most essential knowledge—knowledge of acquaintance; he does not know what the sensation of light is in itself—that is, he has mediate but not immediate knowledge. Now the most that Prof. James can claim is that the present thought lacks knowledge about, but it nevertheless does possess knowledge—knowledge of acquaintance. Prof. James, however, is not altogether unaware of it, for in asserting that" the present moment is the darkest in the whole series," he also tells us that "it may feel its own immediate existence," but he hastens to qualify this last statement of his by adding, "hard as it is by direct introspection to ascertain the fact." Even if it be granted that Prof. James did keep in mind the two kinds of knowledge, and denied to the passing thought only knowledge about, he is still in the wrong; for self-consciousness partakes of the two kinds of knowledge: it is both knowledge about and knowledge of acquaintance.

A close examination of the two theories shows that neither the bundle of associationism nor Prof. James's passing thought gives us a true account of personality. The "pure ego" or personality is not a series, for a disconnected series can not possibly make a unity a person; nor is personality a mere synthesis of passing thoughts, for there may be synthesis or memory in each passing wave of consciousness and still no personality. The consciousness of a dog, of a cat, may fully answer Prof. James's description of the "pure ego." *The central point of the ego or of personality lies in the fact of the thought knowing and critically controlling itself in the very process of thinking, in the very moment of that thought's existence.*

Prof. James is certainly wrong in asserting that in personality the passing thought does not know itself in the moment of thinking. He seems to assume that the knowledge of an object and the knowledge of that knowledge require two distinct pulses of consciousness, two distinct thoughts; but, as we pointed out above in our discussion, if this were the case self-consciousness would have been an impossibility. The fact is that the knowledge of an object and the knowledge of that knowledge *do not require two* distinct moments, but only one and the same moment. Once a thought has come to assert "I feel," the knowledge and the feeling constitute one and the same thought. The pure ego, the "I," taken by itself means consciousness of consciousness. What the "I" asserts is that there is present consciousness of consciousness. "I feel" means that there is consciousness of a feeling along with consciousness of that consciousness. The "I know, and I know that I know," and the "I know that I know that I know," and so on, do not require so many separate thought-moments, but only one and the same moment of self-consciousness.

Prof. James's defective analysis of personality seems to be the result of his imperfect discrimination between the present moment of consciousness and the present time-moment. It is this want of discrimination between the two moments that underlies the ideal structure of Hegelianism; and although Prof. James[3] kicks vigorously against Hegel, he still can not free himself from the influence of that great dialectician. Prof. James, in fact, is a Hegelian at heart.

Moments, Hegel tell us,[4] are in a continuous flux; the *now* and the *here*, the *this* and the *that*, change with each coming moment. No sooner does the moment of consciousness posit its *now*, than the moment is changed and the *now* turns out to be something different. The negation lies on the very face of the moment's affirmation. The moment of consciousness taken in its immediacy can not know itself, because it negates itself in the very act of its affirmation. "*Le moment où je parle est déjà loin de moi.*" It is partly this consideration that Prof. James has in mind when he declares that "the present moment of consciousness is the darkest in the whole series."

Before we proceed further with our discussion it would not be amiss to point out the fact that Prof. James is also guilty of confounding two widely different moments: the present moment of consciousness and the present moment of self-consciousness. This is, in fact, implied by his whole theory of the passing thought with no self-consciousness to back it; and this confusion of the two moments is especially clearly revealed in the "darkness of the present moment of consciousness." Prof. James means by the present moment of consciousness the present thought, the present thinker-that is, the present moment of self-consciousness. Now, even if it be granted that the present moment of consciousness be "the darkest in the whole series," the present moment of self-consciousness is certainly the brightest of all.

Turning now to the Hegelian flux fallacy——a fallacy committed by many a philosopher and psychologist——we find that two qualitatively different moments are lumped together into one, namely, the present time moment and the present moment of consciousness. While in the schema of objective time the present moments are in a continuous flux, the present moments of consciousness are far from being in a parallel incessant change. The moments in the schema of time may go on flowing, but the present moment of consciousness may still remain unchanged nay, it is even fully conceivable that a present moment of consciousness should fill a whole eternity. The radical difference of those two moments is well illustrated in the popular story of the monk, who happened to listen to the song of a bird from paradise for but a single moment and found that meanwhile a thousand years had passed away.

The present moment of consciousness does not change with the change of the present time moment; the two moments are totally different in their nature. Now the moment of consciousness not being a time moment, not being in a continuous flux as the latter is, may include as wen its own consciousness, and thus be a moment of self-consciousness; and as a matter of fact a present moment of self-consciousness does include the knowledge of the present moment of consciousness within the self same present moment.

Prof. James passes a severe criticism on Hume for not making his ego-bundle a little more of a decent whole; he censures Hume for denying the synthetic unity of the pure ego. On similar grounds may Prof. James be criticised for not making his evanescent thinker a little more of a decent person; he may be censured for not seeing that knowledge of the conscious moment within the very present moment of consciousness; in other words, that self-consciousness is of the very essence of the pure ego.

The central point of personality is self-consciousness. A series of moments-consciousness cognized as a unity or synthesis of many moments in one thought, or by one thought, is not at all an indispensable prerequisite of personality. We can fully conceive an eternal moment of self-consciousness with no preceding moments to synthetize, and still such a moment of self-consciousness is no doubt a personality. An ego of such a type is not constituted of a series of moments, and has therefore neither memory nor personal identity; and still such an ego is a person, and possibly the most perfect of persons, since the personality, independent of all time; is completely synthetized by the very nature of its self-conscious being. We can again conceive it being with distinct pulses in each moment of self-consciousness. Each pulse of consciousness, however, being a moment of self-consciousness, is certainly of the nature of personality. We have here an objective series of moments of self-consciousness, originating from the primitive life consciousness, but each moment remaining distinct in itself, not owned, not synthetized by the succeeding moment of self-consciousness. This type of self-consciousness has a series, but no synthesis, no memory, no personal identity. On the other hand, there may be a series of pulses of consciousness, there may be memory, there may be a synthesis of all the preceding moments in each passing moment of consciousness, and still if there is no self-consciousness such a consciousness is certainly no personality. Neither a connected series of moments nor their synthesis is of the essence of personality; it is only consciousness of consciousness, the knowledge of consciousness within the same moment of consciousness; in short, it is only the moment of self-consciousness that makes of a consciousness a personality.

Consciousness and self-consciousness may hypothetically be arranged in the following series of stages or types:

I. *Desultory consciousness*. In this type of consciousness there is no connection, no association, between one moment of consciousness and another; there is certainly no synthesis of moments, and consequently no memory, no recognition, no self-consciousness, no personality. This type of consciousness may have its representatives in the psychic life of the lowest invertebrates.

II. *Synthetic consciousness.* In this type of consciousness there is synthesis of the preceding moments in each passing moment, but there is no recognition. Former experiences are reinstated in consciousness, but they are not recognised as such. Instinctive consciousness falls naturally under this type of mental activity. Memory is certainly present, but it is objective in its nature; it exists only for the observer, not for the individual consciousness itself. The subjective side of memory, the projection of the present experience into the subjective past of the present moment consciousness, is wanting; and, of course, it goes without saying that the synthetic consciousness has no self-consciousness, no personality.

III. *Recognitive consciousness.* In this type of consciousness there is not only an objective synthesis of the preceding moments in each moment of consciousness, but there is also present a subjective synthesis.[5] Former experiences are not only simply reinstated in consciousness, but they are also recognised as such. This type of mental activity may be represented by the consciousness of the higher vertebrate animals. There is here memory, there is the projection of the present into the subjective past, there is recognition, but there is no self-consciousness, no personality.

IV. *Desultory self-consciousness.* This type of selfconsciousness has no synthesis in each present moment of the preceding past moments of self-consciousness.

Such a form of consciousness may be regarded as a series of independent, instable personalities coming like bubbles to the surface of consciousness and bursting without leaving any marked trace behind them. It is evident that this type of personality, although it has a series of moments, has no memory of that series, nor has it any personal identity.

V. *Synthetic self-consciousness.* This form of selfconsciousness has a series of moments, and all the moments in the series can be included in and owned by each present moment of self-consciousness. The moments in the series are intimately linked and intertwined. Each moment synthetizes, owns, knows, and controls the preceding ones. This type of consciousness possesses synthesis, reproduction, recognition, personality, personal identity, and is represented by man's mental activity.

VI. *The eternal moment of self-consciousness.* In this form of self-consciousness there is no series; it is but one moment. Memory and personal identity are not present because they are superfluous, since there is no preceding series to synthetize. This type of personality may transcend the synthetic personality, as the former may contain the whole content of complete lines of series in one eternal moment of self-consciousness. This form of self-consciousness may be considered as the pure type of personality; it is the perfect person.[6]

---

1. Self is often understood by writers as equivalent to personality, while I use the term self to designate mere consciousness.
2. See Lloyd Morgan's Comparative Psychology, chapter Memory in Animals.
3. See James's essay On Some Hegelisms.
4. See Hegel's Phänomenologie, chapter Die sinnliche Gewissheit.

5. It is this type of consciousness that answers Prof. James's description of personality.

6. I must, however, add that this last type of personality is purely hypothetical, and if I brought it here it was simply to emphasize the pure aspect of personality.

11

THE ELEMENTS AND STAGES OF SUBCONSCIOUSNESS

FROM the standpoint gained in our discussion on personality or the "pure ego" we can once more turn to the study of the secondary self. The secondary or subconscious self must not be regarded as an individual; it is only a form of mental life, and as such may belong to one of the three types of consciousness. It may be desultory, synthetic, or recognitive. The secondary consciousness is recognitive at its highest, desultory at its lowest.

The subconscious self is a co-ordination of many series of moments-consciousness. In the subconsciousness series of moments-consciousness form groups, systems, communities, clusters, constellations. This co-ordination of series, however, can be dissolved; each separate series again can be broken up into its constituent moments, which may be endowed with a conscious tendency to reunite at a stated interval. The content of the isolated moment. is not any more represented in the moments of the other series, and is not therefore I known or cognized by them.

The inhibited content knowledge or object consciousness has not disappeared; it is still present in the dissociated moments, and can I be revealed by different
methods.

*Synthesis and catalysis of moments-consciousness are at the
heart of the subconscious.*

The catalysis of moments-consciousness is often
brought about by psychic stimuli under the conditions
of suggestibility——conditions that favour a dissociation of the primary from the secondary consciousness. Once this dissociation is effected, a catalysis of
the constellations of moments-consciousness constituting the subconsciousness may be produced *by* suggestion and by other means. A dissociation of
consciousness may be effected by the impression of a
very powerful stimulus, such as a strong shock. The
conditions of suggestibility——conditions that favour
disaggregation of the upper from the lower consciousness, conditions that lay bare the subconscious
self to the influence of external stimuli——are here
brought about by the overpowering intensity of the
stimulus. An intense, overpowering shock limits the
activity of the voluntary muscles——frequently para-
lyzes them momentarily, and sometimes for an appreciable period of time fixes the attention on the
impression to the exclusion of all else, strongly in-
hibits all other mental activity, and narrows the field
of the upper consciousness——in fact, very often totally removes it. The subconscious self thus emerges.

If the stimulus is too strong even for the secondary self, the disaggregation goes still further, the
subconsciousness becomes disaggregated in its turn,
and falls from the plane of recognitive to that of synthetic consciousness. With a further increase of the
stimulus the dissolution goes on further, the disaggre-

226

gation becomes deeper, and the subconsciousness falls from the level of synthetic to that of desultory consciousness.

Now; if such a disaggregation of moments-consciousness occurs, whatever may be the cause of it, if the moments can not get synthetized, and if new combinations with different psychic contents are formed, then the result is *amnesia*——amnesia for that particular state of moment-consciousness.

We must discriminate between the psychic content that may be characterized as the moment-content of consciousness and the synthesis of that content. It is this synthesis of thc content that constitutes the nature of a moment-consciousness. In short, a moment-consciousness is content *plus* synthesis.

Psychic or moment-contents may be represented in the synthesis of different moments-consciousness, so that while certain moments-consciousness may be entirely cut off from given psychic contents, other moments may bc in full possession of all that material. Thus there may be loss of mental experience and amnesia for certain states of consciousness, and at the same time full presence of that mental experience as well as recollection of it in other states of consciousness.

The relation of the moments-consciousness to the psychic contents and their synthesis by different moments-consciousness at different levels of consciousness may be graphically represented in the following diagram:

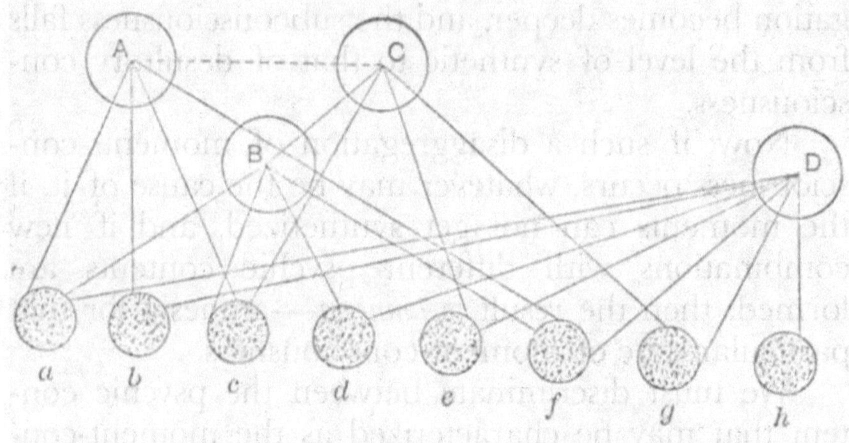

In this diagram the granulated circles *a, b, c, d, e, f, g, h* stand for the moment-content or masses of psychic material, while the nucleated circles A, B, C, D, the centres of which form foci for the convergent lines from different moments-content, stand for momentsconsciousness. A synthetizes *a, b, c, f* ; B synthetizes *a, c, d, f* ; C synthetizes *c, e, g* ; and D synthetizes all the moments-content. Moment-content *c* is represented in all the moments-consciousness, while the rest of the moments-content are represented in different combinations in each of the moments-consciousness.

Furthermore, there may also be communications between the moments-consciousness. Some of the psychic material directly presented to and synthetized by one moment-consciousness may be transmitted to and represented in another moment. Such is, in fact, very often the case. The dotted line that connects A with C represents such a relation.

The moments-consciousness may be connected by association of contiguity, so that if one begins to function, the other moment is also set into activity.

The line connecting Band C represents such a relation.

D represents a moment-consciousness which, although it synthetizes all the moments-content, is altogether dissociated from the rest of moments-consciousness.

This stage of synthesis may be termed primary synthesis, or synthesis of apprehension.

There may be a higher stage of synthesis than the one just considered, and that is when a moment-consciousness synthetizes not only moments-content but also moments-consciousness. This stage of synthesis may be termed secondary synthesis, or synthesis of apprehension and reproduction.

The secondary stage of synthesis may be represented in the following diagram:

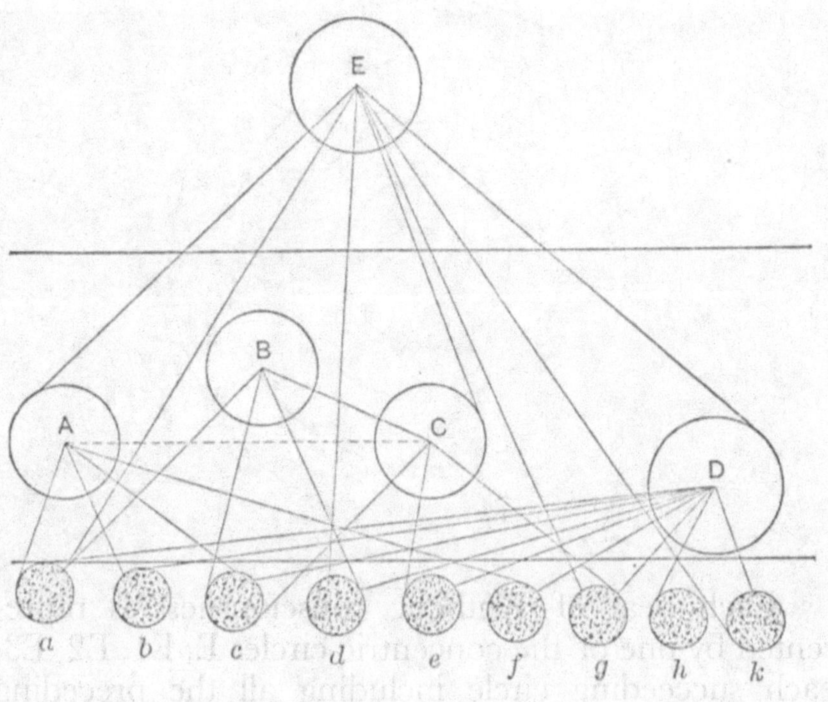

The moment consciousness E in the diagram is represented to be one that possesses synthesis of apprehension and reproduction. Such a moment-consciousness may be termed the synthetic moment-consciousness, because it is in this stage that synthetic consciousness of whole series of moments-consciousness first appears.

The synthetic moment-consciousness may change its synthetized moments-consciousness as well as its moments-content, but still, from the very nature of this type of consciousness, the fluctuations themselves are synthetized in their turn, for each successive beat of synthetic consciousness or each synthetic moment-consciousness synthetizes all the preceding moments. The beats of synthetic consciousness may be graphically represented as follows:

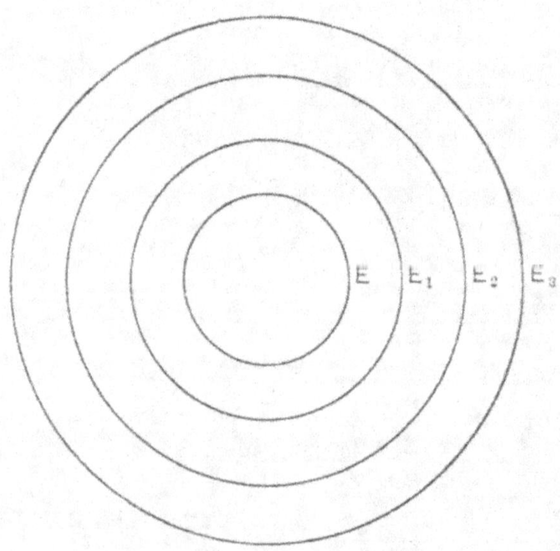

Each beat of synthetic consciousness is represented by one of the concentric circles E, E1, E2, E3, each succeeding circle including all the preceding ones.

In the moment of synthetic consciousness, as we know from a previous discussion, the former synthetic moments are merely reproduced, but they are not recognised as former, as past. It is only an external observer who occupies a higher plane than that of the synthetic consciousness, it is only such an observer who can notice the reproduction in the synthetic moment. There is, then, a higher plane of consciousness where a new synthesis is effected——that of recognition. This synthesis of recognition is the highest stage that mere consciousness, which takes as yet no recognizance of itself, can attain.

The stages of consciousness and their interconnections in relation to the nature and range of growth of the subconscious self are graphically represented in the following diagram:

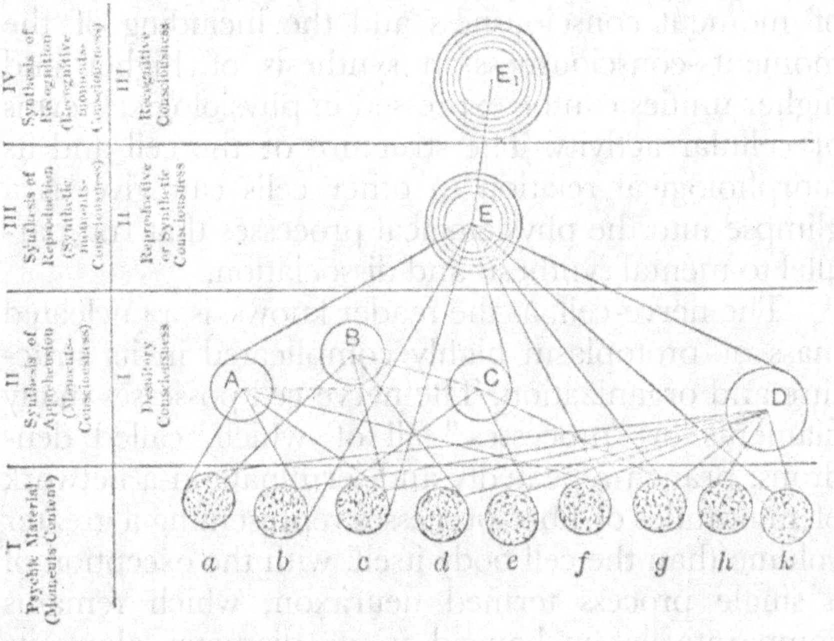

IV Synthesis of Recognition (Recognitive Moments-Consciousness)

III Recognitive Consciousness

III Synthesis of Reproduction (Synthetic Moments-Consciousness)

II Reproductive or Synthetic Consciousness

II Synthesis of Apprehension (Moments-Consciousness)

I Desultory Consciousness

I Psychic Material (Moments-Content)

E_1

E

A   B   C   D

a   b   c   d   e   f   g   h   k

12

THE PHYSIOLOGY AND PATHOLOGY OF SUBCONSCIOUSNESS

THE mental processes of association and aggregation of psychic contents in the synthesis of moment consciousness and the including of the moments-consciousness in synthesis of higher and higher unities can be expressed in physiological terms of cellular activity. The structure of the cell and its morphological relation to other cells can give us a glimpse into the physiological processes that run parallel to mental synthesis and dissociation.

The nerve-cell, as the reader knows, is a nucleated mass of protoplasm highly complicated in its structure and organization. The nerve-cell possesses many filaments or "processes," all of which, called dendrons, branch repeatedly and terminate in a network of multitudes of fibre-processes representing a greater volume than the cell body itself, with the exception of a single process termed neuraxon, which remains comparatively unchanged in its diameter along its whole course and sends out but a few branches called collaterals. The terminals of collaterals and neuro-axons are in their turn split into a comparatively small number of branches called the terminal arborization.

If we inquire as to the connection of nerve-cells with one another, we find that no nerve-cell is anatomically connected with other cells. Every nerve-cell with all its processes forms a distinct and isolated morphological individual. *Every nerve-cell anatomically considered is a complete unit.* The processes coming out from different nerve-cells do not fuse with processes coming out from other nerve-cells, but rather interlace and come in contact, like the electrodes of a battery in forming the electric circuit. Thus neurological investigations point to the highly significant fact that the connections among the nerve-cells are not of an anatomical but of a physiological nature. *The association of nerve-cells is not organic, but functional.*

axons are in their turn split up into a comparatively
small number of branches, and the terminal arborization.

If we inquire as to the connection of nerve-cells
with one another, we find that no nerve-cell is
anatomically connected with other cells. Every nerve-
cell with all its processes forms a distinct and isolated
morphological individual. Every nerve-cell, enumerated by
anatomy, is a complete [illegible] the processes starting out
from different nerve-cells do not fuse with processes
coming out from other nerve-cells, but rather interlace and come in contact [illegible] the electrodes of a battery in forming the electric circuit. Thus neurological
investigations point to the highly significant fact that
the connexions among the nerve-cells are not of an
anatomical but [illegible] a functional nature. For a more
tion of nerve-cells see [illegible]

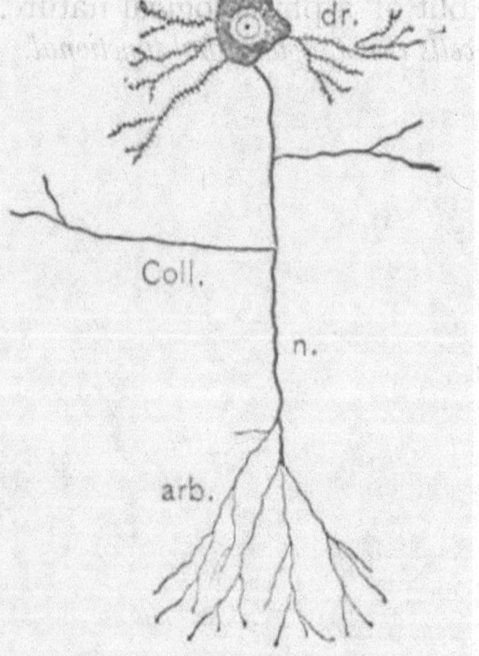

Nerve-cell of cortex: *dr.*, dendrons; *n.*, neuraxon; *coll.*
collaterals; *arb.*, terminal
arborization.

234

Nerve-cells with concomitant psychic moments-content come into contact with other nerve cells accompanied by psychic content by means of their fine terminal processes. This association of cells forms a group whose physiological function has a concomitant mental activity resulting in some form of psychic synthesis. By means of association fibres the groups arc organized into systems, the systems into communities, the communities into clusters, the clusters into constellations, and each of the higher, more complex aggregates is more feebly organized by less stable association fibres. The combination of groups into systems and of these systems into clusters and constellations by means of association fibres have as their psychic concomitants higher and higher forms of mental syntheses.[1] Thus moments-content are synthetized in the unity of moments-consciousness, and the latter are synthetized in their turn in higher and higher unities.

The simpler, the less complicated a group of nerve cells is, and the longer and more frequent their fine processes come in contact, the greater is the tendency of that group to form permanent relations; awl the same holds true of system of cells in communities, clusters, and constellations. We may therefore say that *the organization of a system or constellation of cells is in proportion to the duration and frequency of their associative activity*.

Groups of nerve-cells with a more or less stable function become gradually organized and form a sable organization. The more complex, however, a system of nerve is, the greater is its instability, and in the very highest systems or constellations of clusters the instability reaches its maximum. The instability of a system is in proportion to its complexity. In the very highest constellations the instability is extreme, and there is going on a continuous process of variation. Under the action of the slightest external or internal stimuli, such unstable systems or constellations lose their equilibrium, dissolve and form new systems, or enter into combination with other constellations, On the psychical side we have the continuous fluctuation of the content of attention. *The characteristic trait of the highest type of psycho-physical life under the ordinary stimuli of the environment is a continuous process of association and dissociation of constellations.*

As the stimuli increase in their intensity, be they of an external or internal nature—be they toxic, such as the influence of a poison, or purely mechanical, such as the action of a blow, or be they of a purely internal psycho-physiological character, such as a strong emotion-a process of dissolution sets in, and the highest, the most unstable, the least organized constellations of clusters are the first to dissolve, With the further increase of the intensity of the stimulus the dissolution goes deeper and extends further—the simpler, the more stable, the more organized systems become dissolved, The psycho-physical content, however, does not disappear with the dissolution of the system; the content exists in the less complex forms of cell-associations, and psychically in the simpler forms of mental synthesis.

The same result may be effected by stimuli of less intensity but of longer duration. A durable hurtful stimulus is in fact by far the more detrimental to the life of cell-aggregation. The pathological process of dissociation and disaggregation may be regarded as a function of two factors—*of duration and intensity.*

Such a dissociation is not of an organic but of a

functional character. *The association fibres that connect groups into systems, communities, clusters, constellations contract. The fine processes of the nerve-cells, the dendrons, or the collaterals that touch these dendrons, thus forming the elementary group, retract and cease to come in contact.*[2]

Association fibres combining the highest constellations are the first to give way; they are the latest to arise in the course of psycho-physical evolution, they are the most unstable, the least organized, and are also the first to succumb to the process of dissolution. *The instability of association fibres is proportionate to the complexity and instability if the joined clusters and constellations.*

At the first onslaught of inimical stimuli the cell-communities combined into clusters and constellations by association fibres become dissociated and independent of one another. Cell-communities, being more firmly organized than clusters and constellations, of which they are a part, and acting as a more organized whole, resist longer the action of hurtful stimuli. The association-cells that connect different clustered cell-communities *contract* or *retract* their fine terminal processes, and the cluster is dissolved. As the hurtful stimuli become more intense, the systems within the cell-community, though more firmly organized by association-fibres than the clusters, withdraw in their turn from the action of the hurtful stimuli. The associationcells that combine systems into communities *retract* their terminal processes, and the result is the dissolution of the cell-community into its constituent systems, which have more power of resistance than communities of cells, because systems are far more stable, far better organized. As the stimuli rise in intensity the process of disaggregation reaches the systems and they fall asunder into groups. With the further increase of the intensity of the hurtful stimuli the process of disaggregation affects the group itself, the fine processes of the nerve-cell, the dendrons or collaterals and the terminal arborization of the neuraxon *contract*, withdraw from the hurtful stimuli, as the monocellular organism retracts its pseudopodia from the influence of noxious stimuli. Thus the groups themselves become dissociated, and are dissolved into a number of simple and isolated nervecells. For plan of the organization of brain-cells, see Plate V.

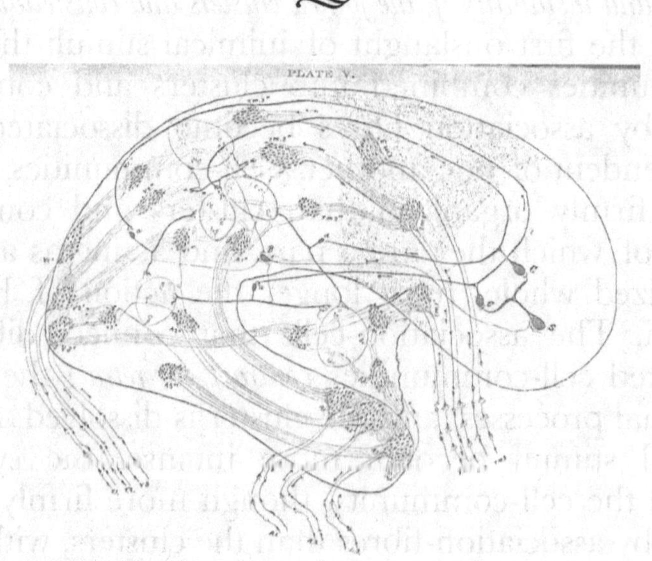

A PLAN OF THE ORGANIZATION OF THE BRAIN CELLS INTO GROUPS, SYSTEMS, COMMUNITIES, CLUSTERS, AND CONSTELLATIONS

Three sets of fibres are represented terminating in the brain cortex, namely, visual fibres V.1, V.2, V.3; acoustic fibres A.1, A.2, A.3; and tacto-motor fibres T.M.1, T.M.2, T.M.3.

The portion of the cortex denoted by the shaded areas in

which these fibres terminate is relatively very small in comparison with the unshaded portions which are not in direct communication with the external world, but subserve the purpose of associating and correlating the impressions derived through sensation. Hence the larger unshaded areas are termed association centres and the smaller shaded regions sensory centres, which in the diagram comprise the visual centre, V.1, V.2, V.3; the acoustic centre A.1, A.2, A.3; and the tacto-motor centre T.M.1, T.M.2, T.M.3. The tacto-motor centre receives tactile and other impressions from the general integument, and also transmits impulses to the voluntary muscles. Each of these centres is in communication with the external world by the ejection fibres, which consist of two sets of fibres——centripetal and centrifugal. In the tacto-motor zone, for instance, the direction of the arrows indicates both the centripetal fibres conveying impressions from the integument and the centrifugal projection fibres conveying impulses to the voluntary muscles.

Groups are constituted by collections of cells in the sensory centres with their projection fibres coming from the sense organs or going to the muscles. Thus three groups are presented in V.1-V.1´, V.2-V.2´, V.3-V.3´. Similar groups are indicated by the same notation for the other sensory centres.

Systems are evolved by the further growth of the groups within the association centres to form more complex combinations with other groups V.1-V.1´-V.1´´, V.2-V.2´-V.2´´, V.3-V.3´-V.3´´, and in a like notation for the other sensory centres.

Groups having entered the partial oceipito-temporal, and median or insular association centres as systems, these are in turn organized into higher units by the formation of communities. This is accomplished by means of the association cells with their fibres, C C C C. Communities are in their turn grouped into higher units——clusters——by means of other association cells. The clusters are indicated by the circles.

Finally, clusters are aggregated into constellations of higher and higher complexity by means of new association cells with their fibres thus, A A A A are elementary constellations; A, somewhat more complex; B and C being still more complex; and, finally, S represents one of the highest forms of constellations.

~

The following experiment, made at my request by Mr. R. Floyd, at the Pathological Institute of the New York State Hospitals, tends to confirm the theory of retractility of the extensions of the ganglion cell protoplasm.

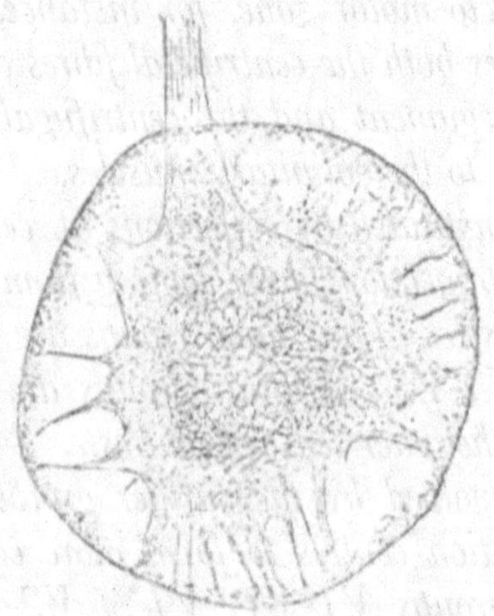

Fig. A.—Retraction of the ganglion cell body (from the cockroach) under the influence of a solution of corrosive sublimate.

Fig. A shows the retraction of one of the ganglion cells of the cockroach in the living state (*Blatta orientalis*) under the influence of a strong toxic reagent, corrosive sublimate. The outer circular zone indicates the normal volume of the cell in the living condition, and the retracted outline of the cell indicates the reduction of the volume after contact with the corrosive sublimate. The protoplasmic network of the cell having become contracted under the influence of this toxic reagent, the inference seems to be presented that the fibrillæ of the dendrons, and perhaps of the axon also, which are continuous with the fibrillar network in the cell-body, may become correspondingly retracted. The dendrons are not shown in the preparation, but the root of the axon with its parallel fibrils continuous with the cell-body network is shown at the right-hand side.

This whole process of dissolution is functional, for the disaggregation occurs only in the different forms of cell combinations. The cell itself, however, with all its processes remains intact and organically sound. With the removal, therefore, of the hurtful stimuli, there is once more a tendency, on account of the habit acquired from previous combination, to form old associations, and the old relations and functions are gradually restored. *In short, until the process of dissolution reaches the individual cell, the process is not of an organic but of a functional character.*

All functional diseases are cases of psycho-physiological disaggregation, and the gravity of the disease is proportional to the amount of dissociation. A functional disease or functional change is a disaggregation of clusters and systems of nerve-cells with their concomitant moments-consciousness and moments-contents. This disaggregation consists in the withdrawal of the simpler and better organized cell-colonies from the more complex systems, and, lastly, in the withdrawal of individual cells from the group or cell-colony. The whole process of dissociation or disaggregation is one of *contraction*, of shrinkage, from the influence of hurtful stimuli. First, the most unstable association-fibres are loosened, and communication is interrupted in the clusters forming the highest and most complex constellations, and then, as the intensity of the stimuli increases, the more stable association-fibres are loosened from the systems they connect. With the further increase of the stimuli the process of disaggregation descends still lower, to the elementary group formed of individual cells; the cells withdraw the terminal processes by which they come in contact with those of other cells in the same group.

In post-hypnotic states, in cases that go under the name of hysteria, in many forms of aphasia, in many obscure mental diseases, in many psychic states subsequent to great mental shocks, in many mental maladies known as the "psychic equivalent of epilepsy,"[3] we meet with cases of different degrees of cell-disaggregations, accompanied by all shades and forms of mental dissociation or amnesia, forms and types which I shall discuss further on. These forms may be spontaneous, as in cases of diseases, or they may be artificial, as in the case of hypnosis. *One psycho-pathological process, however, underlies all the various forms of functional diseases, and that is the process of cell-disaggregation, with its concomitant dissociation of moments-consciousness.*[4]

---

1. The difficulties of how a conglomeration of objective units can possibly give rise to a unity in a synthesis are excellently well discussed by Prof. W. James in the first volume of his Psychology. We take it as a postulate that the very nature of mental activity is *synthesis*.

2. The neuraxon is not retracted as a whole: it may remain practically stationary as far as its whole length is concerned, but the fibrillæ by contracting withdraw the terminal arborizations for minute distances, and the same holds true of the dendrons.

3. See Dr. Van Gieson and Sidis, Epilepsy and Expert Testimony,
   New York State Hospitals Bulletin, April, 1897.
4. I wish here to express my acknowledgment and sincere thanks
   to Dr. Ira Van Gieson, Director of the Pathological Institute
   of the New York State Hospitals, for his kind assistance afforded me in the preparation of the accompanying plate.

13

THE CASE OF THE REV.
THOMAS CARSON HANNA

I MPORTANT as the problem of amnesia is for psychology and psychiatry, no case of amnesia has been studied carefully and experimented on, so as to bring out the inner nature of the subconscious self. Fortunately, a very important case of amnesia recently fell under my care and observation. Dr. S. P. Goodhart, of New York, in making a clinical examination of a case of amnesia and not finding any external signs of organic lesion, had the kindness to refer the case to me for psychological investigation. Thanks to the scientific spirit and excellent facilities for research work at the Pathological Institute of the New York State Hospitals, I was enabled to undertake the work. Dr. Goodhart was so much interested in the case that he gave up much of his time to assist me in my psychological investigations of the intricacies of this case.

This case of amnesia is certainly unique in the annals of psychiatry, because it presents such a rich store of manifold phenomena bearing an intimate relation to many important problems in the science of psychology, and especially because no other case within my knowledge has been so closely and vigilantly watched, so carefully experimented upon, and so many momentous results elicited concerning the nature of the subconscious. From a clinical standpoint, too, this case of amnesia is of the utmost consequence, on account of the methods worked out for the diagnosis of different types of amnesia. From a practical therapeutic stand point the case can not but be of the highest interest, because of the psycho-therapeutic methods first worked out and applied by me to this case in order to effect a complete cure.

I give here but a very brief outline of this extremely interesting case, since a full account of it, together with a discussion of the methods used and the results arrived at, will appear in the State Hospitals Bulletin, published by the New York State Hospitals. For our purpose, meanwhile, a short account of the case will suffice to reveal the presence and the nature of the secondary self, to work out the different forms of subconscious states, and to classify the different types of amnesia to which these states may give rise.

The following is a brief statement of the case:

The patient, Rev. Thomas C. Hanna, of Plantsville, Conn., twenty-five years of age, is a man of extraordinary abilities and high aspirations. He has an excellent university education. He has a good family history, free from any taint of degeneration. He is possessed of a vigorous, healthy constitution and of a strong power of will. On April 15, 1897, Mr. Hanna met with an accident; he fell from a carriage, and was picked up in a state of unconsciousness. When the patient called to himself he was like one just born. He lost all knowledge acquired by him

from the date of his birth up to the time of the accident. He lost all power of voluntary activity, knew
nothing of his own personality, and could not recognise persons or objects. He had, in fact, no idea whatever of an external world. Objects, distance, time did
not exist for him. Movements alone attracted his involuntary attention, and these he liked to have repeated. Nothing remained of his past life, not even a
meaningless word, syllable, or articulate sound. He
was totally deprived of speech. He had lost all comprehension of language. The conversation of the
people around him was to him nothing but sounds,
without any meaning. He had lost all sense of orderli-
ness in his responses to the calls of Nature. The patient was smitten with full mental blindness, with the
malady of complete oblivion. Impressions coming to
him from the external world had lost their meaning;
the patient did not know how to interpret them. He
was like a newborn babe. The patient opened his eyes
on a fresh world. Impressions received by his sense
organs kept his attention busy in the elaboration of
his new world of experience. He did not know, could
not recognise anything from his former life. No object, no person, however intimate and near, awakened
in him even the vaguest sense of familiarity.

The patient had to learn all over again. He soon
regained the use of his voluntary muscles from involuntary movements and instruction. He learned to
use his arms and legs in walking and working, and
acquired a knowledge of objects and their distance;
he no longer attempted to seize his own image in
the mirror, no longer stretched out his hand to
grasp distant trees or far-off shining lights. He
learned to know different articles of food; he no
longer ate apple, core, and stem, nor did he any

more attempt to devour cakes of soap given to him; with a strong intelligence left entirely intact the patient learned things very quickly. His progress in the acquirement of knowledge was such a rapid one that in a few weeks he was fairly able to comprehend his environment and to communicate with people. At first he imitated words and phrases heard, thinking that this would help him to make his wants known to others; then he dropped this method, and by systematic imitation of words in connection with the objects they indicated the patient learned to speak. He also gained a knowledge of reading and writing, in a very imperfect way, though. In reading, he asked for the meaning of nearly every third word, and his writing was like that of a child who had just begun to learn the formation of letters. His reading was extremely slow, hesitating, and his handwriting awkward. He was ambidextrous; he could write equally well with both hands, something the patient could not achieve before the accident.

All knowledge of his life before the accident was totally gone; all his scholarly attainments, all his higher scientific and linguistic acquirements, an the memories of his former experience, seemed to have been wiped out by the destructive violence of the catastrophe. Persons whom he once knew intimately had to be introduced to him again. He could not recognise his parents, nor the young lady to whom he was attached. From a later inquiry it was found that the patient lost his sexual instincts. He bad no idea of the sexual functions and of the difference between men and women. The only life experience known to him dated from the time of the accident. He was practically but a few weeks old, and in this brief period of

time he rapidly passed in his development through all
the stages an infant passes in its slow growth of years.

When I first met the patient I found him in a state
of complete amnesia. To quote from my notes taken
at that time:

"H. has absolutely no recollection of any experience previous to the accident. His former life is completely gone from his memory. He has recollections
only for such events of his life as have occurred since
the injury. The patient is like one just born, a being
that had just entered into life. Patient says 'I know' of
events that have occurred since the accident; of experiences previous to that time he knows from reports,
of what 'others tell him.' He regards the history of his
life before the accident as an experience that had occurred within the life of quite a different person.

"He is but a few weeks old, and no memory of his
previous life spontaneously occurs to him. The accident may be considered as the boundary line separating two distinct lives of the same individual. What
had occurred in his former life before the accident is
unknown to the personality formed after the accident.
Two selves seem to dwell within H. One seems to be dead-
ened, crushed in the accident, and the other is a
living self whose knowledge and experience are but
of yesterday. It seems to be a case of double consciousness, and the patient is now in a secondary
state."

Such was the cursory diagnosis of the case the
very first time I met the Reverend Thomas Carson
Hanna, and I was glad to find that the diagnosis was
fully verified by the results.

The patient was then examined and tested in different ways and was found perfectly normal in all
other respects. No lesion was found anywhere; no ab-

normality could he discovered in his organic or psychomotor life. He was well and healthy. There was not the least disturbance in his sense organs, no sign of peripheral or central injury. His sensibility and reactions to sense stimuli were fully normal.

His intelligence, his power of inference, his acuteness for distinguishing fine points, his persistence in carrying on a long and complicated train of reasoning, were truly remarkable. His sense of number and his perception of form and symmetry were admirable. He showed the superiority of his mind by his inquisitiveness and his great anxiety to learn new things. Although he had not yet learned (in this state) his fractions, nor did he know anything of geometry, he still could solve very complicated problems in a simple way, making the best use of the knowledge he acquired.

The tenacity with which he retained the knowledge once acquired was truly astounding. His memory was extraordinary, and whatever was mentioned to him once was retained by him down to the least detail ever after. His appreciation of the beautiful was keen; his disgust for the ugly was extreme; he shivered and turned away at the sight of deformity. He was extremely sensitive to the harmonious. In his morality he was as pure and innocent as a child. What struck me especially was his patience, and the total absence of any angry moods. The only flaw was the incompleteness of his acquired material. He asked the meaning of the simplest words, did not know the spelling of the most commonplace names, and wondered at trite things of ordinary life, as if witnessing something unusual, something he had "never seen before," to use the patient's own words.

His keen sense of the proportionate, the harmonious, and the musical, his delicate appreciation of the good and the beautiful, his remarkable logical acumen, his great power of carrying on a long train of reasoning, the extraordinary rapidity and facility with which he acquired new knowledge, the immediate use to which he put it, the significant fact that in the course of a few weeks he learned to speak English correctly, pronouncing well and making no mistakes—all that, taken as a whole, confirmed me in the conclusion that the old personality was not crushed to death, that it was only dissociated from the rest of conscious life, and that from the subconscious depth into which it sunk it still exerted a great influence on the newly formed personality of the patient.

To tap the subconscious self and find whether or not the seemingly dead experiences are present there, the patient was asked to relate his dreams.

"I have two kinds of dreams," he answered. "In the one kind the pictures are not clear; I can recall, but I can not see them well. In the other kind of dreams it is so clear that even now I can see them well." The first kind of dreams, the indistinct ones, were those commonplace dreams of everyday life. They were all experiences coming from the patient's life after the accident. The second kind of dreams, however, proved to be of the highest importance; they were rifts through which one could catch a glimpse into the darkness of the subconscious life.

It turned out that the dreams related by the patient, and characterized by him as "clear picture dreams," and afterward as "visions," and which we may term "vivid experiences," in contradistinction to dreams being "faint experiences" if compared to those of the waking life, it turned out that these dreams were real occurrences of the patient's former life now lapsed from his memory. The patient, however, *did not recognise them, as past experiences*. To him they were extraordinarily vivid dreams, strange visions, having taken place within his present life experience and without the least hint as to their qualitative pastness. The meaning of these visions was beyond the patient's ken.

In these visions, incidents, names of persons, of objects, of places, were arising from the depths of the patient's split-off subconscious life, and, reaching the surface of the upper consciousness, were synthetized within the narrowed circle of the patient's waking self. This synthesis in memory, however, lacked the element of recognition in so far as the life previous to the accident was concerned. The patient did remember well the "visions," but he did not refer them to his previous life history; he regarded them as "lively dreams." The different proper names brought up to his memory by the "visions" were to him meaningless, so many empty sounds which could only be understood by the experienced observer, or by his parents, who were acquainted with all the details of his life. Thus, in one of his dreams the patient saw a house on which there was it sign with the following letters (he spelled them out): N-E-W B-O-S-T-O-N J-U-N-C. He could now make out what N-E-W meant, as he had since learned the word "new," but the meaning of the rest of the letters was to him entirely unintelligible and unfamiliar.

The patient's father, who was present at the recounting of the dreams, identified the places described by his son, and found that all the names of the places, persons, and objects were perfectly correct. Mr. Hanna not having heard of all that since the accident, regarded these experiences as "strange dreams" which he could not understand, because he saw in them places, persons, and objects which, according to his own statements, he had "never seen before." The patient, greatly wondered at the comments and amplifications the father was making on "the visions." When the father accidentally happened to mention the name "Martinoe," the patient's amazement knew no bounds. "That is the name of a place I passed in my dream (vision)," the patient exclaimed, "but how do you know it? It is only a dream!"

The subconscious memories of the patient were then tested by different methods, especially by the method which I term "hypnoidization." This method consists in the following procedure: The patient is asked to close his eyes and keep as quiet as possible, without, however, making any special effort to put himself in such a state. He then asked to attend to some stimulus, such as reading or singing. When the reading is over, the patient, with his eyes still shut, is asked to repeat it, and tell what came into his mind during the reading, during the repetition, or after it. Sometimes, as when the song-stimulus is used, the patient is simply asked to tell the nature of ideas and images that entered into his mind at that time or soon after. This method, simple as it is, I find to work wonders, especially in cases of amnesia.

In the case of our patient the hypnoidization brought forth phenomena of the utmost interest and value. Events, names of persons, of places, sentences, phrases, whole paragraphs of books totally lapsed from memory, and in languages the very words of which sounded bizarre to his ear and the meaning of which was to him inscrutable——all that flashed lightninglike on the patient's mind. So successful was this method, that on one occasion the patient was frightened by the flood of memories that rose suddenly from the obscure subconscious regions, deluged his mind, and were expressed aloud, only to be forgotten the next moment. To the patient himself it appeared as if another being took possession of his tongue.

The probing of the patient's subconscious self made it perfectly clear that his old and forgotten memories did not perish, that they were present to the secondary consciousness.

To be still more sure of my conclusion, I arranged with Dr. Goodhart, who assisted me in my psychological examination and investigation of the ease, to watch for the appearance of "the vision." After having watched in vain a whole night, we were at last amply rewarded for our vigilance: we were fortunate enough to be present at the visitation of one of those "visions." Dr. Goodhart was taking notes, while I was trying to insinuate myself by means of questioning into the patient's mind, and lead him on so as to reveal the inner working of his subconscious mental states.

The patient acted out and lived through experiences long forgotten and buried. He was in what may be called a "hypnoidic" state. In these hypnoidal states moments-consciousness not synthetized within the focus of the ego, moments-consciousness dissociated from the main stream of personal life, but present to the less organized and less focalized life of the subconsciousness, emerge from the obscure depths of the mind in focalized clusters, in synthetized systems of moments-consciousness. Outlived personalities with these momentsconsciousness come to life again, run through in a short period the whole cycle of events and actions they had once worked through. These outlived personalities with their moments-content of consciousness become infused with new life activity, only once more to merge into the ocean of disaggregated consciousness and to give place to new focalization, to new resurrected personalities seemingly dead years ago.

By leading questions, without his least knowledge of it, the patient, as if answering to his own thoughts, was induced to tell of his life forgotten in the waking state. Thus the rich store of the subconscious self was laid bare. *The amnesia was only for the self-conscious waking personality, but not for the aggregated totality of moments-consciousness of the subconscious life.*

A week later the patient was transferred, for the sake of further investigation, to the Pathological Institute of the New York State Hospitals, and under the influence of psychic and physiological stimuli[1] fell into a state of double consciousness or double personality. The old memories, instead of rising in the form of hypnoidic and hypnoidal states, rose to the full light of the upper consciousness. The "primary state" included the patient's whole life lip to the time of the accident; the "secondary state" dated from the accident, and included all the knowledge and experience acquired in that state. In the primary state the patient was discussing metaphysics, philosophy, theology, and even once wrote for me a concise statement on the science of pathology; in the secondary state he did not even know the meaning of these terms. In the primary state his handwriting was fine and delicate; in the secondary state it was awkward and childish, and he could only *print* capitals, as he had not yet learned to write them. Whatever he did in one state he could remember only when he again passed into that state. The events of one state were not known to the patient when in the other state. Complete amnesia separated the two states.

In the artificially induced persistent alternation of the two states, all the primary entered into one synthetic unity of consciousness, and so also all the secondary states. By means of the psychic and physiological stimuli used by me, two personalities were crystallized in the depths of his subconsciousness and kept alternating in the upper consciousness. A short interval of complete unconsciousness or of a low desultory consciousness with full anæsthesia and analgesia intervened between the two states. This interval lasted from one to about three minutes. This intermediate state was an attack; it was sudden in its onset, and may be termed *hypnoleptic*.[2]

By means of a method used by me—a method the value of which seems to me to be inestimable for theoretical and practical purposes-the two alternating personalities were finally run together into one.[3] The patient is now perfectly well and healthy, and has resumed his former vocation.

---

1. During the whole course of investigation and treatment of the case hypnosis was not and could not be used. The reasons will be given in the full report of the case.
2. A knowledge of the hypnoidal state is of the utmost value to therapeutics. A discussion of this state will appear in the State Hospitals' Bulletin.
3. An account and discussion of the method of cure will be given in the State Hospitals' Bulletin.

14

FORMS OF SUBCONSCIOUS STATES AND TYPES OF AMNESIA

WITH the case of H. before us, we return once more to the discussion of subconscious states and types of amnesia. In our analysis of consciousness we arrived at the conclusion that consciousness consists of moments consciousness. A moment-consciousness contains as much psychic matter or moments-content as is present within one given synthesis of consciousness. Now, the subconscious includes within it the sum total of all the moments-content and also of an the moments-consciousness in a condition of indifferent association and dissociation.

The subconscious is not a selective activity; it simply stands for the sum total of all the moments-consciousness. In the moment-consciousness, again, selection is absent; it is simply a matter of chance what psychic matter shall enter into the synthesis of the moment consciousness. It is only as we reach the higher plane of psychic life characteristic of the primary self, it is only then that we for the first time meet with selective activity. The primary self, being an active self-conscious synthesis, is *selective* in its nature. Out of a number of sensations, ideas, and feelings the activity of the primary self selects only some, and leaves the rest in the background of consciousness. The primary self has its more or less definite, determinate outlines that constitute its personal character. Only material of a certain kind and quality, only moments-content and moments-consciousness of a definite character fitting into the form activity of the self, only such material is taken up within the circle of its experience; the rest of the material is simply ignored. This leaving out, this ignoring of many moments, ranges through all degrees of synthetic activity, from the laying up of the moments with a view to further use, from the possibility of synthetizing the rejected material up to the total ignoring of it, when the material is entirely resigned, never to be used again because of its total incongruence with the character of the selective activity or because of the weakness within the energy of the synthetic agency. Many mental diseases, and especially those that go under the collective name of hysteria, have as their psychic cause some of those conditions or all of them in different combination and in various degrees of intensity.

This ignoring of mental material, ranging through all shades and degrees, and also the selective synthetic agency, having different degrees of weakness in the energy of its intensive and extensive activity, give rise to dissociation of mental states, to disaggregation of synthetized moments from those that were not taken up in that particular synthesis that constitutes for the time being the patient's principal individuality. All the types and degrees of amnesia depend on the nature and degree of such dissociation or disintegration. Where the dissociation is incomplete the amnesia will also be incomplete.

Moments-consciousness as well as moments-content may drop out from the unity of the synthetic consciousness and produce forgetfulness or amnesia. In such a kind of amnesia, however, the gap formed is felt and appreciated by consciousness as a gap. Glimpses of memory come back and disappear again; the forgotten moments tend to recur time and again. The range of such an amnesia varies greatly, from simple forgetfulness of some few details to the oblivion of many important events. This type of amnesia may be characterized as reproductive or recurrent.

Where the dissociation, however, is complete, the amnesia in regard to the disaggregated new synthetized material is total. Under conditions that bring about a disruption in consciousness the whole moment of synthetic self-consciousness may in a disaggregated form fall into the region of desultory moments-consciousness, and very frequently with a tendency to combine and emerge at the first favorable opportunity to the surface of the primary consciousness. Meanwhile, another series of moments-content and of moments-consciousness rise to the level of the upper consciousness and become synthetized in another different moment that takes the place of the disaggregated one. Between the two moments there is a break, a gap; fragmentary reproduction of the one by the other is not impossible; if induced by certain methods, the recognition element may be present, but may also be totally lacking. This form of amnesia may be termed *irretraceable*.

Many of the former moments-consciousness and moments content may come up in this newly formed moment consciousness, still the moment, on the whole, is new and different synthesis. Hence we may say that *irretraceable amnesia is the possible manifestation of the phenomena of double consciousness.*

We may put it down as a law, that *the degree of amnesia is proportional to the amount of psychophysiological disaggregation.*

The psycho-physiological process of dissolution may extend still further and deeper. From a disaggregation of systems of moments-consciousness the process may pass into a disintegration of the moments-content themselves, and the amnesia then is absolute; for a disintegration of the moment content itself practically means a total loss of that psychic content and the impossibility of its reinstatement in the synthesis of moment consciousness.

The physiological side of amnesia is to be found in the disaggregation of clusters of cells into their constituent systems and groups. This disaggregation is due to the violent, hurtful impressions of strong stimuli that effect a contraction of these systems and groups joined by association fibres into clusters. Under the influence of some strong injurious stimulus a whole system or group may withdraw from a constellation of co-ordinate systems of cells, but in such a way that the contraction is effected only in relation to some of the systems——that is, only some of the association paths get interrupted, while through other paths the system still stands in connection with the cluster or constellation. There will, of course, be amnesia, but it will be of a vacillating, unstable character, because the connection of the disaggregated system can be effected in an indirect way through other systems. Such amnesia will be *reproductive*. The easiness with which this reproduction can be brought about is in inverse proportion to the extent of disaggregation effected, in inverse proportion to the number of interrupted association paths.

If, however, the system has contracted completely, and has fully withdrawn from the cluster of systems so that all association paths are interrupted, the result is complete irretraceable amnesia.

In irretraceable amnesia the system that has withdrawn is perfectly sound, only it possesses groups of cells of a less complex nature, and the former connections can be again reinstated under favorable circumstances. Should, however, the hurtful stimulus be of such a nature as to destroy a whole system of cells, then the amnesia effected is *absolute*. The connections can not any more be reinstated, because the system itself is destroyed.

The process of disaggregation setting in under the action of strong and hurtful stimuli is not something new and different in kind from the usual; it is a continuation of the process of association and dissociation normally going on in the higher constellations. The one process gradually passes into the other with the increase of the intensity or duration of the hurtful stimulus. Both processes are of one and the same nature. A further continuation of the process of disaggregation passes into that of cell destruction, which, accepting Dr. Ira Van Gieson's terminology of cell disintegration, may be characterized as cytoclasis[1]

The process may be represented as follows:

Psychologically, we find that different degrees of

amnesia shade into each other imperceptibly, and that between the two extremes—namely, that of normal forgetfulness and that of absolute amnesia—there exists a whole uninterrupted series of gradations of amnesia, forming a continuous progression.

This may graphically be represented as follows:

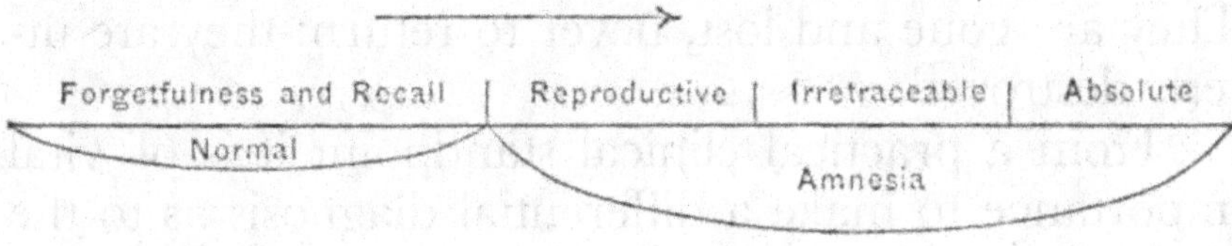

We may now no co-ordinate the two series and graphically represent them by two parallel lines.[2]

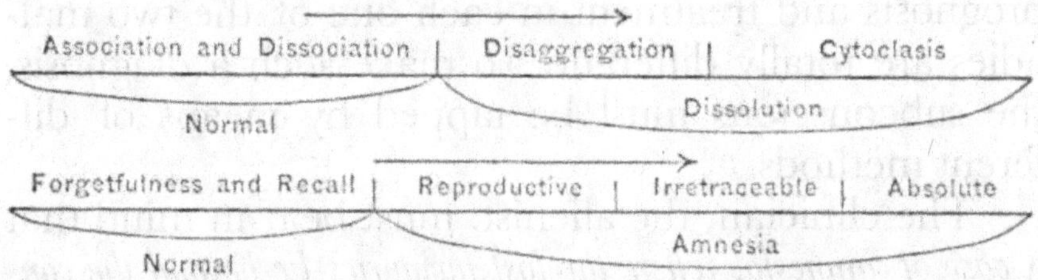

In reproductive or recurrent amnesia the patient must make a special effort to bring out the dissociated experiences, and the strength of the effort is proportional to the amount of dissociation. In irretraceable amnesia the patient can by no effort of will bring back the lost memories, but they emerge under artificial conditions, such as in the state of hypnosis or in the induction of slight hypnoidal states, when isolated ideas and sensations, fragments of experiences, without being recognised as past, emerge to the surface of consciousness; also in hypnoidic states, when

all the memories are found to be present. The case of
Hanna is a fair example. In the hypnoidic states, as
the "vision dreams," the patient proved to know
everything he had forgotten in his seemingly normal
waking state.

In absolute amnesia, however, there are no means
by which the lost memories may be restored; no psychic condition can reinstate them in consciousness.
They are gone and lost, never to return; they are utterly destroyed.

From a practical clinical standpoint it is of vital
importance to make a differential diagnosis as to the
kind of amnesia. In a case of amnesia with no possibility on the side of the patient, no matter how strong
the efforts are, to bring up the lost memories, it is of
the utmost importance to find out whether it is a case
of irretraceable or a case of absolute amnesia, as the
prognosis and treatment in each one of the two maladies are totally different. To make such a diagnosis,
the subconscious must be tapped by means of different methods.

The clinician, the alienist, must bear in mind that
a *case of amnesia, where the lost memories lie beyond the control of the patient, may be irretraceable, disaggregative, and
therefore curable, or absolute, cytoclastic, and therefore completely incurable.*

Turning now to irretraceable or disaggregative
amnesia, we find that hypnotic, hypnoid[3], hypnoidic,
and hypnoidal states reveal the presence of lost memories in the depths of the subconscious self. Memories
which the upper personality is unable to recall, and
which seem to be altogether obliterated, suddenly'
emerge to the surface of consciousness with the removal of the upper layers of mental activity. In hypnosis the removal of the waking consciousness is

followed by a state of high reflex suggestibility characteristic of the indefinite nature of the secondary self. In the hypnoidic state such suggestibility is absent, because another quasi-personality emerges with a more or less definite character, a personality that is inaccessible to direct suggestion. The hypnoidic state, however, is amenable to indirect suggestion. By means of indirect suggestion it is even possible entirely to remove this hypnoidic personality, and have it replaced by another one, which in its turn may be treated in ike manner.

The character of the hypnoidic individuality is some outlived phase of the patient's personal life. Such states may also be induced in hypnosis, but then the hypnoidic state is vague and ill defined. More frequently the hypnoidic state may be fully brought about in post-hypnotic or what may be termed hypnonergic states. I could effect such an analogous state in my somnambulic subjects by post-hypnotic suggestion. The difference between the post-hypnotic or hypnonergic and the true spontaneous hypnoidic state consists in the relation of the subject to external impressions. In the hypnonergic state the subject receives external impressions directly and refers them to some external source. He hears, sees, feels, perceives things that happen around him, and frequently carries on very animated conversations on different topics. Even in the case of post-hypnotic negative hallucinations, the patient is still fully alive to other not inhibited sense impressions that reach him from all sides. Quite different is the true hypnoidic state. The sense organs of the patient are closed to the impressions of external stimuli. He does not perceive anything that takes place around him. His environment is that of the past, and in it he lives and moves.

Shut up within one of his past lives, he remains insensible to the world of his objective present. If by chance any impressions do reach the subject, they are at once worked into his present hallucinatory life experience. If the patient is touched, squeezed, pricked, he feels nothing at all; he is totally anæsthesic and analgesic, and still within his "vision" he may be extremely sensitive to pain, shiver from cold, complain of fatigue, and tortures of pricking sensations caused by a strong gale blowing icicles into his face. Of such a nature were the visions in the case of Hanna.

The patient hears none of the conversation carried on in his presence. When the patient is spoken to on subjects not directly related to his resurrected life experience, he makes no reply; he simply does not hear. Only when he is addressed on something relating to the experience he is passing through, it is only then that he makes a reply. He does not realize, however, that it is some one else who speaks to him; his replies to questions are to him either answers to his own thoughts, or sometimes——a case very rare——he seems to converse with some imaginary person within his hypnoidic state.

No suggestions are taken by the hypnoidic personality. It is fully rational in relation to the environment in which it lives. Thus, in one of his hypnoidic states Rev. Thomas C. Hanna lived through a terrible accident that happened to him once. He was on Mount Jewett, Pa. The wind blew high. Lightning rent the sky, thunder crashed overhead. The gale gained strength and became a tempest. Broken branches and trees were falling on all sides. "There is an old woman with a child!" he exclaimed. "Oh, it is terrible! it is terrible!" he moaned. "We must run! We must run! I must drag the woman. Thunder! It is terrible! Save the woman! I am so cold! My heart is so weak! Oh, it is terrible! We must run! we must run!" To my question whether he knew Miss C., the answer of the hypnoidic personality was highly interesting" and instructive. "*Don't know her yet*——acquainted with her a year later. From Mount Jewett to her is a year." (This was found to be correct.) When I suggested to him that his friend S. was with him, he laughed me to scorn. "That is impossible!" he exclaimed; "S. is many miles away from here." I asked for the date. He gave the date in which the event took place. "It is August now," he said. When I insisted that it was May (the actual time when the vision occurred), the hypnoidic personality became impatient, raised its hand, struck the bed with great force, and exclaimed: "I am sure it is now August. You can not make me crazy! "

All the time the patient was sitting up in his bed, with his eyes firmly shut, blind and deaf to all impressions that had no relation to the "vision." By indirect leading questions this particular personality gradually dwindled away, and lo! a new personality appeared on the scene——a boy personality.

The Rev. Thomas C. Hanna became a boy of thirteen. The scenery changed completely. He was on Umbrella Island. It was sunset, it was "beautiful." He was expected for supper, but he was on the water, rowing and fishing.

On awakening from his hypnoidic state the patient remembered the "vision" very clearly; he could reproduce it, as if it were impressed on his mind in images of fire. He could not recognise the experiences of his vision as events that had taken place in his past life; he did not know that I or anyone else conversed with him and led him to give answers; nor did he remember any of the many statements to my indirect questioning he had made in his hypnoidic state. He could not remember the answers he gave me on the suggestion that his friend S. was with him; he did not know anything of the quarrel we had about the date; nor did he remember anything of the interesting information he gave me about the events of his life, such as the date of his acquaintance with Miss O. He could only remember, and that with extraordinary clearness and distinctness, everything that directly related to the "vision" itself.

Left to itself the hypnoidic personality tends to disappear, to fall back into the undifferentiated mass of moments-consciousness of the subconscious self, for the hypnoidic personality is unstable in its nature. Unstable, however, as the hypnoidic personality is, it is in closer contact with the subconscious life than is the waking self. The hypnoidic personality is in possession of facts, experiences, memories, of which the upper central consciousness is entirely ignorant. Absolute amnesia, where there is full destruction of psychic experience, is the only type of amnesia that may touch the hypnoidic personality; all other forms of amnesia are maladies of the upper self.

The hypnoidal states are of an entirely different nature. They are sudden intrusions of isolated momentsconsciousness into the upper regions of the waking personality, and can be induced by post-hypnotic suggestion, as well as by methods of hypnoidization. Like the hypnoidic, the hypnoidal states are outlived experiences, but, unlike the hypnoidic state, they are not outlived personalities. The hypnoidal states are bits, mere fragments of past experiences.

In hypnoidal states past, outlived experiences heave up into the upper consciousness from the depths of the subject's subconscious life. The subject does not welcome these experiences as his own; he does not recognise them as belonging to the stream of his conscious life once lived through; they are volcanic eruptions from the subconscious life.

The hypnoidal differ from the hypnoidic states in four very important points:

1. They can be and usually are artificially induced by the method of hypnoidization. The hypnoidic can not be artificially induced; they are always spontaneous.

2. The upper consciousness takes direct cognizance of the hypnoidal states in the moment of their appearance. The hypnoidic states are not directly cognized by the upper consciousness; the latter is always absent when the hypnoidic states are present.

3. The experience of hypnoidal states is vague, and tends to disappear from the upper consciousness the next moment after its occurrence. The experience of the hypnoidic state is inscribed on the mnemonic tables of the upper consciousness in letters of fire.

4. While the hypnoidic states form complete systems of experiences, whole personalities, the hypnoidal states are mere bits, chips of past experiences.

In both states, hypnoidic and hypnoidal, we find, however, one common trait, and that is the emergence of moments-consciousness that may be known and recalled, whether directly or indirectly, by the primary self. These experiences, as we pointed out, are not remembered as past; they are not regarded as experiences that had taken place within the former life history of the patient.

The most important element of memory—namely, recognition—is here totally absent; for memory is the reproduction and recognition of one's past conscious experience. Hence, where this recognition element is lacking, there true memory is also absent. The reproduction of past experience without the element of recognition, a condition of mind characteristic of hypnoidic and hypnoidal states in their relations to the upper consciousness, may be termed *recognitive amnesia.*

In contradistinction to this type of amnesia, there is another one where not only recognition but even the synthesis of reproduction is absent. Such a type may be termed *synthetic amnesia.*

Irretraceable amnesia may be recognitive or synthetic.

The dissociated moment may come and go, may suddenly emerge, to the surprise of the patient, to the upper stream of consciousness, be synthetized, sometimes even recognised, and then be lost again. Such a lapse of memory may be termed *simple amnesia.*

Where the loss of memory is for events of a certain period, as an hour, a day, a month, or even several years, and where all events before and after that gap can be recalled, then we have that type of amnesia which is characterized as *localized amnesia.*

If the loss of memory is only for certain systems of events, while other events that happened at the same time can be fully recalled, such a loss is termed *systematized amnesia.*

When the lost content remains unaltered during the whole course of the disease, the amnesia is *stable.*

If the amnesia sets on at intervals, it is *periodic.*

If psychic states keep on alternating, each one being completely amnesic for the other, such as is the case in double-consciousness, then the amnesia is *alternating.*

When the content of memory is continually decreasing, ending at last in a more or less total loss of it, such as we find in general paralysis, then the amnesia is *progressive*.

The dissociation in consciousness may he in relation to sensations. The patient experiences the sensation but does not comprehend its meaning. This may he termed *sensory* or *perceptual* amnesia. This form of amnesia may be limited to one or two classes of sensations, or may extend to all of them.

If the amnesia is of one sense, it may be called *local*; if of all of them, *total sensory amnesia*.

Where the dissociation occurs in the motor consciousness or motor centres, the amnesia is *motor*. This type may he again *local* or *total*.

If the amnesia is of the whole life experience, as it is in the case of Rev. H., it may he termed *general*.

If, however, the amnesia is of but a part of life experience, as, for instance, in cases of aphasia, or of localized amnesia, it may he termed *special*.

If the cause of the amnesic state is some intense mechanical stimulus, such as a fall or a blow on the head, the amnesia is *traumatic*.

Amnesia is *toxic* when the cause is some extrinsic poison absorbed by the organism, as, for instance, in the case of alcoholic intoxication.

Amnesia is *autotoxic* when the poison that causes the disease is periodically developed by the organism itself, on account of its defective working and imperfect elimination of waste products. Such cases of amnesia may occur in the status epilepticus, in the states of mind that go under the name of psychic equivalent of epilepsy, which are found interspersed in the series of typical epileptic motor attacks that are accompanied by a mental activity that can rise no higher than the most elementary desultory moment-consciousness.

If amnesia is the result of fatigue, of nervous exhaustion, or of the instability of central organization, it may be termed *asthenic*.

Amnesia is *emotional* or *pathematic* when the cause of it is an intense emotion.

These types of amnesia occur spontaneously in many mental diseases, and can also be produced artificially by hypnotic suggestion. Whether artificial or spontaneous, the mechanism of these types is at bottom the same—it is a disaggregation or disintegration of moments-consciousness.

Thus there are three types of amnesia, if regarded from the standpoint of extensiveness:

1. Reproductive.
2. Irretraceable or disaggregative.
3. Absolute or cytoclastic.

According to intensiveness, there are three types of amnesia:

1. Simple.
2. Recognitive.
3. Synthetic.

According to the lost content, amnesia has six types:

1. General.
2. Special.
3. Localized.
4. Systematized.
5. Sensory, local or total

6. Motor, local or total.

According to stability or fluctuation of content amnesia has four types:

1. Stable.
2. Periodic.
3. Alternating.
4. Progressive.

Etiologically, or according to cause, there are five types of amnesia:

1. Traumatic.
2. Toxic.
3. Autotoxic.
4. Asthenic.
5. Emotional or pathematic.

A summary of all the principal forms of subconscious states and of all the types of amnesia gives the following table:

Forms of subconscious states:

1. Hypnotic.
2. Somnambulic.
3. Hypnonergic.
4. Hypnoid.
5. Hypnoidic.
6. Hypnoidal.
7. Hypnoleptic.

Types of amnesia:

1. Reproductive or recurrent.

2. Irretraceable or disaggregative.
3. Absolute or cytoclastic.
4. Simple.
5. Recognitive.
6. Synthetic.
7. Localized.
8. Systematized.
9. Sensory, local or total.
10. Motor, local or total.
11. General.
12. Special.
13. Stable.
14. Periodic.
15. Alternating.
16. Progressive.
17. Traumatic.
18. Toxic.
19. Autotoxic.
20. Asthenic.
21. Emotional or pathematic.

---

1. See Dr. Van Gieson's article, The Toxic Basis of Neural Diseases, State Hospitals' Bulletin, No. 4.
2. The physiological process of association and dissociation corresponds to the psychological process of forgetfulness and recall; the process or disaggregation, to the forms of reproductive and irretraceable amnesia. Cytoclasis is concomitant with absolute amnesia.
3. By the term "hypnoid" I indicate the coexistence of two or more fully independent functioning constellations of moments-consciousness such as is presented in the phenomena of automatic writing and of hysteria. An experimental study of cases of hypnoid states and the method of their complete and permanent cure will appear in The State Hospitals' Bulletin.

15

THE CHARACTER OF THE SUBCONSCIOUS SELF

THE problem that interested me most was to come into closer contact with the subwaking self. What is its fundamental nature? What are the main traits of its character? Since in hypnosis the subwaking self is freed from its chains, untrammelled by the shackles of the upper controlling self; since in hypnosis the underground self is more or less exposed to our view, it is plain that experimentation on the hypnotic self will introduce us into the secret life of the subwaking self; for, as we pointed out above, the two are identical. Now I have made an kinds of experiments, bringing subjects into catalepsy, somnambulisms, giving illusions, hallucinations, post-hypnotic suggestions, etc. As a result of my work one central truth stands out clear before my mind, and that is the extraordinary plasticity of the subwaking self. If you can only in some way or other succeed in separating the primary controlling consciousness from the lower one, the waking from the subwaking self, so that they should no longer keep company, you can do anything you please with the subwaking self. You can make its legs, hands, any limb you like, perfectly rigid; you can make it eat pepper for sugar; you can make it drink water for wine; feel cold or warm; hear delightful music; feel pain or pleasure; see oranges where there is nothing; nay, you can make it even eat them and feel their taste. In short, you can do with the subwaking self anything you like. The subwaking consciousness is in your power like clay in the hands of the potter. The nature of its plasticity is revealed by its complete suggestibility. Unlike clay, however, it can not be hardened into any permanent and durable form.

I wanted to get an insight into the very nature of the subwaking self; I wanted to make personal acquaintance with it. "What is its *personal character?*" I asked. How surprised was I when, after close interrogation, the answer came to me that there could possibly be no personal acquaintance with it, for the *subwaking self lacks personality*. Under certain conditions a cleavage may occur between the two selves, and then the subwaking self may rapidly grow, develop, and attain the plane of self-consciousness, get crystallized into a person, and give itself a name, imaginary or borrowed from history. But this newly crystallized personality is, as a rule, extremely unstable, ephemeral, shadowy in its outlines, tends to subside, to become amorphous, again and again gets formed, rising to the surface of life, then sinks and disappears for evermore. The two selves blend, and once more form one conscious individuality.

The following account by an automatic writer[1] is extremely interesting from our point of view. I bring the account in full, as I find it of great value.

"The experiment," writes Mr. A., "was made Easter, 1883, on one day, and, after an interval of a week, continued on three consecutive days. Upon the first day I became seriously interested; on the second puzzled; on the third I seemed to be entering upon entirely novel experiences, half awful, half romantic; upon the fourth the sublime ended painfully in the ridiculous.

"FIRST DAY.

"*Ques*. Upon what conditions may I learn from the unseen?

"Ans. My hand immediately moved, though not to a very satisfying issue.

"Q. What is it that now moves my pen?

"A. Religion.

"Q. What moves my pen to write that answer?

"A. Conscience.

"Q. What is religion?

"A. Worship.

"Q. What is worship?

"A. W b w b w b w b.

"Q. What is the meaning of w b?

"A. Win, buy.

"Q. What?

"A. Know(ledge).

"Here I knew the letters which were to follow, and the pen made a sudden jerk, as if it were useless to continue.

"Q. How?

"A.———.

We find here the secondary self emerging from its prison, giving unintelligent and unintelligible answers, as one dazzled by the light of day.

"SECOND DAY

"*Ques*. What is a man?
"*Ans*. Flise.
"Q. What does F stand for?
"A. Fesi.
"Q. l?
"A. le.
"Q. i?
"A. Ivy.
"Q. s?
"A. sir.
"Q. e?
"A. eye.

"'Fesi le ivy sir eye.'

"Q. Is this an anagram?
"A. Yes.
"Q. How many words in the answer?
"A. 4.
"This was made out as:

'Every life is yes.'"

The secondary self could not stand long the mid-day light of the waking consciousness, and plunged once more into the depths of the obscure regions, whence it came.

"THIRD DAY

"*Ques*. What is man?
"*Ans*. Sefi Haslesbli lies.
"Q. Is this an anagram?
"A. Yes.
"Q. How many words in the answer?

"A. v (5).
"Q. What is the first word?
"A. See.
"Q. What is the second word?
"A. e e e.
"Q. Must I interpret it myself?
"A. Try.
"Presently I got out:

'Life is the less able.'

"I do not know whether any other interpretation can be given to the letters, but these fulfil the requirements; and the action of the pen, assisting in the process of interpretation, pointing to the letters, accepting these and rejecting those combinations, left no doubt in my mind that I had hit the meaning.

"*But now I was so astonished at the apparently independent will and intellect manifested* in forming the above anagrams that it was not without something of awe that I put:
"Q. Who art thou?
"A. Clelia.
"Q. Thou art a woman?
"A. Yes.
"Q. Hast thou ever lived upon the earth?
"A. No.
"Q. Wilt thou?
"A. Yes.
"Q. When?
"A. Six years.
"Q. Wherefore dost thou then speak with me?
"A. E if Clelia el.
"I made out, 'I Clelia feel.'

"But upon my asking whether this was right Clelia
wrote again, thus,

'E if Clelia e l. 20.'

"Q. Is 20 ;your age?
"A. ∞ (She was eternal).
"Q. Then 20 what?
"A. Words. . . .

"FOURTH DAY

"*Ques*. Wherefore dost thou speak with me?
"*Ans*. (Wavy line. Repetition and emphasis):
Wherefore dost *thou* speak with me?
"Q. Wherefore dost thou answer me?
"A. (Wavy line) Wherefore dost *thou* answer *me*?
"Q. Do I answer myself?
"A. Yes.
"Q. Is Clelia here?
"A. No.
"Q. Who is, then, now here?
"A. Nobody.
"Q. Does Clelia exist?
"A. No.
"Q. With whom did I speak yesterday?
"A. No one.
"Q. Why didst thou lie?
"A. (Wavy line) Why didst *thou* lie?
"Q. Do souls exist in another world?
"A. M b.
"Q. What does M b mean?
"A. May be.
"Q. What was the last answer of yesterday again?
"A. Eif Clelia o el.

278

"I. e., 'I feel no Clelia.'

"Or the original may have been:

"I Clelia flee.'

"And the 20 meant *no*, negativing my interpretation.

"My pen now became altogether wild, sometimes affirming and sometimes denying the existence of Clelia, and finally performed as follows:

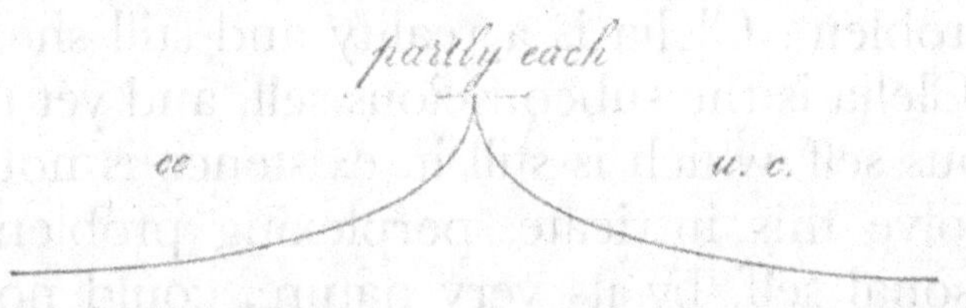

"I wrote ce. and u. c., and placed my pen in the middle. It refused to point to either, but upon my writing 'partly each' above, my pen underlined my words."

This case beautifully illustrates the evolution and dissolution——the birth, life, and death——of the personality acquired by the subwaking self. At first the secondary subwaking self lacked rationality in its answers; soon it gathered round itself more consciousness, intelligence, rationality, and even rose for an instant into the high plane of self-consciousness; but there it could not maintain itself long, and once more it subsided into the obscure regions of subpersonal life, whence it emerged possessing none the less memory of what had passed before. The subwaking self of the fourth day is fully justified in saying that Clelia does not exist. Who, then, speaks? Nobody——that is, no personality, no independent self-conscious being, but only the subpersonal, secondary, subwaking self, an unconscious cerebration, if you please.

And still Clelia did speak, Clelia did exist, there was a self-conscious being that communicated with Mr. A.; but how could the subpersonal self convey the idea that Clelia, the personal being, is not anything apart from itself, from the subwaking self? The subwaking self exists, but Clelia——what is she by herself? Nobody, nothing. The subwaking self in the darkness of its impersonality could not grapple with the puzzling problem. Clelia is a reality and still she has no being. Clelia is the subconscious self, and yet the subconscious self which is still in existence is not Clelia. How solve this intricate, perplexing problem? The subpersonal self, by its very nature, could not grasp the situation, and it grew bewildered, and became agitated, and the pen ran riot, now affirming, now denying the existence of Clelia, at last assenting to the significant suggestion "ce. and u. c.——partly each." The subwaking self was helped out from its seemingly insurmountable difficulty.

The subwaking self is devoid of all personal character; it is both subpersonal and impersonal. And when it attains the plane of self-consciousness and the conditions are favourable to its remaining there it is always roaming about, passing through the most fantastic metamorphoses, assuming with equal case all kinds of personalities without regard to time, station, sex, or age. In automatic writing and kindred phenomena the sub waking, subpersonal self is now Luther, now Mme. Pompadour, now Mozart, now Charlemagne, now Aristotle, Plato, and now an Indian brave or squaw. With marvelous plasticity, with an unequaled placidity, it assumes indifferently all kinds of character and of person, for it has no individuality. This impersonality of the hypnotic self is clearly revealed in the following hypnotic experiments performed by me in the Pathological Institute of the New York State Hospitals:

Mr. V. F. was brought by me into a deep hypnotic condition, and a post-hypnotic suggestion of personality metamorphosis was given to him.

Experimenter. I will wake you up and you must write by the aid of the automatic recorder, "I am to become Sidis, and Miss B. (the librarian of the Institute, who was then present at the experiments) will be yourself, V. F." You will ask her how her health is, how she is getting on with her work. Then you will hypnotize her. You must tell her to sit down in the hypnotic chair, and if she does not want to you must compel her. You must carry out my commands. On awakening, you will forget everything. (Wakes up.)

A few seconds later a sudden change passed over his all being, and he abruptly turned to Miss B. with

"How do you do? How are you getting on with your work? "

B. Pretty well.

Subject. Sleep well?

B. Yes.

Sub. Have dreams?

B. No.

Sub. Get up early?

B. Yes.

Sub. How early?

B. About seven.

Sub. Well, that is better than you used to do. You used to get up at ten.

I then walked up to the subject and addressed him by his name, V. F. With a wave of his hand and with a half-humourous, half-ironical smile of the man who knows better, he pointed to Miss B., saying, "This is V. F."

Exp. Pardon me, what is your name?

Sub. (with a smile). My name is Dr. Sidis, and——let me see-your name is Miss B. Will you sit down, Miss B.?

I did not tell the subject to take me for Miss B., but it seems that by the process of exclusion he had to take me for that lady.

Sub. (turns to Miss B.). Now I am going to hypnotize you.

He leads Miss B. over to the hypnotic chair, but as she does not want to sit down he pushes her down by force. Miss B. laughs and puts her hands over her face. .

Sub. Now put your hands down and compose yourself.

Miss B. laughs.

Sub. (impatiently). What are you laughing at? Just concentrate your mind on sleep.

Miss B. continues laughing.

Sub. Now what is the matter?

Exp. I think Mr. V. F. docs not want to be hypnotized.

Sub. (angrily). I have him under my control; possibly your standing there might interfere and affect him. (Turns to Miss B.) Here, now, don't purse your mouth up like that. Miss B. still continues laughing.) "What is the cause of all this? You must not allow yourself to get worked up. Sleep, sleep, sleep. (Then suddenly raises her hand to see whether it is cataleptic.)

As the lady began to feel rather uncomfortable, I went up to the subject, passed my hand over his face,

and he at once passed into the usual passive somnambulic trance.

Exp. What is your name?

Sub. Dr. Sidis.

Exp. No, your name is not Sidis, but V. F. What is
your name?

Sub. V. F.

Later on, when I asked the subject how he
could take me for Miss B., "Miss B. for himself, and
himself for Sidis, he simply answered: "I felt like
being Dr. Sidis, and there I saw V. F., for some reason
or other, dressed in female attire. I took you for Miss
B. I did not and could not question myself. I was very
angry when you interfered and suggested that Mr. V.
F. did not want to be hypnotized. I felt like showing
you out of the room, asking you to mind your own
business there in the library room, but then I changed
my mind and simply asked you to step aside."

Dr. H. Deady, Chief Associate in Pathology
at the Pathological Institute of the New York State
Hospital, gives the following account of an experiment in personality metamorphosis performed by me
in his presence:

"Mr. V. F., the subject, a man as to whose
health and good character I can fully testify, was hypnotized by Dr. B. Sidis in my presence. Dr. Sidis gave
the subject a suggestion that on awakening and
hearing four raps he should become myself, Dr.
Deady, and that he should take me for himself, for V.
F. The subject was then awakened. For a few minutes
he looked perfectly normal; for more than four or five
minutes the subject kept up an animated conversation, smoked and joked freely. When the conversation
reached its height of animation and interest, Dr. Sidis
gave the signal. So faint and indistinct were the raps

that they would have entirely escaped my notice had I not known of the suggestion. It seemed to me that the subject did not hear the raps, but he did hear them after all. A moment later a profound change suddenly passed over his face; something was struggling up into his mind. At first Mr. V. F. looked as if dazed; his eyes lost their natural lustre and expression, as if darkness set on them, as if the mind became enshrouded by a dense cloud. A few seconds late!" and everything was clear again. The subject looked at me fixedly and smiled. He was myself, Dr. Deady. He assumed my role completely. He began to besiege me with questions—questions which I had put to him when he was in his waking state. Perfectly oblivious to the presence of other people in the room, his whole attention was engrossed by me, whom he evidently took for himself, for V. F. A few minutes later he excused himself for leaving the room, pleading urgent work in the office. Without attracting his attention, I followed him at a distance. He entered my office, sat down at my desk, but was at a loss what to do. A letter was lying on my desk; he took it, opened it, read it through carefully, was lost in thought for a second or two, as if trying to remember something, but, not succeeding, put the letter back in the envelope. At this turn Dr. Sidis came into the office, and I returned to the Pyschological Laboratory where the experiments were made. Through a telephone that connects this e laboratory with the office I had the following conversation with Mr. V. F.:

"*Deady*. I wish you would order an ounce of tannic acid for me.

"*Subject*. Who is that?

"*D*. Dr. Y.

"*Sub*. Who is Dr. Y?

"*D*. One of the men working in the institute.

"*Sub*. Who is going to pay for it?

"*D*. The office, I suppose.

"*Sub*. Well, I do not know about that; I'll have to see about it. Where shall I get it?

"*D*. Send to any of the druggists.

"*Sub*. Well, I'll see about that.

"*D*. Say, there is a man out here—says his name is V. F.—wants to see you.

"*Sub*. What does he want?

"*D*. I do not know.

"*Sub*. I have no time to bother with him. Tell him to come some other time; tell him to go paint pictures. (The subject is an artist.)

"*D*. He can't paint.

"*Sub*. I know that, but I would not tell him so. Tell him to stay where he is, or to go to Jericho. I am busy.

"*D*. All right. Good-bye.

"Dr. Sidis then induced the subject to return to the room; a young lady was waiting there to make Dr. Deady's (that is, the subject's) acquaintance. "When in the room he acted Dr. Deady to life. I say 'acted,' but it was not that; he seemed to feel like Dr. Deady, he was Dr. Deady, and as such he introduced himself to Miss S., who had entered the room during his hypnotic sleep, and whom he had never met nor heard of before. When asked about the institute, the subject began to enlarge on the scope and purpose of the institution, of the pathological work on sunstroke cases done by Dr. Van Gieson and his associates, and of the knowledge the medical profession really needs. When asked about Mr. V. F. (myself), whose presence he seemed totally to ignore, he gave a merciless and cutting but truthful account of himself, an account which he would otherwise not have given in the presence of a strange young lady. The conversation then turned on hypnotism, and the subject related two of my cases as happening within his medical experience. So true to life, so complete was the subject's mimicry of my personality, that he almost expressed my inmost thoughts. . . . As the subject happens to live in the same house with me, I availed myself of the opportunity to watch the after-effects of the experiments. Dr. Sidis, it seemed, did not sufficiently remove the suggestions given to the subject during hypnosis. Mr. V. F. evidently was not in his normal state; something was working in him. When left alone he began to converse with himself; he wanted to know 'who he was not.' Next day the subject was hypnotized again by Dr. Sidis, and the after-effects entirely vanished. Mr. V. F. felt better and happier than ever."

I may add to Dr. Deady's account that before dehypnotizing the subject I suggested to him that he was Mr. V. F., but that on awakening he would not remember what had transpired during hypnosis. The suggested amnesia did not remove the Deady personality, but simply suppressed it into the region of the subconscious. Hence the after-effects, hence the fact of *double personality*.

The phenomena of personality-metamorphosis are still clearer revealed in the following experiments:

I hypnotized Mr. A. Fingold and brought him into a deep somnambulic state. I gave him a pencil and paper and asked him to sign his name, He signed it in English. "You are ten years old," I suggested. The subwaking self instantaneously changed and became a boy of ten, "Sign your name," I commanded. My friends present at the experiments, and myself, were surprised to see the hand changing its direction, and instead of writing from left to right, started from right to left. The subject signed his name not in English but in the modern rabbinical script used by the Eastern Jews; the subject knew no other alphabet when he was of that age. His brother, Mr. J. F., who was also present at the *séance*, wondered at the writing, as it curiously resembled the actual childish handwriting of the subject.[2]

"You are a boy of seven. "Write a letter to your father." The following is the specimen he wrote:

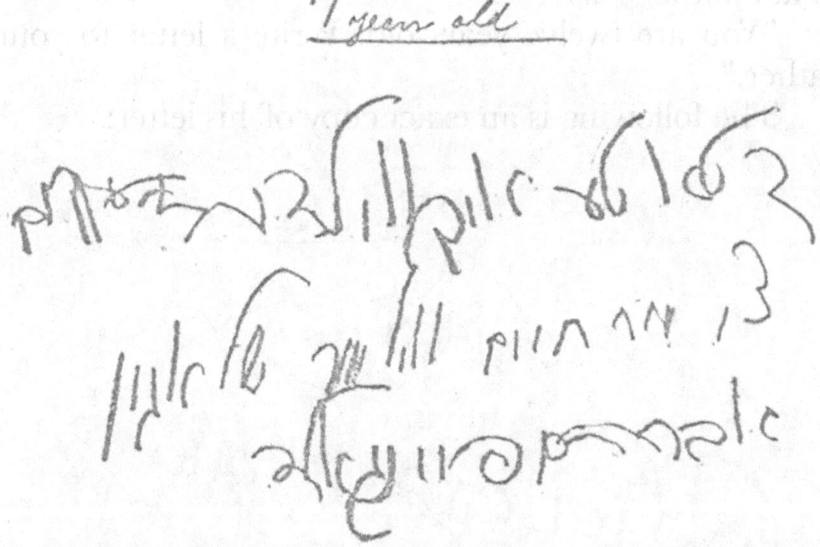

This means:
"Papa,[3] I want you to come to me. Chaim[4] wants to lick me. AB. FINGOLD."

The following is a faithful reproduction of the subject's writing:

The same kind of experiment I repeated on Mr. F. at another *séance*.

"You are twelve years old. Write a letter to your father."

The following is an exact copy of his letter:

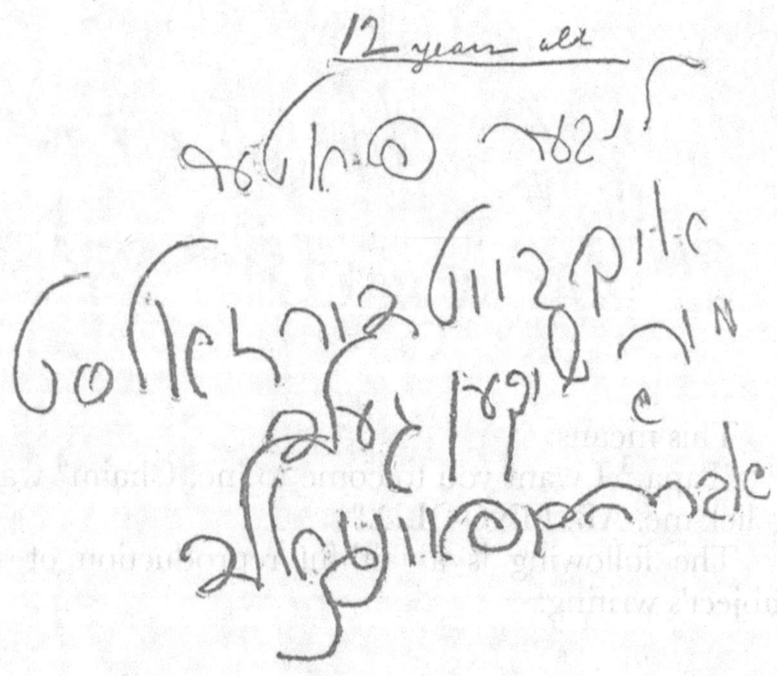

The translation of it is :

"DEAR FATHER:
"I ask of you to send me money.

"A. FINGOLD."

And now began a metamorphosis of personalities.

Experimenter. What is your name?

Subject. Ab. Fingold.

Exp. No, no. Your name is not Fingold. Your name is Sam Finestein. Who are you? What is your name?

Sub. Ab. Fingold.

Exp. (in a commanding voice). You are San Finestein, and you are thirty years old.

Sub. Sam Finestein.

Exp. How old are you?

Sub. I am thirty years old.

Exp. What is your occupation?

Sub. I have none for the present. I live on interest.

Exp. Are you married?

Sub. No.

Exp. (hesitatingly). But I heard you were married.

Sub. No, I am not, and shall never court one unless she be rich.

Exp. (hesitatingly). But, Mr. Finestein, I was told you bad two children. Are you a widower?

Sub. (in an angry tone). I want you to understand that I am not married and never was.

Exp. Have you ever met a man by name of Ab. Fingold?

Sub. Yes, I think I did.

Exp. Can you tell me anything about him?

Sub. Very little; I met him but once. If I am not

mistaken, he is a cigar-maker. He complains of headaches (the subject's disease).

Exp. And how are you?

Sub. Oh, I am well.

Exp. Can you tell me anything more about Ab. Fingold?

Sub. I told you I met him but once.

Exp. Have you met a man by name J. Fingold? (The subject's brother.)

Sub. Yes, I did. Is he not Mr. Ab. Fingold's brother?

Exp. Yes. Can you tell me anything about him?

Sub. People say he is an honest man, but that is all I know of him. He is to me a stranger.

Exp. From what country do you come?

Sub. From Russia.

Exp. How long are you from Russia?

Sub. Fifteen years. (Correct. He came here when he was fifteen years old, and being now thirty, he was just fifteen years from Russia.)

Exp. What is the name of the city you came from?

Sub. Brest-Litovsk. (Correct.)

Exp. Where do you live now?

Sub. 37 Main St., Allston. (A fictitious address. The subject lives in Boston.)

Exp. You are Jacob Aaronson, and you are sixty years old. Who are you?

Sub. Jacob Finestein.

Exp. (emphatically). You are Jacob Aaronson, and you are sixty years old. Who are you?

Sub. Jacob Aaronson.

Exp. How old are you?

Sub. Sixty years.

Exp. What is your business?

Sub. I retired from business.

Exp. (hesitatingly). Have you any money of your own?

Sub. You are too inquisitive.

Exp. Are you married?

Sub. Oh, no, I would not marry again.

Exp. Again? Have you been married once?

Sub. Yes; that was about forty years ago, but my wife died two years after marriage, and I made up my mind not to marry again. She was a loving wife. I shall go to my grave a widower.

Exp. Would not you like to make your will?

Sub. I do not expect to die so soon. Although my hairs are gray, still I am strong enough.

Exp. Have you met a man by name Sam Finestein?

Sub. I think I met him about thirty years ago. (Subject was now sixty, and as Sam Finestein he was but thirty.)

Exp. What do you think of Sam Finestein? He says he does not want to court any girl unless she is rich.

Sub. You know we have not much to think of such a fellow.

Exp. Have you met one by name Ab. Fingold?

Sub. Let me see——let me see——let me see (trying hard to recollect). It is a long while since I saw him last——about forty years. (The subject is twenty years of age.)

Exp. Can not you tell me anything about him?

Sub. I can not tell you anything about him; it is a long while since I met him last. I had no business with him. I met him but once. He did me no harm, nor has he done me any good.

Exp. Where do you come from?

Sub. From Russia.

Exp. How long are you from Russia?

Sub. Forty-five years. (45 + 15 = 60.)

Exp. Would you like to tell me the amount of money you possess?

Sub. What for do you want to know it?

Exp. It is good to know for the sake of reference——for the sake of business.

Sub. But I do no business.

Exp. (hesitatingly). Still I should like to know.

Sub. (decisively). I shall not tell you. It is rather suspicious. What do you want to know it for? It is suspicious.

I made him then pass through a whole series of events. I suggested to him he had a poor nephew. He promised to start "the poor fellow" into business——to give him five hundred dollars. He was, however, better than his word, and gave the nephew one thousand dollars. "What can one do with five hundred dollars," he said.

Exp. (hesitatingly). Would not you like to sign a check all one thousand dollars?

Sub. (decisively). I shall sign no checks. I give cash money. (He produced from his pocket imaginary money.)

Exp. Would not you like to enter into business, Mr. Aaronson?

Sub. I worked enough in my life. Let young people do the work.

During the time of his being J. Aaronson he behaved like an old invalid, rocking himself slowly and comfortably, speaking in a low, drawling tone, and assuming an air of superior knowledge and experience in his conversation with his nephew, telling the latter, "You talk like a young man."

Exp. What is your name? Who are you?

Sub. Jacob Aaronson.

Exp. (authoritatively). No, you are not Aaronson! Who are you?

Sub. Sam Finestein.

Exp. (authoritatively). No, you are not Finestein! Who are you?

Sub. Ab. Fingold.

I gave him now a post-hypnotic suggestion that after awakening, when he will see me rub my hands, he will become Sidis and take me for Fingold. I woke him up. He felt all right; spoke to his brother. I began to rub my hands. Something began to struggle within him. He looked at me hard, fixedly. I went on rubbing my hands. He rose from his chair and became Sidis, addressing me as Fingold. It would take up too much space to describe all he did and said; I can only say that he *mimicked me to perfection*. My friends could not restrain themselves from laughing. He then proceeded to hypnotize me, doing it in a careful and guarded way. He rubbed my head, telling me: "You have no headaches—the pain is gone. I took away the pain. You feel well, comfortable, cheerful," and so on. He then took a chair, placed it near mine, sat down, took my hand in his, and said: "I give you five minutes to sleep. The sleep will refresh you, and you will wake up strong, healthy, and in good spirits." He took out his watch and looked at the time. At the end of the five minutes he gave me again the suggestion of feeling well, etc., and commanded me to count till five, and wake up. I did not count. He raised his voice, and in a tone full of authority commanded, "Count till five, and wake up!" I counted till five, but did not open my eyes. "Wake up! wake up fully!" he urged. I kept my eyes closed. He felt my pulse; put his ear to my chest. "Be quiet! Be quiet!" he soothed me.

Then suddenly in a loud, impressive voice, emphasizing each word, he authoritatively commanded, "Count till five, and wake up!" I counted, and opened my eyes. All the time I watched him closely from the corner of my eye; his face bore an air of unrivalled gravity. Mr. Fingold's subwaking self assumed the Sidis-personality, and for the time being it was Sidis.

I went behind his chair, passed my hand over his face, and simply said, "Sleep!" He closed his eyes and passed into a passive state.

Exp. What is your name? "Who are you?

Sub. Dr. Sidis.

Exp. No, you are not Dr. Sidis! Who are you? Sub. Jacob Aaronson.

Exp. No, you are not Jacob Aaronson! "Who are you?

Sub. Sam Finestein.

Exp. No, you are not Sam Finestein! Who are you?

Sub. Ab. Fingold.

"When Mr. Fingold awoke he did not remember anything. "I slept a long time," he remarked. I then put my hand to his forehead and told him, "Try hard, you can remember everything." A flood of facts and items poured into his consciousness.

In the presence of two Boston High School instructors, Mr. S. and Mr. E., I made similar experiments on their former pupil Mr. W. Mr. W. was now a boy of six; now a boy of twelve; now a Mr. Thomas Davis, a labourer in a sugar factory, thirty years of age, married, and having two children; now teacher of rhetoric; now Mr. E. The change from one personality to the other was instantaneous, and the acting was lifelike. The subwaking self actually passed through the experience of each personality it assumed; it lived that particular life, it was that personality.

When Mr. W. awoke he remembered everything. It was a dream. He remembered how he worked nights in the sugar factory, remembered the looks of the factory. He did work there. He remembered the house in which he lived with his wife and the two "kids," as he named his children. He remembered he was a teacher of rhetoric examining and censuring his idle class, and that he was Mr. E.

The dreaming, subpersonal, subwaking self is chameleon in its nature; it is almost absolutely plastic; it can get metamorphosed into all kinds of beings, it can assume indifferently and instantaneously all sorts of characters and personalities, for it has no personality of its own. Once a personality is assumed, the subwaking self mimics it to perfection. Quick as lightning, like an evil genius, the subwaking self gets into possession. of all ideas and clusters of associations that relate to that assumed personality, embodies, incarnates itself in them, and struts about a different person.

Subpersonal and impersonal as the subwaking self is, it has a rich store of memories, and as it gets crystallized into a new person it takes up memories adapted to that assumed personality. Thus, Mr. F. was Sam Finestein, thirty years of age; he was fifteen years from Russia, because he left that country when he was about fifteen years old. As Jacob Aaronson he was sixty years of age; he was forty-five years from Russia, and again for the same reason.

Recently I suggested to A. Fingold a fictitious personality of a Thomas Mc Vane. He told me he was Irish; came from Dublin; was a bricklayer; was a devout Catholic; went to church every Sunday; spoke of

the "Holy Pope" in terms of reverence and awe; upbraided his sons for being great drunkards.

The subwaking self is impersonal, and still it possesses memory of all the personalities it has assumed.
In the case of Mr. F., as well as in the case of my
other subjects, the emphatic denial of each subsequent personality brings immediately to light the
precedent one. The personalities lived through form a
chain of contiguous memories. The subwaking self
seems to know only one kind of association—that of
contiguity.

---

1. Myers, Some So-called Spiritualistic Phenomena, Proceedings
   of the Society for Psychical Research, November, 1884.
2. While the subject lost his capacity for writing English, he still
   understood it perfectly well, since the commands and suggestions were given to him in English. This seems to indicate
   that the motor memory is especially subject to suggestion.
3. He wrote, instead of "father," the word "*tate*" (a word mostly
   used by Russian Jewish children).
4. A name in common use among the Russian Jews.

16

SUBCONSCIOUSNESS AND INSANITY

BEFORE we proceed to sum up the characteristics of the subconscious self I think it would be well to show of what importance the phenomena of post-hypnotic suggestion in general, and those of transformation of personality in particular, are in relation to many forms of insanity. There is, for instance, a form of mental alienation known under the name of "insistent ideas." From some source unknown to the patient an idea rises into consciousness with a persistency that can not be overcome. The idea haunts the patient like a ghost. A concrete case will bring this disease clearly before the mind of the reader.

A young man of intelligence, of good education, and free from hereditary tendency to neurotic affections, was pursuing his studies at college, when one day he heard his companions talking of the mysterious fatality connected with the number thirteen. An absurd idea took possession of his mind. "If the number thirteen is fatal," he thought to himself, "it would be deplorable if God were thirteen." 'Without attaching any importance to this conception, he could not prevent himself from thinking of it continually, and at each instant he accomplished mentally an act which consisted in repeating to himself "God thirteen," He began to attach a certain cabalistic value to this formula, and attributed to it a preservative influence. "I know perfectly well," he said, "that it is ridiculous that I should think myself obliged to imagine 'God thirteen' in order to save myself from being thirteen," but nevertheless the intellectual act was repeated without ceasing. Very soon he began to apply the same mysterious word to eternity, to the infinite, and similar ideas. His life was thus passed in mentally saying, "God thirteen! The infinite thirteen! Eternity thirteen!" The patient was fully aware of the absurdity of the idea, but still that idea continued to rise from the depth of his mind and insert itself into all his mental operations.

In impulsive insanity we meet with a similar state of mind. A seemingly unaccountable impulse suddenly seizes on the mind of the patient, an impulse which is sometimes so overwhelming that restraint is simply unthinkable. No sooner does the impulse come into consciousness than it works itself out with fatal necessity. It is a kind of emotional automatism. A young man, for instance, at the sight of a black silk dress is suddenly possessed by an impulse to ruin silk dresses, and he is bound to carry out his work of destruction whenever he is confronted with a dress of that material. "I was altogether excited by the sight of that handsome silk dress, and it was impossible for me to resist. I do not know why the idea ever came into my mind." A young lady at the sight of a have shoulder is suddenly seized by the impulse to bite, and she straightway sinks her teeth into the flesh of her victim.[1]

"E. D.," writes Dr. Stearns, "has been insane for several months. . ." He appeared to improve, when on one occasion, while he was standing in his room, his attendant advanced toward him with the intention of passing, when the patient suddenly drew back and struck the attendant a blow which brought the latter to the floor" Immediately after it was over the patient apologized, and said he was very sorry and quite ashamed of himself; he could not tell what had led him to strike, especially his attendant, with whom he was in the most pleasant relations, but the concept suddenly flashed upon and filled his mind as he saw him approach, and the impulse to strike became irresistible."[2]

Pyromania, or the impulse to incendiarism, kleptomania, or the impulse to steal, homicidal or suicidal impulses—all of them belong to that peculiar form of mental alienation that may be characterized as impulsive insanity.

Whence rise those insistent ideas, those imperative conceptions, those mysterious, unaccountable impulses? We can not ascribe these phenomena to the mechanism of associative processes; we can not say that some of the links in the chain of association became abnormally predominant, because those impulses are felt emphatically as having no connection with the association process going on in the consciousness of the patient. Those impulses are psychical parasites on the patient's consciousness. *Ideas, impressions implanted in the subconscious self, when accidentally dissociated from the upper personality, rise to the periphery of consciousness as insistent ideas, imperative concepts, and uncontrollable impulses of all sorts and descrip-*

tions. In hypnotic, and especially in post-hypnotic, suggestion we find the key to all forms of conceptual and impulsive insanity.

When my subject, Mr. A. Fingold, was in a deep hypnosis and his subconsciousness was laid bare, I suggested to him that when he will wake up and hear a knock he shall drive away his brother and Mr. H. L. from the sofa on which they were sitting and lie down there. When Fingold woke up and the signal was given, he rushed to the sofa with such impetuosity that his brother was frightened and left the place at once. Mr. H. L. was rather tardy in his retreat. The subject angrily caught hold of his arm and pushed him away with such violence that poor Mr. H. L. flew to the opposite wall. The subject then stretched himself out on the sofa and felt satisfied. As in the case of impulsive insanity, the suggested impulse set on suddenly and was enacted with a like emotional automatism.

Experiments of like nature I have also performed on other subjects, and with like results. *The suggested ideas buried in the depths of the subconsciousness frequently rise to the surface of the subject's active life, and are realized with all the vehemence and fatality of an irresistible insane impulse.*

The post-hypnotic suggestion may manifest itself in a different form. Instead of a sudden onset it may develop slowly, grow, and finally become uncontrollable. I hypnotized Mr. V. F., and suggested to him that a few minutes after awakening he should sit down on Miss B.'s chair; that if she would not like to leave he should make her go. A few minutes after awakening, Mr. V. F. turns to Miss B., whose acquaintance he made at the beginning of the experiments, with the following request:

V. F. May I sit on your chair?

B. Why do you want my chair? There are other chairs in the room; can't you take one of them?

V. F. Well, you take this one, will you?

B. No; I am very well satisfied with this one. Won't that one do you just as well?

V. F. No. I wish you would give it to me—won't you?

B. No.

V. F. I think that one over there will be much more comfortable. I would rather have this one.

B. Why can't you let me sit here?

V. F. I can, but I would like to have the chair. I could throw you out, hut that would not be exactly square; but at the same time I want that chair.

B. Won't any other chair answer?

V. F. Yes, any other chair would answer my purpose just as well.

V. F. No, no claim or right, but I want it. Let me have it, won't you? You just like to tease me.

B. Why do you think so? To keep one's chair is not teasing.

V. F. You see, it works this way: you don't want the chair, and you know I want it, but you won't let me have it, and that amounts to teasing.

B. Why do you want it?

B. That is very little reason.

V. F. Yes, very little. You don't simply want to keep what you have; you don't want to give it to me. That is your reason, is it not?

B. I am more comfortable here.

V. F. You are only teasing me. I can see your eyes twinkle. You look at Dr. Sidis and see what he thinks about it.

B. I won't give you this chair.

V. Is that your only reason?

B. What is your reason?

V. I have no reason. I have only a sneaking sort of desire to sit down in the chair.

The desire kept on growing. The subject pleaded for a seat in the chair with more and more urgency. He must have this particular chair, happen what may. The desire became an irresistible impulse. Mr. V. F. took a piece of cord, tied it round the much-longed-for chair, and exclaimed: "Now I will show you a modern Stonewall Jackson, If you don't get up I shall pull you down. I'll count three." He counted one, two, and when he came to three he gave a strong pull, and pulled ant the chair from under Miss D. and sat down on it in great haste.

The evolution of the impulse was here a gradual one. Each rebuff served only to increase the intensity of the impulse, until at last the impulse became irresistible and the craved-for object as taken by main force. Thus we see that insistent ideas, imperative conceptions, and insane impulses in general work through the mechanism of the subconscious. An idea sunk into the disaggregated subconsciousness, like a post-hypnotic suggestion, struggles up as an insane impulse.

The phenomena of the subconscious give us an insight into the nature of paramnesia. Paramnesia, or illusions of memory, may be divided into positive or additive and negative or subtractive. In positive or additive paramnesia the patient recognises a new perception as having taken place within his former experience. The patient meets strangers as' old familiar acquaintances. Thus Jensen reports the case of a patient complaining to him: "Doctor, I feel so very strange to-day. When I stand like this and look at you, then it seems to me as if you had stood there once before, and as if everything had been just the same, and as if I knew what was coming."

An interesting case of paramnesia is reported by Dr. Arnold Pick in the Archiv für Psychiatrie for 1870. An educated man who seems to have understood his disease, and who himself gave a written description of it, was seized at the age of thirty-two with a singular mental affection. If he was present at a social gathering, if he visited any place whatever, if he met a stranger, the incident with all the attendant circumstances appeared so familiar that he was convinced of having received the same impression before, of having been surrounded by the same persons or the same objects, under the same sky and the same state of weather. If he undertook any new occupation, he seemed to have none through with it at some previous time and under the same conditions. The feeling sometimes appeared the same day, at the end of a few moments or hours, sometimes not till the following day, but always with perfect distinctness.[3]

Sander brings the case of an in valid who, upon learning of the death of the person whom he knew, was seized with an indefinable terror, because it seemed to him that he knew of the event before. "It seemed to me that at some time previous, while I was lying here in this same lied, X. came to me and said, 'Müller is dead.' I replied, 'Müller has been dead for some time.'"[4]

Similar cases of paramnesia occur also in normal life. Prof. Royce, in an interesting article, hallucinations of Memory and Telepathy,[5] called attention to "a not yet recognised type of instantaneous hallucination of memory, consisting in the fancy at the very moment of some exciting experience that one has expected it before its coming." According to Prof. Royce, many facts of telepathy recorded by Gourney in his book The Phantasms of the Living belong to this last type of paramnesia.

In subtractive paramnesia, on the contrary, the patient has a false memory as to an event that had actually taken place in his experience. He is sure that the event has never occurred to him. Thus Wernicke brings the case of a patient who assaulted a public official and afterward could not be convinced that he had ever done anything like it, although he remembered well everything that happened at that time.

How shall we explain these interesting phenomena of paramnesia? We can not possibly agree with Ribot, who thinks that paramnesia is due to the fact that the memorial image evoked by the present perception is more vivid than the perception itself, and the result is that the present experience as the weaker and fainter one is considered a copy of the more vivid memorial image.

It does not require a deep insight to see the weakness of such a forced explanation. First of all, Ribot is wrong in identifying pastness with faintness. A faint perception is not a past perception. Second, even if we accept the proposition that faintness gives the feeling of pastness, Ribot is still wrong in his explanation. He simply did not analyze well the phenomena of paramnesia. In paramnesia the present perception has about it all the vivid feeling of presentness; what is added to it is the feeling that the perception has been experienced formerly. Were Ribot's account the true one, the present perception would not have been felt as present, but as past, and the evoked memorial image instead would have been felt as present, which is not the case. Besides, such a process would give rise not to paramnesia but to mere illusion. *The phenomena of paramnesia are due to a disaggregation effected within the consciousness of the patient.*

The disaggregated subconsciousness, on account of its wider range of sensibility, or on account of the temporary inhibition of the upper consciousness, gets the perception first, and after some appreciable interval it is transmitted with a feeling of pastness to the upper consciousness, which by this time already has its own direct perception. The present perception of the upper consciousness is then *recognised*——recognised as familiar, as having already been before within the experience of the patient. This transmitted message coming from the secondary to the primary self may be more or less instantaneous, or it may come some time after, as in the interesting case of the patient reported by Dr. Pick.

Subtractive paramnesia admits of still easier explanation if regarded from the standpoint of the subconscious. The disaggregated secondary consciousness possesses itself of certain details in experience that never reached the primary consciousness. The patient therefore with full right asserts that he is sure that the given details had never occurred within his self-conscious experience.

Subtractive paramnesia is analogous to the phenomena of negative hallucination which occur in posthypnotic or hypnonergic states.[6]

Turning now to demonomania and paranoia, we once more encounter the underground working of the subconscious self. In paranoia we find that an insistent idea or an imperative concept, often accompanied by illusions and hallucinations, and detached from the main stream of consciousness, gets inserted into the associative processes of the primary self. The idea soon gathers round itself cluster's of other ideas and forms a system tinged with emotional colour. The insistency and uncontrollableness of this slowly evolving disaggregated cluster give it all the characteristics of an *external* reality. Hence we have a more or less stable delusion of a systematized order. Ideas and impulses coming from the disaggregated subconscious self are projected outward, and ascribed to the activity of an external agency. Hence the ideas of persecution by hidden, mysterious enemies.

With the evolution of that subconscious cluster the primary self is weakened, a new specious personality is formed within the depths of the subconscious, a personality which rises to the surface of consciousness and occupies the whole field of mental vision, the old self existing in the background as memory. Hence we have the last stage of paranoia, known as the stage of transformation of personality.

To give the reader an idea of the mental malady known as paranoia, I select two cases from the reports sent to me for the Pathological Institute of the New York State Hospitals by Dr. Spellman, of Manhattan Hospital, Ward's Island, New York:

"Patient, B. F. Hunter, was admitted in 1895, aged thirty-seven. Memory perfect. He gives a full account of himself up to the year 1892. 'In 1892,' says the patient, 'I lived with Mr. C. Mr. C. went to the country, and I was to look after the place. One hot summer day when I was asleep a sharp, distinct voice called me. I went to look for the caller, but there was none outside. There was a man who lived in the house and who took care of the property. He would leave in the morning and come back at night. I asked him if he had called during the day, and he said he had not. At night I went down to my house and said to my wife:

"Something very queer has happened. I heard a sharp, distinct voice call me, and when I looked out of the window I saw no one." Another time, about half past twelve in the night, I heard again a sharp, distinct voice call me, "Ben! Ben!" and when I looked out of the window I could see no one. This was the third time I had been called.

"'During Cleveland's second term, in 1892, one night while I lay in bed I saw Grover Cleveland in the Executive Mansion. Some other party stood behind me and said to me, "What do you see?" I said, "I see Grover Cleveland." "Go and tell him," said the person behind me, "that he will be the next President of the United States." About the 8th of March I sent a long letter to Mr. Cleveland. I don't know exactly what I said, but here are a few of the words: "On a certain day of the month God notified me to tell you that you would be the next President of the United States, and so you are. When God tells his servant to tell a man such things as I have told you there is something behind it unknown to human beings."

"'The next year, 1894, I wrote letters to all the governors of the States to the following effect: "It is hereby known to all nations, people, and things that there is a prophet among the people with bad tidings from God. Very respectfully, B. F. Hunter."

"'Last June, 1896, it was revealed to me that I was the prophet Nebuchadnezzar.'"

The other case reported by Dr. Spellman is also characteristic of paranoia, and points to the subconscious source whence the delusion originates.

"Solomon Monroe. Admitted January 6, 1897, aged thirty-four; nativity, Germany; salesman; Protestant; single; temperate. No hereditary tendencies are known to exist. The cause of attack is supposed to be lack of food. The patient states emphatically that he is Jesus Christ, and his general demeanour corresponds to his statement. He states as follows: 'I have told you that I am Jesus Christ. I have been Jesus Christ since my birth. I have not always known it, but found it out about six weeks before I came here. I received my proper enlightenment. I was educated in the common schools of Germany. Since coming to New York, about four and a half years ago, I have followed out a religions train of thought, teaching Bible classes, etc. I had hope; birthmarks on my body—viz., scars on my face and sign of a cross on my forehead and hands—confirmed my belief. I was anointed on my head. This anointment came during the night. Later the revelations came through my sight and ears. I have them now days and nights. God my Father holds constant communication with me. I am the same Christ treated of in the Holy Word, and this is my second coming. Father, Father, the Holy Spirit has always been within me.' The patient eats and sleeps well, and aside from his general exaltation of demeanour appears as other people."

The phenomena of personality-metamorphosis in hypnotic and post-hypnotic or hypnonergic states reproduce on a smaller scale the condition of paranoia. "We find in them the growth of systematized delusions culminating in the phenomenon of personality-metamorphosis. The reader is already acquainted with these facts from our previous experiments, and there is no use for me to bring here more of them. One thing is clear from the experiments, and that is the fact that the phenomena of personality metamorphosis are due to a specious parasitic personality formed within the depth of the disaggregated, whether by hypnotization or by disease—subconscious self. *Dissociation of the subconscious is a requisite of paranoia.*[7]

Prof. Josiah Royce, in his remarkable paper on Some Observations on the Anomalies of Self-Consciousness,[8] maintains that self-consciousness is social consciousness, and whenever the derangement is in the mass of ideas involving social relationship there necessarily happens a transformation of personality. That may be. But Prof. Royce must still explain the fact why this change in the social consciousness should be felt as induced by mysterious revelations, uncontrollable, heavenly inspirations, and the activity of hidden agencies. How does it happen that an uncontrollable element, a "sort of non-ego," is formed within "the ego" of the patient? How do insistent ideas, imperative conceptions, irresistible impulses, seize on the consciousness of the patient? What is the source of the strange elements out of which paranoia evolves? This source is the disaggregated subconscionsness.[9]

When my work was already complete Prof. James called my attention to the recent work of Wernicke, Grundriss der Psychiatrie,[10] in which the author discusses the phenomena of paranoia. It is interesting to observe that Dr. C. Wernicke is so near to the solution of the problem and still he does not see it in its full light. He characterizes paranoia as a "sejunction" of consciousness; He tells us that in the state of paranoia the patient is vexed by what Wernicke calls "autochthonic ideas"——ideas that arise from the depth of the patient's "sejuncted" mind, and which the patient projects outside him. I heartily agree with Dr. Wernicke, and I am glad to find that the work of such a great physiologist and psychiatrist falls in the same line with my own investigations. What, however, Dr.

Wernicke does not see is the full meaning of "sejuncted consciousness," the fact that *paranoia is essentially a diseased hypnoidic state*, a pathological condition of the subconscious self.

The subconscious self must not be conceived as any distinct being; it is rather a diffused consciousness of any strength of intensity with a content rich and varied. The subconscious, as we have pointed out, is impersonal. Occasionally, however, it reaches the plane of self-consciousness, but then soon subsides again into its former impersonal obscurity. The subconscious self may become crystallized into a personality, but this personality is ephemeral, transient in its nature. Suppose, now, that the subconscious or secondary self is easily dissociated from the primary self or conscious personality; suppose, further, that within the bosom of the subconscious a new personality is in the process of formation——a personality no longer of an evanescent character, but of a stable nature——we shall then have a case of decomposition of personality. The newly forming parasitic personality will again and again obtrude itself on the primary consciousness, and time and again it will be beaten back into its subconscious obscurity. The patient will then consider himself as having a devil within him, a demon that fights and tempts his honest personality. If the parasitic personality grows in strength or the primary personality is weakened the patient may regard himself as double——the two personalities are of equal rank. It is not, however, only one personality, but two, three, and even more coexistent personalities may be formed within the womb of the subconscious. We have, then, the cases of the mental malady known under the name of demonomania.

Demonomania is a special form of paranoia; it is

a decomposition of personality; it is the formation of new personalities within the depths of the subconscious. The patient claims to he possessed by a demon. The evil spirit sometimes recounts what be did on earth, and what be has done since he left it for the infernal regions. The attack throws the patient into a fury of excitement, into violent convulsions. In the presence of a stranger, especially of a priest, the violence of the convulsions is greatly increased. When the crisis is over the patient looks about with a somewhat astonished air, and returns to the work in which he was engaged at the beginning of the fit. The patient does not remember what he had said or done during the attack. In very rare cases, where there is memory, the patient asserts: "I know "well that he (the devil) has said so, or done so and so, but it was not I. If my mouth has spoken, if my hand has struck, it was he who made me speak and caused the blows." The patient is sometimes possessed not by one demon, but by many demons. The patient feels and hears them moving in his body.

S., forty years of age, is devoured by two demons who have taken up their abode in her haunches and come forth through her cars. Devils have made several marks upon her person, and her heart is daily displaced. She shall never die, though the devil may tell her to go and drown herself. She has seen the two devils by which she is possessed. They are cats, one of which is yellow and white, and the other black. She puts tobacco, wine, and particularly grease, upon her head and in her ears, to exorcise the devil. She walks constantly with naked feet in fair and rainy weather, and while walking picks up whatever comes in her way. She mislays her clothing; eats largely. She sleeps not; is filthy, emaciated, and her skin very much sunburnt. There is no coherence in the system of ideas that constantly occupies her mind.

A young man at Charenton has a *dracq* in his abdomen. The dracq or destiny enters his head, tortures him in a thousand ways during the day, and particularly in the night addresses and threatens him. If I ask this unfortunate young man what this *dracq* may be, "I know nothing about it," he replies, "but it is a destiny that has been imposed upon me, and everything has been done to deliver me from it, but without success."[11]

Prof. James, in his article, Notes on Automatic Writing,[12] brings a very interesting case of personality or ego decomposition akin to demonomania, or demoniacal possession. The case is reported by Dr. Ira Barrows, of Providence. The record begins in the nineteenth year of the patient's age, and continues for several years. It runs as follows:

"*September 17, 1860.*——Wild with delirium. Tears her hair, pillow-cases, bedclothes, bath sheets, nightdress, all to pieces. Her right hand prevents her left hand, by seizing and holding it, from tearing out her hair, but she tears her clothes with her left hand and teeth.

"*29th.*——Complains of great pain in right arm, more and more intense when suddenly it falls down by her side. She looks at it in amazement. Thinks it belongs to some one else; positive it is not hers. Sees her right arm drawn around her spine. Cut it, prick it, do what you please to it, she takes no notice of it. Complains of great pain in the neck and back, which she now calls her shoulder and arm; no process of reasoning can convince her to the contrary. To the present time, now nearly five years, the hallucination remains firm. She believes her spine is her right arm, and that her right arm is a foreign object and a nuisance. She believes it to be an arm and a hand, but treats it as if it had intelligence, and might keep away from her. She bites it, pounds it, pricks it, and in many ways seeks to drive it from her. She calls it 'Stump,' 'Old Stump.' Sometimes she is in great excitement and tears, pounding Old Stump. Says Stump has got this or the other that belongs to her. The history of September is her daily and nightly history till October 25th.

"*November 12th.*——From eleven to twelve at night sits up, apparently asleep, and writes with her paper against the wall. After she wakes seems to be unconscious of what she has written.

"*From November 20th to January 1, 1861*, raving delirium; pulls her hair nearly all out from the top of her head. The right hand protects her against the left as much as possible.

"*February 1st to 11th.*——Under the influence of magnetism writes poetry; personates different persons, mostly those who have long since passed away. When in the magnetic state, whatever she does and says is not remembered when she comes out of it. Commences a series of drawings with her right paralyzed hand, Old Stump. Also writes poetry with it. Whatever Stump writes, or draws, or does, she appears to take no interest in; says it is none of hers, and that she wants nothing to do with Stump or Stump's. I have sat by her bed and engaged her in conversation, and drawn her attention in various ways, while the writing and drawing has been uninterrupted.

"*March 1861.*——She became blind.

"*January 4, 1862.*——Is still blind; sees as well with eyes closed as open: keeps them closed much of the time. Draws in the dark as well as in the light. Writes poetry chiefly with the right hand, and often while it is dark. The hand writing differs greatly in different pieces.

"*January 10th.*——When her delirium is at it height, as well as at all other times, her right hand is rational, asking and answering questions in writing; giving directions; trying to prevent her tearing her clothes; when she pulls out her hair it seizes and holds her left hand. When she is asleep it carries on conversation; writes poetry; never sleeps; acts the part of a nurse as far as it can; pulls the bedclothes over the patient, if it can reach them, when uncovered; raps on the headboard to awaken her mother (who always sleeps in the room) if anything occurs, as spasms, etc.

"*January, 1863.*——At night and during her sleep Stump writes letters, some of them very amusing; writes poetry, some pieces original. Writes Hasty Pudding, by Barlow, in several cantos, which she had never read; all correctly written, but queerly arranged——e.g., one line belonging in one canto would be transposed with another line in another canto. She has no knowledge of Latin or French, yet Stump produces the following lines:

"Sed tempus recessit, and this was all over,
Cum illi successit, another gay rover;
Nam cum navigaret in his own cutter,
Portenturn apparet, which made them all
   flutter.
"Et horridus anguis which they behold,
Haud dubio sanguis within them ran cold;
Tringinta pedes his head was upraised,
Et corporis sedes in secret was placed.
"Sic serpens mancbat, so says the same joker,

Et sese ferebat as stiff as a poker;
Tergum fricabat against the old lighthouse,
Et sese liberabat of scaly detritus.
"Tunc plumbo percussit thinking he hath him,
At serpens exsiluit full thirty fathoms,
Exsiluit mare with pain and affright,
Conatus abnare as fast as he might.
"Neque ille secuti? no, nothing so rash,
Terrore sunt muti he'd made such a splash;
Sed nunc adierunt the place to inspect,
Et squamas viderunt, the which they collect.
"Quicumque non credat and doubtfully rails,
Adlocum accedat, they'll show him the scales;
Quas, sola trophea, they brought to the shore;
Et causa est ea, they couldn't get more.

"Stump writes both asleep and awake, and the writing goes on while she is occupied with her left hand in other matters. Ask her what she is writing, she replies, 'I am not writing; that is Stump writing. I don't know what he is writing. I don't trouble myself with Stump's doings.' Reads with her hook upside down, and sometimes when covered with the sheet. Stump produces two bills of fare in French.

"Upon this one subject of her right arm she is a monomaniac. Her right hand and arm are not hers. Attempt to reason with her, and she holds up her left arm and says: 'This is my left arm. I see and feel my right arm drawn behind me. You say this Stump is my right arm. Then I have three arms and hands.' In this arm the nerves of sensation are paralyzed, but the nerves of motion preserved. *She* has no will to move it. She has no knowledge of its motion. This arm appears to have a separate intelligence. When she sleeps, it writes or converses by signs. It never

sleeps; watches over her when she sleeps; endeavours
to prevent her from injuring herself or her clothing
when she is raving. It seems to possess an independent
life."

Prof. James, who is in possession of the full
record, adds "that Old Stump used to write to Miss
W. in the third person as Anna."

Instead of being possessed by an evil spirit, as is
usually the rule in Catholic countries, this patient was
possessed by a good spirit, who took care of the patient and watched over her, and who, like spirits in
general, claimed to be clairvoyant. This good spirit
was probably a peculiarly crystallized personality
formed of the sane remnants of the patient's subconscious self.

In the Journal of Nervous and Mental Diseases[13]
Dr. Irving C. Rosse describes the following interesting
case of triple personality:

"M. L., age thirty-five; brasier; single; nativity,
Connecticut; education, common school; religion,
Roman Catholic. No hereditary or atavistic an-
tecedents of note. His habits from earliest manhood
have been of a kind that it would be charitable to designate simply as irregular. Alcoholic, nicotinic, and
venereal excesses have been followed by persistent
masturbation and constant erotic tendency.

"Nothing unusual occurred in his life until about
1884, when he got to drinking, became nervous,
sleepless, and finally had *mania a potu*, with a series of
epileptiform convulsions. His physicians prescribed
more whisky and a hypodermic of morphine, which
did not quiet him altogether, and while lying on the
bed a 'picture form' appeared on the wall and gradually assumed the form of Lucifer, whose voice issued
forth, saying, 'Who has hold of your blood—God, or

the devil?' (the beginning of the delusional state as near as can be ascertained). Leaping from the bed, lie ran to a priest's house for protection from the Evil One. Subsequently was sent to a private asylum for four weeks; afterward under asylum treatment on three different occasions, about three years in all; finally, escaping and getting drunk, was arrested for using profane language on the street, and spent four weeks in jail. Regaining his liberty, worked as porter, Lucifer still pursuing him, but not so "troublesome as formerly. On speaking to a priest about the delusion, the patient was advised to stop drink. Shortly after went to New York, where he kept up his bad habits. At length returned to his home in Connecticut, insulted his mother, sister, and a young woman visitor, owing to which erotic conduct he was compelled to quit the paternal roof, ultimately bringing up in Boston, where he enlisted. in the Marine Corps. This last act was voluntary, and not the outcome of Lucifer's instigation as were the preceding acts, especially those of a criminal or sinful nature; but when asked by an examining officer if there had been anything the matter with him that would tend to disqualify him for military service, Lucifer spoke up and said 'No,' After enlisting he kept up his bad habits. He was transferred to Washington, where his erotic habits and eccentric conduct, particularly his speaking aloud to himself and gesticulating wildly while communing with Lucifer, attracted the attention of officers and men, and led to his being sent to a hospital.

"M. L. speaks of himself as au innocent person who is controlled by a spirit whom he calls 'the young man,' and who in his turn is under the influence of Lucifer, or, at any rate, is engaged in a continual struggle with the latter for supremacy in controlling the actions of L. The young man abuses himself sexually at times, but L. is not responsible for these actions. He does not see Lucifer, but hears him talking and roaring like a lion when opposed and angered. Lucifer tells him to kill the writer or other person finding out L.'s business, but he resists that advice.

"The patient is generally well conducted, and when not assisting at work about the ward will go to a secluded place, where he can be heard upbraiding Lucifer in a loud tone for attempting to control his speech and actions against his will, and tempting him to do things that he knows to be improper. The patient dwells a great deal on the importance of religious duties, earnestly wishes to comply with the rules of the Church, and believes that Lucifer can finally be expelled or chased out by a species of exorcism.

"Patient's memory is fair as regards dates, but he is indifferent to surroundings and to recent occurrences, political or other. Knew when Mr. Cleveland was President; don't know who is now and don't care, his only concern being to get his personality out of trouble, as he feels that he has to answer to God for being the cause of them. For the past six years he has been in league with Lucifer to 'down' L., but for the last six months he has endeavoured to give up his dealings with Lucifer awl to assist L. to return to God. He, as the' young man,' wants to become L.'s good angel. Formerly he was L.'s bad angel or evil counsellor, owing to some sinful act which placed him in Lucifer's power. At each attempt to emancipate himself from the power of Lucifer the latter tantalizes him in every conceivable way. He says Lucifer is afraid of God, but tries to bluff L. into the belief that God does not know and see all things. The patient keeps religious souvenirs about him, which displease Lucifer and induce 'kicking' on his part."

The phenomena of insistent concepts, of imperative ideas, of impulsive mania, of paramnesia, of paranoia and demonomania, can be fully reproduced in our laboratories. From the way we induce the phenomena artificially we can learn how they originate spontaneously. To bring about insistent concepts, irresistible impulses, and all kinds of changes of the ego, we must dissociate the secondary subconscious self from the primary controlling consciousness; we must then inoculate the subconscious self with the idea, impulse, or specious personality, and make a deep cleft between the two selves by enforcing amnesia, otherwise the suggestion will simply rise as a memory. Once, however, disaggregation is enforced, we can easily induce all kinds of insistent ideas, imperative concepts, all forms of irresistible impulses, all sorts of changes of personality; and we may assert that all these forms have at their basis a disaggregation of consciousness, a dissociation of the primary and secondary subconscious selves.

---

1. W. Hammond, A Treatise on Insanity.
2. H. P. Stearns, Mental Diseases.
3. Ribot, Diseases of Memory.
4. Archiv für Psychiatrie, 1873, vol. iv.
5. Mind, xiii.
6. Subtractive paramnesia is a form of amnesia. For a fuller discussion of amnesia see Chapters XXI-XXIII.
7. The theory of Ribot, that metamorphosis of personality is due to a fundamental change in common sensibility, is more fanciful than it is commonly supposed, for that fundamental change remains yet to be proved. There may be a change in common sensibility without a transformation of personality, and also a transformation of personality without a change in common sensibility. Besides, Ribot's theory can not account

for the phenomena of coexistent double or multiple personality.

8. The Psychological Review, November, 1895.
9. I may add that in a private talk with me Prof. Royce admitted that we must look for that source to the subconscious.
10. Theil II, Die Paranoischen Zustände, 1896.
11. Esquirol, Mental maladies.
12. Proceedings of the American Society for Psychological Research, vol. i.
13. March 1892.

17
THE TRAITS OF THE SUBCONSCIOUS SELF

WE are now in a position to characterize the underground self.

The subwaking self is stupid; it lacks all critical sense. A thing must be told to it plainly in all details, and even then it follows more the letter than the spirit of the suggestion. I remind the reader of Prof. W. James's subject who smoked but "one" pipe the whole day, and also of my own subject, who, on being suggested not to have any slight headache, next day came complaining of violent pain. The lack of critical sense is well brought out in the following experiment:

"Mr. V. F. is hypnotized and is suggested to be Sam Smith, a bootblack, ten years of age.

Exp. What is your name?

Sub. Sam Smith.

Exp. Your occupation?

Sub. A bootblack.

Exp. How old are you?

Sub. Ten years,

Exp. What is your father's name?

Sub. (Gives his father's correct name.)

Exp. How is it that your name is Sam Smith and your father's is different?

Sub. I do not know.

On another occasion I made the following experiment on the same subject:

Exp. Are you alive?

Sub. Yes.

Exp. No, you are dead.

Sub. Yes, I think I am dead.

Exp. How long is it since you died?

Sub. A few days ago.

Exp. From what disease?

Sub. I do not know; just died.

Exp. Can you hear and feel me?

Sub. Yes.

Exp. But how can you feel if you are dead?

Sub. I do not know.

The subwaking self is ready to take any suggestion, no matter how ridiculous or painful the suggestion is.

Mr. Y. F. is hypnotized and is suggested that on awakening he should light the gas and bow to the light whenever the door is opened. On awakening he at once rushes to light the gas, and is at last satisfied when he sees the flame.

Exp. What did you light the gas for?

Sub. I do not know, unless I wanted to light my pipe.

Exp. But you have no pipe.

Sub. That is true, but then I can light a cigarette. (Takes a cigarette from my table, lights it, and begins to puff.)

The reason here given by the subject is extremely stupid, because he could far easier light directly the cigarette with the match, and, besides, the gas jet was so high up that he had to give a good jump to reach it.

I then opened the door. The subject bowed to the light. I opened the door again; again the subject bowed to the gas jet. Each opening of the door was followed by a polite bow to the fire.

Exp. Why do you bow to the fire?

Sub. I do not know. I suppose I am practising. I do not know. I feel like a chump while I am doing it.

Exp. Why are you doing it? Can you give any reason?

Sub. None, except that I want to.

Exp. Have you any desire to do it?

Sub. Yes, I think it is a nice thing to do.

I take the hand of the subject, put it on the table, and tell the hypnotic self that the pencil is a lighted candle, the flames issuing from the point. When I now touch any part of the subject's body with the point of the pencil the self screams from great pain. I tell the self," You have a toothache," and he does get the ache.

The subwaking self is extremely credulous; it lacks all sense of the true and rational. "Two and two-make five." "Yes." Anything is accepted if sufficiently emphasized by the hypnotizer. The suggestibility and imitativeness of the subwaking self was discussed by me at great length. What I should like to point out here is the extreme servility and cowardliness of that self. Show hesitation, and it will show fight; command authoritatively, and it will obey slavishly.[1]

The subwaking self is devoid of all morality; it

will steal without the least scruple; it will poison; it
will stab; it will assassinate its best friends without the
least scruple. When completely cut off from the
waking person it is precluded from conscience.[2]

The subwaking self dresses to fashion, gossips in
company, runs riot in business panics, revels in the
crowd, storms in the mob, and prays in the camp
meeting. Its senses are acute, but its sense is nil. Association by contiguity, the mental mechanism of the
brute, is the only one that it possesses.

The subwaking self lacks all personality and individuality; it is absolutely servile; it works according to
no maxims; it has no moral law, no law at all. To be a
law unto one's self, the chief and essential characteristic of personality, is just the very trait the subwaking
self so glaringly lacks. The subwaking self has no will;
it is blown hither and thither by all sorts of incoming
suggestions. *It is essentially a brutal self.*

The primary self alone possesses true personality,
will, and self-control. The primary self alone is a law
unto itself—a person having the power to investigate
his own nature, to discover faults, to create ideals, to
strive after them, to struggle for them, and by continuous, strenuous efforts of will to attain higher and
higher stages of personality.

> Zwei Seelen wohnen, ach! in meiner Brust,
> Die eine will sich von der andern trennen:
> Die eine hält, in derber Liebeslust,
> Sich an die Welt, mit klammernden Organen;
> Die andre hebt gewaltsam sich von Dust
> Zu den Gefilden hoher Ahnen.
>
> — FAUST

1. This is well illustrated in the experiments on my subject A. Fingold, see Chapter XXIV.
2. See an interesting article by Liébault in the Zeitschrift für Hypnotismus for April and May, 1895.

SOCIETY

1
SOCIAL SUGGESTIBILITY

SUGGESTIBILITY is a fundamental attribute of man's nature. We must therefore expect that man, in his social capacity, will display this general property; and so do we actually find the case to be. What is required is only the condition to bring about a disaggregation in the social consciousness. This disaggregation may either be fleeting, unstable——then the type of suggestibility is that of the normal one; or it may become stable——then the suggestibility is of the abnormal type. The one is the suggestibility of the crowd, the other that of the mob. In the mob direct suggestion is effective, in the crowd indirect suggestion. The clever stump orator, the politician, the preacher, fix the attention of their listeners on themselves, interesting them in the "subject." They as a rule distract the attention of the crowd by their stories, frequently giving the suggestion in some indirect and striking way, winding up the long yarn by a climax requiring the immediate execution of the suggested act. Out of the infinite number of cases, I take the first that comes to my hand: On August 11, 1895, at Old Orchard, Me., a camp meeting was held. The purpose was to raise a collection for the evangelization of the world. The preacher gave his suggestions in the following way:

"The most impressive memory I have of foreign lands is the crowds, the billows of lost humanity dashing ceaselessly on the shores of eternity. . . . How desperate and unloved they are—no joy, no spring, no song in their religion! I once heard a Chinaman tell why he was a Christian. It seemed to him that he was down in a deep pit, with no means to get out. [Story.] Have you wept on a lost world as Jesus wept? If not, woe unto you. Your religion is but a dream and a fancy. We find Christ testing his disciples. Shall he make them his partners? Beloved, he is testing you to-day. [Indirect suggestion.] He could convert one thousand millionaires, but he is giving us a chance. [Suggestion more direct than before.] Have we faith enough? [A discourse on faith follows here.] God can not bring about great things without faith. I believe the coming of Jesus will be brought about by one who believes strongly in it. . . . Beloved, if you are going to give grandly for God you have got faith. [The suggestion is still more direct.] The lad with the five loaves and the two small fishes [story]——when it was over the little fellow did not lose his buns; there were twelve baskets over. . . . Oh, beloved, how it will come back! . . . Some day the King of kings will call you and give you a kingdom of glory, and just for trusting him a little! What you give to-day is a great investment. . . . Some day God will let us know how much better he can invest our treasures than we ourselves." The suggestion was effective. Money poured in from all sides, contributions ran from hundreds into thousands, into tens of thousands. The crowd contributed as much as seventy thousand dollars.

A disaggregation of consciousness is easily effected in the crowd. Some of the conditions of suggestibility work in the crowd with great power and on a large scale. The social psychical scalpels are big, powerful; their edges are extremely keen, and they cut sure and deep. If anything gives us a strong sense of our individuality, it is surely our voluntary movements. We may say that the individual self grows and expands with the increase of variety and intensity of its voluntary activity; and conversely, the life of the individual self sinks, shrinks with the decrease of variety and intensity of voluntary movements. We find, accordingly, that the condition of limitation of voluntary movements is of great importance in suggestibility in general, and this condition is of the more importance since it, in fact, can bring about a narrowing down of the field of consciousness with the conditions consequent on that contraction—all favourable to suggestibility. Now nowhere else, except perhaps in solitary confinement, are the voluntary movements of men so limited as they are in the crowd; and the larger the crowd is the greater is this limitation, the lower sinks the individual self. Intensity of personality is in inverse proportion to the number of aggregated men. This law holds true not only in the case of crowds, but also in the case of highly organized masses. Large, massive social organisms produce, as a rule, very small persons. Great men are not to be found in ancient Egypt, Babylon, Assyria, Persia, but rather in the diminutive communities of ancient Greece and Judea.

This condition of limitation of voluntary movements is one of the prime conditions that help to bring about a deep, a more or less lasting dissociation in the consciousness of the crowd—the crowd passes into the mob-state. A large gathering on account of the cramping of voluntary movements easily falls into a state of abnormal suggestibility, and is easily moved by a ringleader or hero. Large assemblies carry within themselves the germs of the possible mob. The crowd contains within itself all the elements and conditions favourable to a disaggregation of consciousness. What is required is only that an interesting object, or that some sudden violent impressions should strongly fix the attention of the crowd, and plunge it into that state in which the waking personality is shorn of its dignity and power, and the naked subwaking self alone remains face to face with the external environment.

Besides limitation of voluntary movements and contraction of the field of consciousness, there are also present in the crowd, the matrix of the mob, the conditions of monotony and inhibition. When the preacher, the politician, the stump orator, the ringleader, the hero gains the ear of the crowd, an ominous silence sets in, a silence frequently characterized as "awful." The crowd is in a state of overstrained expectation; with suspended breath it watches the hero or the interesting, all-absorbing object. Disturbing impressions are excluded, put down, driven away by main force. So great is the silence induced in the fascinated crowd, that very frequently the buzzing of a fly, or even the drop of a pin, can be distinctly heard. All interfering impressions and ideas are inhibited. The crowd is entranced, and rapidly merges into the mob-state.

The great novelist Count Tolstoy gives the following characteristic description of a crowd passing into the entranced condition of the mob: "The crowd remained silent, and pressed on one another closer and closer. To bear the pressure of one another, to breathe in this stifling, contagious atmosphere, not to have the power to stir, and to expect something unknown, incomprehensible, and terrible, became intolerable. Those who were in the front, who saw and heard everything that took place, all those stood with eyes full of fright, widely dilated, with open mouths; and straining their whole strength, they kept on their backs the pressure of those behind them."[1]

The following concrete cases taken from American life will perhaps show clearly the factors that work in the entrancement of the crowd, and will also disclose the disaggregation of consciousness effected in the popular mind.

One of the American newspapers gives the following sensational but interesting account of feminine crowds entranced by Paderewski. There is a chatter, a rustling of programmes, a waving of fans, a nodding of feathers, a general air of expectancy, and the lights are lowered. A hush. All eyes are turned to a small door leading on to the stage; it is opened. Paderewski enters. . . . A storm of applause greets him, . . . but after it comes a tremulous hush and a prolonged sigh, . . . created by the long, deep inhalation of upward of three thousand women. . . . Paderewski is at the piano. . . . Thousands of eyes watch every commonplace movement [of his] through opera glasses with an intensity painful to observe. He the idol, they the idolators. . . . Toward the end of the performance the most decorous women seem to abandon themselves to the influence. . . . There are sighs, sobs, the tight clinching of the palms, the bowing of the head. Fervid exclamations: 'He is my master!' are heard in the feminine mob." In this highly sensational report the paper unconsciously describes all the conditions requisite to effect a disaggregation of consciousness.

The conditions of crowd entrancement are clearly revealed in the following case:

In 1895 a "modern Messiah," a "Man-Christ" by name of Francis Schlatter, appeared in this country. He worked miracles. People believed in his divine, supernatural power. Men, women, and children flocked to him from all sides, and Schlatter did cure many of them of "the ills of the flesh" by "mere laying on of hands," as the hypnotizer treats the entranced subject or the one he intends to entrance. A disaggregation of consciousness was easily effected in the manipulated crowd of believers, the subwaking reflex self emerged, and Schlatter's suggestions took effect. A reporter describes the scene as follows:

"Men, women, and children, with the imprint of mental illness upon their faces were on all sides. . . . Every moment the crowd was augmented, . . . and soon the place was a sea of heads as far as the eye could see. [Limitation of voluntary movements.] . . . Then a sudden movement went through the assemblage, and even the faintest whisper was hushed. [Monotony, inhibition.] . . . Schlatter had come." [Concentration of attention.] The reporter, as the individual of the crowd, fell into the trance condition characteristic of the person in the mob. "As I approached him," writes the reporter, "I became possessed of a certain supernatural fear, which it was difficult to analyze. My faith in the man grew in spite of my reason." The waking, controlling, thinking, reasoning self began to waver, to lose its power, and the reflex, subwaking consciousness began to assert itself.

"As he released my hands my soul acknowledged some power in this man that my mind and my brain (?) seemed to fight against. When he unclasped my hands I felt as though I could kneel at his feet and call him master."

The suggestion given to the entranced crowd by the "master" spreads like wildfire. The given suggestion reverberates from individual to individual, gathers strength, and becomes so overwhelming as to drive the crowd into a fury of activity, into a frenzy of excitement. As the suggestions are taken by the mob and executed the wave of excitement rises higher and higher. Each fulfilled suggestion increases the emotion of the mob in volume and intensity. Each new attack is followed by a more violent paroxysm of furious demoniac frenzy. The mob is like an avalanche: the more it rolls the more menacing and dangerous it grows. The suggestion given by the hero, by the ringleader, by the master of the moment, is taken up by the crowd and is reflected and reverberated from man to man, until every soul is dizzied and every person is stunned. In the entranced crowd, in the mob, everyone influences and is influenced in his turn; every one suggests and is suggested to, and the surging billow of suggestion swells and rises until it reaches a formidable height.

Suppose that the number of individuals in the crowd is 1,000, that the energy of the suggested idea in the "master" himself be represented by 50, and that only one half of it can be awakened in others; then the hero awakens an energy of 25 in every individual, who again in his or her turn awakens in everyone an energy of 12.5. The total energy aroused by the hero is equal to 25 X 1,000 = 25,000. The total energy of suggestion awakened by each individual in the crowd is equal to 12.5 X 1,000, or 12,500 (the hero being included, as he is, after all, but a part of the crowd). Since the number of individuals in the crowd is 1,000, we have the energy rising to as much as 12,500 X 1,000; adding to it the 25,000 produced by the ringleader, we have the total energy of suggestion amounting to 12,525,000 !

The mob energy grows faster than the increase of numbers. The mob spirit grows and expands with each fresh human increment. Like a cannibal it feeds on human beings. In my article A Study of the Mob [2] I point out that the mob has a self of its own; that the personal self is suppressed, swallowed up by it, so much so that when the latter comes once more to the light of day it is frequently horrified at the work, the crime, the mob self had committed; and that once the mob self is generated, or, truer to say, brought to the surface, it possesses a strong attractive power and a great capacity of assimilation. It attracts fresh individuals, breaks down their personal life, and quickly assimilates them; it effects in them a disaggregation of consciousness and assimilates the subwaking selves. Out of the subwaking selves the mob-self springs into being. The assimilated individual expresses nothing but the energy [of the] suggestion, the will of the entranced crowd; he enters fully into the spirit of the mob. This can be well illustrated by a curious incident describing the riots of the military colonists in Russia in 1831, taken from the memoirs of Panaev:

"While Sokolov was fighting hard for his life I saw a corporal lying on the piazza and crying bitterly. On my question, 'why do you cry?' he pointed in the direction of the mob and exclaimed, 'Oh, they do not kill a commander, but a father!' I told him that instead of it he should rather go to Sokolov's aid. He rose at once and ran to the help of his commander. A little later when I came with a few soldiers to Sokolov's help, I found the same corporal striking Sokolov with a club. 'Wretch, what are you doing? Have you not told me he was to you like a father?' To which he answered: 'It is such a time, your honor; all the people strike him; why should I keep quiet?' "

To take another interesting example: During the Russian anti-Jewish riots in 1881 the city of Berditchev, consisting mainly of Jewish inhabitants, suffered from Jewish mobs. One day a Jewish mob of about fifteen thousand men, armed with clubs, butchers' knives, and revolvers, marched through the streets to the railway station to meet the Katzapi.[3] To the surprise of intelligent observers, many Christians were found to participate in this Jewish mob.

An interesting case of this kind is brought by the Rev. H. C. Fish in his Handbook of Revivals:

"While a revival was in progress in a certain village a profane tavern keeper swore he would never be found among the fools who were running to the meetings. On hearing, however, of the pleasing mode of singing his curiosity was excited, and he said he did not know but he might go and hear the singing, but with an imprecation that he would never hear a word of the sermon. As soon as the hymn before the sermon was sung he leaned forward and secured both ears against the sermon with his forefingers. Happening to withdraw one of his forefingers, the words, 'he that hath ears to hear let him hear,' pronounced with great solemnity, entered the ear that was open and struck him with irresistible force. He kept his hand from returning to the ear, and, feeling an impression he had never known before, presently withdrew the other finger and hearkened with deep attention to the discourse which followed." The tavern keeper was fascinated, drawn into the mob of true believers, was converted, and, in the words of the Rev. H. C. Fish, "became truly pious."

The power of suggestion possessed by the revival meeting is well brought out in another case related by the Rev. H. C. Fish: [4]

"An actress in one of the English provincial theatres was one day passing through the streets of the town when her attention was attracted by the sound of voices. Curiosity prompted her to look in at an open door. It was a social (revival) meeting, and at the moment of her observation they were singing:

> Depth of mercy! can there be
> Mercy still reserved for me?

She stood motionless during a prayer which was offered. . . . The words of the hymn followed her. . . . The manager of the theatre called upon her one morning and requested her to sustain the principal character in a new play which was to be performed the next week. . . . She promised to appear. The character she assumed required her on her first entrance to sing a song, and when the curtain was drawn up the orchestra immediately began the accompaniment. But she stood as if lost in thought (she seemed to have fallen into a trance), and as one forgetting all around her and her own situation. The music ceased, but she did not sing, and, supposing her to be overcome by embarrassment, the band again commenced. A second time they paused for her to begin, but still she did not open her lips. A third time the air was played, and then with clasped hand and eyes suffused with

338

tears she sang not the words of the song," but the verses suggested to her at the revival meeting:

Depth of mercy! can there be
Mercy still reserved for me?

"The performance," the Rev. H. C. Fish naïvely adds, "was suddenly ended."

The extreme impulsiveness of the mob self is notorious. No sooner is a suggestion accepted, no matter how criminal, how inhuman it might be, than it is immediately realized, unless another suggestion more in accord with the general nature of suggestions in which the mob self was trained, interferes and deflects the energy of the mob in another direction. The following interesting case will perhaps best illustrate my meaning.

On February 6, 1896, at Wichita Falls, Texas, a mob of several thousand men attacked the jail where two bank robbers were confined. The mob battered the jail doors and forcibly took possession of the two prisoners. The two men were taken to the bank which they attempted to rob the day before. An improvised scaffold was erected. The first impulse of the mob was to burn the prisoners. Roasting was the programme. This inquisitorial mode of execution "without shedding human blood" was by suggestion changed to hanging, the way of execution commonly in use in this country to inflict capital punishment, the way of murder common to all American lynching mobs.

The consciousness of the mob is reflex in its nature. In the entranced crowd, in the mob, social consciousness is disaggregated, thus exposing to the direct influence of the environment the reflex con-

sciousness of the social subwaking self. The subwaking mob self slumbers within the bosom of
society.

------

1. Voina i Mir. (War and Peace.)
2. Atlantic Monthly, February, 1895.
3. A Malo-Russian term for Veliko-Russians. In all anti-Jewish
   riots Veliko-Russiuns were the ringleaders.
4. Handbook of Revivals.

2

SOCIETY AND EPIDEMICS

WHEN animals, on account of the great dangers that threaten them, begin to rove about in groups, in companies, in herds, and thus become social, such animals, on pain of extinction, must vary in the direction of suggestibility; they must become more and more susceptible to the emotional expression of their comrades, and reproduce it instantaneously at the first impression. When danger is drawing near, and one of the herd detects it and gives vent to his muscular expression of fear, attempting to escape, those of his comrades who are most susceptible reproduce the movements, experience the same emotions that agitate their companion, and are thus alone able to survive in the struggle for existence. A delicate susceptibility to the movements of his fellows is a question of life and death to the individual in the herd. Suggestibility is of vital importance to the group, to society, for it is the only way of rapid communication social brutes can possibly possess. Natural selection seizes on this variation and develops it to its highest degree. Individuals having a more delicate susceptibility to suggestions survive, and leave a greater progeny which more or less inherit the characteristics of their parents. In the new generation, again, natural selection resumes its merciless work, making the useful trait of suggestibility still more prominent, and the sifting process goes on thus for generations, endlessly. A highly developed suggestibility, an extreme, keen susceptibility to the sensori-motor suggestions, coming from its companions, and immediately realizing those suggestions by passing through the motor processes it witnesses, is the only way by which the social brute can become conscious of the emotions that agitate its fellows. The sentinel posted by the wasps becomes agitated at the sight of danger, flies into the interior of the nest buzzing violently, the whole nestful of wasps raises a buzzing, and is thus put into the same state of emotion which the sentinel experiences.

Suggestibility is the cement of the herd, the very soul of the primitive social group. A herd of sheep stands packed close together, looking abstractedly, stupidly, into vacant space. Frighten one of them; if the animal begins to run, frantic with terror, a stampede ensues. Each sheep passes through the movements of its neighbour. The herd acts like one body animated by one soul. Social life presupposes suggestion. No society without suggestibility. Man is a social animal, no doubt; but he is social because he is suggestible. Suggestibility, however, requires disaggregation of consciousness; hence, society presupposes a cleavage of the mind, it presupposes a plane of cleavage between the differentiated individuality and the undifferentiated reflex consciousness, the indifferent sub waking self. Society and mental epidemics are intimately related; for the social gregarious self is the suggestible subconscious self.

The very organization of society keeps up the disaggregation of consciousness. The rules, the customs, the laws of society are categorical, imperative, absolute. One must obey them on pain of death. Blind obedience is a social virtue.[1] But blind obedience is the very essence of suggestibility, the constitution of the disaggregated subwaking self. Society by its nature, by its organization, tends to run riot in mobs, manias, crazes, and all kinds of mental epidemics.

With the development of society the economical, political, and religious institutions become more and more differentiated; their rules, laws, by-laws, and regulations become more and more detailed, and tend to crimp the individual, to limit, to constrain his voluntary movements, to contract his field of consciousness, to inhibit all extraneous ideas—in short, to create conditions requisite for a disaggregation of consciousness. If, now, something striking fixes the attention of the public—a brilliant campaign, a glittering holy image, or a bright "silver dollar"—the subwaking social self, the demon of the demos, emerges, and society is agitated with crazes, manias, panics, and mental plagues of all sorts.

With the growth and civilization of society, institutions become more stable, laws more rigid, individuality is more and more crushed out, and the poor, barren subwaking self is exposed in all its nakedness to the vicissitudes of the external world. In civilized society laws and regulations press on the individual from all sides. Whenever one attempts to rise above the dead level of commonplace life, instantly the social screw begins to work, and down is brought upon him the tremendous weight of the socio-static press, and it squeezes him back into the mire of mediocrity, frequently crushing him to death for his bold attempt. Man's relations in life are determined and fixed for him; he is told how he must put on his tie, and the way he must wear his coat; such should be the fashion of his dress on this particular occasion, and such should be the form of his hat; here must he nod his head, put on a solemn air; and there take off his hat, make a profound bow, and display a smile full of delight. Personality is suppressed by the rigidity of social organization; the cultivated, civilized individual is an automaton, a mere puppet.

Under the enormous weight of the socio-static process, under the crushing pressure of economical, political, and religious regulations there is no possibility for the individual to determine his own relations in life; there is no possibility for him to move, live, and think freely; the personal self sinks, the suggestible, subconscious, social, impersonal self rises to the surface, gets trained and cultivated, and becomes the hysterical actor in all the tragedies of historical life.

Laws and mobs, society and epidemics—are they not antagonistic? In point of fact they are intimately, vitally interrelated, they are two sides of the same shield.

Under normal conditions social activity no doubt works wonders; it elaborates such marvellous products as language, folklore, mythology, tribal organization, etc.—products that can only be studied and admired by the intellect of the scientist. When, however, the social conditions are of such a nature as to charge society with strong emotional excitement, or when the institutions dwarf individuality, when they arrest personal growth, when they hinder the free development and exercise of the personal controlling consciousness, then society falls into a hypnoid condition, the social mind gets disaggregated. The gregarious self begins to move within the bosom of the crowd and becomes active; the demon of the demos emerges to the surface of social life and throws the body politic into convulsions of demoniac fury.

---

1. "The Vast majority of persons," writes F. Galton, "of our race have a natural tendency to shrink from the reponsibility of standing and acting alone;' they exalt the vox *populi,* even when they know it to be the utterance of a mob of nobodies, into the *vox Dei,* and are willing slaves to tradition, authority, and custom."

3

STAMPEDES

M ENTAL epidemics, panics, stampedes occurring in social animals, are especially interesting from our point of view. In the Journal of Mental Science for January, 1872, Dr. W. Lauder Lindsay brings a few cases of stampedes among cavalry horses. Of these stampedes four deserve our special attention. Three were English, one was Russian.

On Monday August 30, 1871, a stampede happened among the horses of the First Life Guard, encamped on Cove Common, near Aldershot. The Daily Telegraph of September 1, 1871, gives the following description of the panic: "A sudden noise frightened the horses of two officers and caused them to start from their pickets, followed by six troop horses. A panic then seized on the whole line; three hundred horses broke loose simultaneously, running, in all directions, some dragging the cords and pins, and all wearing their saddle cloths. . . . Almost every open route had been taken by the fugitives. . . At one point the troop dashed against the closed toll-gate and smashed it to pieces, while . . . many plunged against stakes or other obstructions, seriously injuring themselves. Several dropped down dead within an hour; some were drowned in the canal, and others were captured in a crippled state." "Who could have thought," exclaims the Times, "that horses would go mad, like Goldsmith's dog, to gain some private end of their own? and yet, what other conclusion can we form? . . . A sedate and virtuous body of three hundred horses suddenly going mad, running over one another, kicking and fighting among themselves, and committing suicide by all the means in their power. . . The three hundred horses . . . became frenzied with the same unity of purpose."

On September 2, 1871, a second stampede occurred to the horses of the Second Dragoon Guards, also encamped on Cove Common. This time the stampede was on a somewhat smaller scale than the first one. According to the Daily News of September 4, 1871, seventy-six horses suddenly broke loose from the right wing of the regiment and galloped madly in all directions. The vast expanse of common ground in the locality is intersected by the Basingstoke Canal and numerous ditches, into which many of the animals plunged or fell, and were with difficulty rescued from drowning or suffocation."

Next day, September 3d, a still smaller stampede of forty only occurred in the same camp to the horses of the Tenth Hussars. The epidemic was rapidly losing ground, and vanished altogether with the third stampede.

If now we inquire after the immediate or exciting cause in all these stampedes, we find it invariably to be some very trivial accident, in itself utterly disproportionate to the effect produced. Thus the first stampede was caused by a flock of geese that disturbed the repose of the chargers, and the second was brought about by "a runaway horse from an adjacent camp." The exciting cause was insignificant; what, then, was the predisposing cause?——The natural social suggestibility of horsekind. Compare now these equine stampedes with similar stampedes or panics among men. The following case may serve as a good illustration:

In the Year 1761 the citizens of London were alarmed by two shocks of an earthquake, and the prophecy of a third, which was to destroy them altogether. A crack-brained fellow named Bell, a soldier in the Life Guards, was so impressed with the idea that there would be a third earthquake in another month that he lost his senses and ran about the streets predicting the destruction of London on the 5th of April. Thousands confidently believed his prediction and took measures to transport themselves and their families from the scene of the impending calamity. As the awful day approached the excitement became intense, and great numbers of credulous people resorted to all the villages within a circuit of twenty miles, awaiting the doom of London. Islington, Highgate, Hampstead, Harrow, and Blackheath were crowded with panic-stricken fugitives, who paid exorbitant prices for accommodation to the housekeepers of these secure retreats. Such as could not afford to pay for lodgings at any of those places remained in London until two or three days before the time, and then encamped in the surrounding fields, awaiting the tremendous shock which was to lay the city all level with the dust. The fear became contagious, and hundreds, who had laughed at the prediction a week before, packed up their goods when they saw others doing so and hastened away. The river was thought to be a place of great security, and all the merchant vessels in the port were filled with people, who passed the night between the 4th and 5th on board, expecting every instant to see St. Paul's totter and the towers of Westminster Abbey rock in the wind and fall amid a cloud of dust.

Stampedes have their leaders just as mobs have their instigators, as political parties have their bosses, and as great movements have their saints and heroes. Each great stampede has its political boss, its "runaway horse," its hero who is obeyed blindly and devotedly followed even to the point of self-destruction. The suggestion of the hero is fatal in its effects. The special correspondent of The Scotsman, in commenting on the English stampedes, truly remarks: "It is always one or two horses which begin the mischief; and if they were quieted at once, the contagion of the panic would be arrested."

If not counteracted, the suggestion given by the boss of the stampede is simply irresistible, and is carried out in a spirit of perfectly blind, slavish obedience. This can be clearly seen in the Russian St. Petersburg stampede of 1871. The Times correspondent gives the following account of it:

"On the second night of the campaign an unlucky accident occurred. . . . A regiment of the Empress's Cuirassiers of the Guard, nine hundred strong, . . . had arrived at their cantonments. One of the squadron of horses became alarmed, broke away, was followed by the next squadron, and, a panic seizing them all, in one instant the whole nine hundred fled in wild disorder. . . . Two things were very remarkable in this stampede. In the first place, they unanimously selected one large, powerful horse as their leader, and, with a look at him and a snort at him which they meant and he understood as *après vous*, they actually waited until he dashed to the front, and then followed in wild confusion. When I tell you that some of the horses were not recovered till they had gone one hundred and twenty miles into Finland, you may imagine what the panic was.

"The second remarkable thing is the way that some of them were stopped. In one solid mass they dashed on for miles, and then came directly, at right angles, on a river. In front of them was a bridge, but on the other side of the bridge was a sort of *tête du pont* and a small picket of cavalry. The horse which led would not face the bridge, seeing the cavalry at the other end, but turned to one side, dashed into the stream, and the whole nine hundred horses swam the river together. As they emerged and flew wildly on, the commander of the picket bethought him of a ruse, and ordered a bugler to blow the appel. This is always blown when the horses are going to be fed. . . . All the old horses pricked up their ears, wavered, stopped, paused, turned round and trotted back. . . . This severed the mass. . . . The rest was broken up."

Those who live in a democracy and have the interests of the country at heart may well ponder on these stampedes. From our standpoint these stampedes are very interesting and highly instructive, because they clearly show the extreme suggestibility to which the social brute is constantly subject.

4

MEDIÆVAL MENTAL
EPIDEMICS

THE phenomena of history lie open before us. Looking back to the middle ages, we find them to be times in which abnormal social suggestibility was displayed on a grand scale—times full of mobs, riots, of blind movements of vast human masses, of terrible epidemics ravaging Europe from end to end. They were ages peculiar for the seemingly strange fact that whole cities, extensive provinces, great countries were stricken by one mental disease. Men went mad in packs, in tens of thousands. An obscure individual in some remote country place went off into fits of hysterics, and soon nations were struggling in convulsions of hysterical insanity.

The middle ages appear to us as dark and brutal. We consider ourselves vastly superior to the mediæval peasant, burgher, and knight, with their superstitions, religious fervor, with their recurrent mental epidemics. But might we not meet with a similar fate at the hands of our descendants? Might not a future historian look back to our own times with dismay, if not with horror? He might represent our "modern civilized" times as dark, cruel, brutal; times of the St. Bartholomew butchery and other Protestant massacres; times of the Thirty Years' War, of the Seven Years' War, of the terrors of the French Revolution, of the brutal Napoleonic wars; times of the absurd tulip craze in Holland, of great commercial manias and business bubbles, and of still greater industrial panics and crises; times of Salvation armies, Coxey mobs, of blind religious revivals, of mental epidemics and plagues of all sorts and descriptions.

Different as mediæval society is from our own, it is still at bottom of like nature. A close inspection of it will therefore help us to see clearer into the nature of our own social life.

The life of the mediæval individual was regulated down to its least details by rigid laws, orders, and commands. The guild, the order, the commune, and the church all had minute regulations, rules, and prescriptions for the slightest exigencies of life. Nothing was left to individual enterprise; even love had its rules and customs. Society was divided and subdivided into classes and groups, each having its own fixed rules, each leading its own peculiar, narrow, dwarfish life. The weight of authority was crushing, social pressure was overwhelming, the inhibition of the individual's will was complete, and the suggestible, social, subwaking self was in direct relation with the external environment.

A brief review of the chief mental epidemics of that time will at once show us the extreme suggestibility of mediæval society.

The most striking phenomenon in mediæval history is that of the Crusades, which agitated European nations for about two centuries, and cost them about seven million men. People were drawn by an irresistible longing toward the Holy Sepulchre, which fascinated their mental gaze, ,just as the butterfly is blindly drawn toward the candle. This attraction of devout Christians by the Holy Sepulchre manifested itself in pilgrimages, which at first were rare, but gradually spread, and became a universal mania. Bishops abandoned their dioceses, princes their dominions, to visit the tomb of Christ.

At the time of its highest tide, the flood of pilgrims was suddenly stopped by the Seljukian Turks, who conquered Palestine about 1076. As a maniac, when thwarted in his purpose, becomes raving and violent, so did Europe become when the floodgates of the pilgrim torrent were stopped, and only drops were let to trickle through. European humanity fell into a fit of acute mania which expressed itself in the savage ecstasy of the first Crusade.

Peter the Hermit and Pope Urban II were the heroes who first broke the ice, and directed the popular current to the conquest of the Holy Land. The fiery appeals of the emaciated, dwarfish hermit Peter carried everything before them. The frenzy which had unsettled the mind of the hermit was by him communicated to his hearers, and they became enraptured, entranced with the splendid schemes he unfolded.

Meantime Pope Urban II convoked two councils, one after another. At the second council, that of Clermont, the pope addressed a multitude of thousands of people. His speech was at first listened to in solemn silence. Gradually, however, as he proceeded, sobs broke out. "Listen to nothing," he exclaimed, "but the groans of Jerusalem! . . . And remember that the Lord has said, 'He that will not take up his cross and follow me is unworthy of me.' You are the soldiers of the cross; wear, then, on your breast or on your shoulders the blood-red sign of him who died for the salvation of your soul!" The suggestion was irresistible. Leaving the fields and towns, agricultural serfs and petty traders displayed intense eagerness to reach the Holy City. If a rational individual interfered with a word of warning, their only answer was the suggestion of the pope, "He who will not follow me is unworthy of me." The whole world of Western Christendom fell into a deep somnambulic condition. This state of social somnambulism was naturally accompanied by its usual phenomena, by illusions, hallucinations, and delusions——in other words, by religious visions and miracles.

Heinrich von Sybel, in speaking of the first Crusade, tells us that "we can hardly understand such a state of mind. It was much as if a large army were now to embark in balloons, in order to conquer an island between the earth and the moon, which was also expected to contain the paradise." Swarms of men of different races, with their wives and daughters, with infants taken from the cradle, and grandsires on the verge of the grave, and many sick and dying, came from every direction, all of them ready to be led to the conquest of the Holy Land. Peter the Hermit, Walter the Penniless, and Gottschalk became the heroes, the ringleaders of the mobs, which were cut to pieces before they reached Palestine. Then followed an army led by pilgrim princes, who succeeded in conquering the Holy Land, and founded there a Christian kingdom; but this kingdom was unstable, and it fell again and again into the hands of the unbelievers, and crusade after crusade was organized, each being a weaker copy of the preceding, until

1272, when the crusade epidemic was completely at an end.

During the same period of time there were also western crusades against the Arabians in Spain and against the unfortunate Albigenses in southern France. In the crusade against the Albigenses, according to Albert von Stade, a peculiar religious mania broke out among women; thousands of them, stark naked and in deep silence, as if stricken with dumbness, ran frantically about the streets. In Lüttich many of them fell into convulsions of ecstasy.

The abnormal suggestibility of mediæval society was most clearly seen in the crusades of children; about 1212, between the fourth and fifth crusades, Stephen, a shepherd boy at Cloyes, in imitation of his elders, began to preach to children of a holy war. Stephen soon became the rage of the day; the shrines were abandoned to listen to his words. He even worked miracles. The appeal of Stephen to the children to save the Holy Sepulchre aroused in the young a longing to join him in the holy pilgrimage.

The crusade epidemic rapidly spread among the little ones. Everywhere there arose children of ten years, and some even as young as eight, who claimed to be prophets sent by Stephen in the name of God. When the "prophets" had gathered sufficient numbers, they began to march through towns and villages. Like a true epidemic, this migration-mania spared neither boys nor girls; according to the statements of the chroniclers, there was a large proportion of little girls in the multitude of hypnotized children.

The king, Philip Augustus, by the advice of the University of Paris, issued an edict commanding the children to return to their homes; but the religious suggestions were stronger than the king's command,

and the children continued to assemble unimpeded. Fathers and mothers brought to bear upon the young all the influence they had to check this dangerous migration- mania, but of no avail. Persuasions, threats, punishments were as futile as the king's command. Bolts and bars could not hold the children. If shut up, they broke through doors and windows, and rushed to take their places in the processions which they saw passing by. If the children were forcibly detained, so that escape was impossible, they pined away like migratory birds kept in seclusion.

In a village near Cologne, Nicolas, a boy of ten, began to play at crusade, preaching. Thousands of children flocked to him from all sides. As in France, all opposition was of no avail. Parents, friends, and pastors sought to restrain them by force or appeal; but the young ones pined so that, as the chroniclers say, their lives were frequently endangered, as by disease, and it was necessary to allow them to depart. Hosts of children assembled in the city of Cologne to start on their pilgrimage to the Holy Land. There they were divided into two armies, one under the leadership of Nicolas, the boy-prophet, the other under some unknown leader. The armies of the little crusaders, like Coxey's army of our own times, were soon reduced in numbers by mere lack of food.

After many tribulations the army led by Nicolas, considerably reduced in size, reached Rome, where the pope, Innocent III, succeeded in diverting this stream of little pilgrims back to Germany. Ruined, degraded, and ridiculed, the poor German children reached their homes; and when asked what they in reality wanted, the children, as if aroused from a narcotic state, answered that they did not know.

The other German army had a worse fate. After

untold sufferings and enormous loss of numbers, they reached Brindisi, where they were treated with extreme cruelty. The boys were seized by the citizens and sold into slavery, and the girls were maltreated and sold into dens of infamy.

The French little crusaders met with a similar fate. When, after a long and fatiguing journey, they at last reached Marseilles, two pious merchants voluntarily offered to provide vessels to convey the children to Palestine. Half of the vessels suffered shipwreck, and the rest were directed to the shores of Africa, where the little pilgrims were delivered into the hands of the Turks and Arabians. The two pious merchants were slave dealers.

A contemporary chronicler[1] describes the children's crusade epidemic in the following barbaric, doggerel Latin verse:

> Hic vide perigrinacioncm et qualiter per
>   incantacinnes sunt decepti,
> Illis temporibus stupendum quid crevit.
> Mundoque mirabilis truffa inolevit.
> Nam sub boni specie malum sic succrevit.
> Arte quiden magiclt iata tatc aevit.
> . . . . . .
> Talis devocio ante hec non est audito.
> Aures cunctis pruriunt virgnes ornantur.
> Annos infra scdecim evangelizantur.
> Concurrentes pucri ccrtant et seqllantur.
> Et romorew viderant casso consolantur.
> Ungarus Theutunicus Francus sociantur.
> Boemus Lombardicus Brittoque canantur.
> Flandria Vestfalia amnes federantur.
> Friso cum Norwagia cuncti conglobantur
> Prurit pes et oculus pucros venantur.

Risum lctus occopat digne lamentantur.

No sooner did the crusade epidemic abate than another one took its place, that of the flagellants. In 1260 the flagellants appeared in Italy, and from there spread all over Europe. "An unexampled spirit of remorse," writes a chronicler, "suddenly seized on the minds of the people. The fear of Christ fell on all; noble and ignoble, old and young, and even children of five, marched on the streets with no covering but a scarf round their waists. They each had a scourge of leather thongs, which they applied to their limbs with sighs and tears with such violence that blood flowed from their wounds."

As the flagellant epidemic was dying away, a terrible plague arose, and this time a deadly one—that of the black death. While the black death was doing its merciless, destructive work, a frenzy of anti-Semitic mania seized on European nations; they brutally burned and slaughtered the unfortunate Jews by thousands, sparing neither sex nor age. The black death over, the dancing mania began. About the year 1370 thousands of dancers filled the streets of European cities. So virulent was this epidemic that peasants left their ploughs, mechanics their workshops, and housewives their domestic duties, to join the wild revels. Girls and boys quitted their parents, and servants their masters, to look at the dancers, and greedily imbibed the poison of mental infection.

In Italy the dancing mania took a somewhat different form. There a belief spread that he who was bitten by a tarantula (a species of spider whose sting is no more harmful than that of the ordinary wasp) got dangerously sick, and could not be cured unless he danced to the tune of the tarantella. Nothing short of death itself was expected from the wound which those insects inflicted; and if those who were bitten escaped with their lives, they were pining away in a desponding state of lassitude. Many became weak-sighted, lost the power of speech, and were insensible to ordinary causes of excitement. At the sound of musical instruments the patients awoke from their lethargy and started a most passionate dance. Tarantism became the plague of Italy. Crowds of patients thronged the streets of the Italian cities, and danced madly to the merry tune of the tarantella. The epidemic reached such a height and became so widely spread that few persons could claim to be entirely exempt from it. Neither youth nor age was spared. Old men of ninety and children of five were alike attacked by it.

Social suggestibility is individual hypnotization written large. The laws of hypnosis work on a great scale in society. Hypnotic suggestion is especially effective if it accords with the character of the subject. The same holds true in the case of social hynotization. Each nation has its own bent of mind, and suggestions given in that direction are fatally effective. The Jew is a fair example. Religious emotions are at the basis of his character, and he is also highly susceptible to religious suggestions. The list of Jewish Messiahs is inordinately long. It would take too much space to recount the names of all the "saviours" who appeared among the Jews from the second destruction of the temple down to our own times. A few strong cases, however, will suffice. In the year 1666, on Rosh Hashanah (Jewish New Year), a Jew, by name Sabbathai Zevi, declared himself publicly as the long-expected Messiah. The Jewish populace was full of glee at hearing such happy news, and in the ardour of its belief, in the insanity of its religions intoxication, shouted fervently, "Long live the Jewish King, our Messiah!" A maniacal ecstasy took possession of the Jewish mind. Men, women, and children fell into fits of hysterics. Business men left their occupations, workmen their trades, and devoted themselves to prayer and penitence. The synagogues resounded with sighs, cries, and sobs for days and nights together. The religious mania became so furious that all the rabbis who opposed it had to save their lives by flight. Among the Persian Jews the excitement ran so high that all the Jewish husbandmen refused to labour in the fields. Even Christians regarded Sabbathai with awe, for this event took place in the apocalyptic year. The fame of Sabbathai spread throughout the world. In Poland, in Germany, in Holland, and in England, the course of business was interrupted on the exchange by the gravest Jews breaking off to discuss this wonderful event. The Jews of Amsterdam sent inquiries to their commercial agents in the Levant, and received the brief and emphatic reply, "It is He, and no other!"

Whenever the messages of the Messiah came, there the Jews instituted fast days, according to the cabalistic regulations of Nathan the prophet, and afterward abandoned themselves to gross intemperance. The Jewish communities of Amsterdam and Hamburg were especially conspicuous for their absurd religious extravagances. In Amsterdam the Jews marched through the streets, carrying with them rolls of the torah, singing, leaping, and dancing as if possessed. Scenes still more turbulent, licentious, and wild occurred in Hamburg, Venice, Leghorn, Avignon, and in many other cities of Italy, Germany,

France, and Poland. The tide of religious mania rose so high that even such Jearned men as Isaac Aboab, Moses de Aguilar, Isaac Noar, the rich banker and writer Abraham Pereira, and the Spinozist, Dr. Benjamin Musaphia, became ardent adherents of the Messiah. Spinoza himself seemed to have followed these strange events with great interest.

The tide of religious mania rose higher and higher. In all parts of the world prophets and prophetesses appeared, thus realizing the Jewish belief in the inspired nature of Messianic times. Men and women, boys and girls, wriggled in hysterical convulsions, screaming praises to the new Messiah; many went raving about in prophetic raptures, exclaiming: "Sabbathai Zevi is the true Messiah of the race of David; to him the crown and kingdom are given!"

The Jews seemed to have gone mad. From all sides rich men came to Sabbathai, putting their wealth at his disposal. Many sold out their houses and all they possessed, and set out for Palestine. So great was the number of pilgrims that the price of passage was considerably raised. Traffic in the greatest commercial centres came to a complete standstill; most of the Jewish merchants and bankers liquidated their affairs. The belief in the divine mission of Sabbathai was made into a religious dogma of equal rank with that of the unity of God. Even when Sabbathai was compelled by the Sultan to accept Mohammedanism the mystico-Messianic epidemic continued to rage with unabated fury. Many stubbornly rejected the fact of his apostasy: it was his shade that had turned Mussulman.

After Sabbathai's death a new prophet appeared, by the name of Michael Cordozo. His doctrine, in spite of its manifest absurdity, spread like wildfire. "The Son of David," he said, "will not appear until all Israel is either holy or wicked." As the latter was by far the easier process, he recommended all true Israelites to hasten the coming of the Messiah by turning Mohammedans. Great numbers with pious zeal complied with his advice. As individual man may be foolish and mischievous, but as a social brute he is absurd and dangerous.

---

1. Anon. Chron. Rhythmicum, in Rauch's Rerum Austriacarum Scriptores.

5
DEMONOPHOBIA

ABOUT the end of the fifteenth century the germs of a fearful epidemic got lodged within the subconscious mind of Western humanity. Demonophobia, the fear of demons, the fear of witchcraft, got possession of the mind of European nations. Whole populations seemed to have been driven crazy with the fear of the devil. For more than a century and a half did the epidemic of demonophobia rage with an overwhelming fury. No one was exempt from this malady of truly infernal origin. The old and the young, the ignorant and the learned, were stricken by it alike.

In all European countries the same absurd opinions and insane ideas prevailed as to the power of impious and malicious people, especially of old women, to effect supernatural mischief, to fly through space, to change themselves into dogs, cats, wolves, and goats, to kill, worry, or terrify men, women, and children for their pastime, and to feed on the flesh of the latter at horrid banquets presided over by devils.[1]

Europe seemed to have become a vast asylum of paranoics, of monomaniacs, possessed with the fear of persecution by infernal agencies. Weak-minded persons, old, helpless, demented men and women, hysterical subjects, and insane patients with a disposition to form delusions were accused, or accused themselves, of having entered into intimate relationship with imps, incubi, succubi, and even of having had direct intercourse with the archfiend himself. So strong were the suspicions of this peculiar acute form of social *paranoia persecutoria* that neither beauty nor tender age could serve as protection.

The pope, Innocent VIII, in his bull of 1488 made a strong appeal to his Catholic fold to rescue the Church of Christ from the power of Satan. He preached a crusade against the atrocious, unpardonable sin of witchcraft. The land must be purified of this great evil. Those servants of the devil, the sorcerers and witches, commit the horrible crime of having intercourse with impure spirits; moreover, they delight in mischief and evildoing; they blast the corn of the field, the herbs of the orchard, the grapes of the garden, and the fruits of the trees; they afflict with diseases man and beast. Sorcery must be wiped out from the face of the earth.

The appeal of the pope made a strong impression on the minds of the people, and the malady of demonophobia was fairly under way. On all sides men sprang up who made it their sole business to discover and burn sorcerers and witches. Sprenger, the author of *Malleus Maleficarum,* with true German thoroughness, even worked out a whole system of rules by which the inquisitors in other countries might best discover the guilty. The inquisitors, for instance, were required to ask the suspected whether they had midnight meetings with the devil; whether they attended the witches' sabbath; whether they could raise whirlwinds; whether they had had sexual intercourse with Satan. To elicit affirmative answers, tortures of the most excruciating kinds were employed.

Pious and zealous inquisitors set at once to their deadly work. Cumanus, in Italy, burned forty-one poor women in one province alone; and Sprenger, in Germany, burned numbers of them; his victims amounted to as many as nine hundred in a year. The German commissioners appointed by the pope, Innocent VIII, condemned to the stake upward of three thousand victims.

The new commissioners for the extermination of witchcraft appointed by each successive pope still further increased the virulence of the epidemic. One was appointed by Alexander VI in 1494, another by Leo X in 1521, and a third by Adrian VI in 1522. The epidemic of demonophobia increased from year to year, and the spirit of persecution grew in vigour and intensity. In Geneva alone five hundred persons were burned in the years 1515 and 1516. Bartholomew de Spina informs us that in the year 1524 no less than a *thousand* persons suffered death for witchcraft in the district of Como, and that for several years afterward the average number of victims exceeded one hundred annually. One inquisitor, Remigius, took great credit to himself for having during fifteen years convicted and burned nine hundred. The inquisitor of a rural township in Piedmont burned the victims so plentifully and so fast that there was not a family in the place which had not its dead to mourn.

The Reformation helped little to alleviate this witchcraft mania; on the contrary, it only served to intensify this truly demoniacal malady. The spirit of persecution was even stronger in Protestant than in Catholic countries. In Luther's Table Talk we find the following item:

"August 25, 1538. The conversation fell upon witches, who spoil milk, eggs, and butter in farmyards. Dr. Luther said: *'I should have no compassion on these witches; I would burn all of them.'*"

In France, fires for the execution of witches blazed in almost every town. Children were torn away from their parents and wives taken from their husbands and cruelly sacrificed to the Moloch of demonophobia. The people became so strongly possessed with the fear of persecution by infernal agencies that in 1579 a great alarm was raised in the neighbourhood of Melun by the increase of witches, and a council was to devise some measures to stay the evil. A decree was passed that all witches and consultors with witches should be punished with death; and not only those, but also fortune-tellers and conjurers. In the following year the Parliament of Rouen took up the same question, and decreed that the possession of a *grimoire*, or book of spells, was sufficient evidence of witchcraft, and that all persons on whom such books were found should be burned alive. Three councils were held in different parts of France in the year 1583, all relating to demonophobia.

From the Continent the epidemic spread to England. In 1562 the statute of Elizabeth declared witchcraft as a crime of the highest magnitude. An epidemic terror of witchcraft seized on the English mind, and this epidemic spread and grew in virulence with the growth of Puritanism.

In Scotland the germs of the epidemic were diligently cultivated by the preachers of the Reformation. In 1563 the ninth parliament of Queen Mary passed an act that decreed the punishment of death against witches and consulters of witches. The Scotch nation was smitten with an epidemic fear of the devil and his infernal agents. Sorcerers and witches were hunted out and tortured with a truly demoniacal cruelty. As a fair example of the cruelties and tortures practised on the poor unfortunates convicted of witchcraft may be taken the case of Dr. Fian, a petty schoolmaster of Tranent.

Dr. Fian was accused of sorcery. He was arrested and put on the rack, but he would confess nothing, and held out so long unmoved that the severe tortures of the *boots* was resolved upon. He fainted away from great pain, but still no confession escaped his lips. Restoratives were then administered to him, and during the first faint gleam of returning consciousness he was prevailed upon to sign a full confession of his crime. He was then remanded to his prison, from which he managed to escape. He was soon recaptured and brought before the Court of Judiciary, James I, the demonologist, being present. Fian denied all the circumstances of the written confession which he had signed; whereupon the king, enraged at his stubborn wilfulness, ordered him once more to the torture. Dr. Fian's finger nails were riven out with pincers, and long needles thrust, their entire length, into the quick. He was then consigned again to the boots, in which he continued "so long, and abode so many blows in them that his legs were crushed and beaten together as small as might be, and the bones and flesh so bruised that the blood and marrow spouted forth in great abundance."

The social malady of demonophobia kept on growing among the Scotch, and the spirit of persecution grew in violence from year. From the passing of the act of Queen Mary till the accession of James to the throne of England, a period of thirty-nine years, the average number of persecutions for witchcraft in Scotland was two hundred annually, or upward of seventeen thousand victims.

Witch-finding in Scotland became a regular trade, and hundreds of ruffians carried on this profession with great profit. It was believed that the devil put his mark on his servants in the shape of an anæsthetic, or rather analgesic, spot—a spot free from pain. Such anæsthetic spots, as we know, exist in hysterical subjects, and can be easily induced by suggestion. The witch-finders, armed with long pins, roamed about the country, pricking the flesh of supposed criminals. Once the anæsthetic spot was found the person was doomed to death. So acute was the social mental malady of demonophobia that no one once accused of relations with the devil was acquitted. To be accused of witchcraft meant to be guilty of it, and to be guilty of witchcraft was certain death.

In the year 1597 King James I published his famous—or infamous—treatise on demonology. "Witches," says the king, "ought to be put to death, according to the law of God, the civil and imperial law, and the municipal law of all Christian nations: yea, to spare the life, and not strike whom God bids strike, and so severely punish in so odious a treason against God, is not only unlawful, but doubtless as great a sin in the magistrate as was Saul's sparing Agag." He says also that the crime is so abominable that it may be proved by evidence which would not be received against any other offenders—young children who knew not the nature of an oath and persons of an infamous character being sufficient witnesses against them. To be, however, more sure, James gives us well-tried tests for the discovery of witches and sorcerers. "Two good helps," says James, "may be used: the one is the finding of their mark and the trying of the insensibleness thereof; the other is their floating on the water; for, as in a secret murther, if the dead carcass be at any time thereafter handled by the murtherer, it will gush out of the blood, as if the blood were crying to Heaven for revenge of the murtherer (God having appointed that secret supernatural sign for trial of that secret unnatural crime); so that it appears that God hath appointed (for a supernatural sign of the monstrous impiety of witches) that the water shall refuse to receive them in her bosom that have shaken off them the sacred water of baptism and wilfully refused the benefit thereof; no, not so much as their eyes are able to shed tears (threaten and torture them as you please) while first they repent (God not permitting them to dissemble their obstinacy in so horrible a crime); albeit the womankind especially be able otherwise to shed tears at every light occasion when they will, yea, although it were dissembling like the crocodiles."

With the accession of James, the demonologist, to the throne of England, the epidemic of demonophobia burst forth among the English with renewed vigour and with more intense fury than ever. In 1604 the first parliament of King James passed a bill to the effect "that if any person shall use, practise, or exercise any conjuration of any wicked or evil spirit, or shall consult, covenant with, or feed any spirit, the first offence to be imprisonment for a year and standing in the pillory once a quarter; the second offence to be death."

This act of James I against witchcraft was passed

when Lord Bacon was a member of the House of Commons and Lord Coke was attorney-general. That act was referred to a committee which had the spiritual guidance of twelve bishops of the Church of England.

As a rule, however, the minor punishment was but rarely inflicted. Nearly all of the records report cases of accused hanged and burned *alive and quick*. During the long period of social cataclysms from the reign of James I to that of Charles II, the epidemic of demonophobia continued to rage with unabated fury. Dr. Zachary Grey, in a note to "Hudibras," informs us that he himself perused a list of three thousand witches executed in the time of the Long Parliament alone. During the first eighty years of the seventeenth century the number executed has been estimated at five hundred annually, making a total of forty thousand.

Among the English inquisitors, Matthew Hopkins, the witch-finder, greatly distinguished himself for his insane passion of witch persecution. He claimed to have a thorough knowledge of "such cattle," as he called the witches, and soon assumed the title of "Witch-finder Generall." He travelled through the counties of Norfolk, Essex, Huntington, and Sussex for the sole purpose of finding out the servants of tile devil.[2] The most favourable test, however, with him was that of swimming. The hands and feet of the suspected persons were tied together crosswise, the thumb of the right hand to the toe of the left foot, and the thumb of the left hand to the toe of the right foot. The unfortunates were then wrapped up in a large blanket and laid upon their backs in a pond or river. If they sank and were drowned, they were innocent; but if they floated, they were guilty of witchcraft and were burned "alive and quick."

Another favourite method of Hopkins, "the Witch-finder Generall," was to tie the suspected witch in the middle of a room to a chair or table in some uneasy posture. He then placed persons to watch her for four-and-twenty hours, during which time she was kept without food and drink. In this state one of her imps will surely come and visit her and suck her blood. As the imp might come in the shape of a moth or a fly, a hole was made in the door or window to admit it. If any fly escaped from the room, and the watchers could not catch it and kill it, the woman was guilty, and she was sentenced to death. Thus a poor old woman was found guilty, because four flies appeared in the room, and she was made to confess that she had in her employ four imps named "Hemazar," "Pye-wackett," "Peck-in-the Crown," and "Grizel-Greedigut."

In the seventeenth century the social malady of demonophohia reached its acme of development. The epidemic was in full swing. "The world seemed to be like a large madhouse for witches and devils to play their antics in." The terror of mysterious evil agencies fell on the spirits of men. The demon of fear seemed to have obsessed the mind of European humanity. Continental Europe, especially France, Germany, and Switzerland, suffered greatly from the epidemic. High and low were attacked by this malady without any discrimination. In fact, the more learned one was the stronger was the malady, the more acute was the fear of inimical mysterious agencies. Social *paranoia persecutoria* seemed to have become chronic.

· · ·

The great Bodinus, the highest authority of the seventeenth century, tells us that "the trial of the offence [witchcraft] must not be conducted like other crimes. Whoever adheres to the ordinary course of justice perverts the spirit of the law, both divine and human. He who is accused *of sorcery should never be acquitted, unless the malice of the persecutor be clearer than the sun;* for it is so difficult to bring full proof of this secret crime, that out of a million of witches not one "would be convicted if the usual course were followed."!

Thousands upon thousands of victims were cruelly sacrificed to that insane fear of evil spirits. Nuremberg, Geneva, Paris, Toulouse, Lyons, and many other cities, brought on the average an annual sacrifice of two hundred; Cologne burned three hundred and the district of Bamberg four hundred witches and sorcerers annually.

The list of trials of the city of Würzburg for only two years, from 1627 to 1629, may serve as an illustration of the diabolical work done by that insane spirit of demonophobia. Hauber, who has preserved the list in his *Acta et Scripta Magica,* says, in a note at the end, that it is far from being complete, and that there were a great many other burnings too numerous to specify. This list of executions contains the names of one hundred and fifty-seven persons who were burned in the course of two years in twenty-nine burnillgs, averaging from five to six at a time. It comprises three play actors, four innkeepers, three common Counicilmen of Würzburg, fourteen vicars of the cathedral, the burgomaster's lady, an apothecary's wife and daughter, two choristers of the cathedral, Göbel Babelin, the prettiest girl in the town, and the wife, the two little sons, and the daughter of the councillor Stalzenberg. At the seventh of these recorded burnings the victims are described as a wandering boy twelve years of age, and four strange men and women. Thirty of the whole number appear to have been vagrants of both sexes. None escaped. All fell victims to the insane suspicions of religious *paranoia persecutoria.*

The spirit of persecution did not spare even the little ones. The number of children on the list is great. The thirteenth and the fourteenth burnings comprise a little girl of nine, another child (a younger sister), their mother, and their aunt, a pretty young woman of twenty-four. At the eighteenth burning the victims were two boys of twelve and a girl of fifteen. At the nineteenth, the young heir of Rutenhahn, aged nine, and two other boys, one aged ten and the other twelve. Whoever had the misfortune of falling under the suspicion of practising witchcraft, of dealing with spirits, was lost. Nothing could save him from the homicidal fury of religious demonophobia.

So acute was the malady of demonophobia that nonsensical jargon uttered by poor crazed creatures scared people out of their wits. Thus at Amsterdam a crazy girl confessed that she could cause sterility and bewitch pig and poultry by merely repeating the magic words *Turius und Surius Inturius.* She was hanged and burned. One insane person was condemned to the stake by the magistrate of Wüzburg for uttering the followillg formula:

Lalle, Bachera, Magatte, Baphia, Dajam,
Vagath Heneche Ammi Nagaz, Adamator,
Raphael Immanuel Christus, Tetra-
grammaton,
Agra Jad Loi. König! König!

People were condemned to the flames for pronouncing meaningless words, such as

Anton, Lalle, Sabalos, Aado, Pater, Aziel,
Adonai Sado Vagoth Agra, Jad,
Baphra! Komm! Komm!

It was considered an unpardonable sin, a heinous crime that could only be expiated by the *auto-da-fé*, to repeat the following gibberish:

Zellianelle Heotti Bonus Vagotha,
Plisos Sother osech unicus Beelzebub,
Dox! Comm! Comm![3]

The wave of the epidemic ran so high that even little children who in their play happened to repeat those awful incantations were seized by the authorities, tried for witchcraft, found guilty, and condemned the flames.

On American ground we find the same malady of demonophobia blazing up in the celebrated trials of Salem witchcraft. On the accusation of a few hysterical girls,[4] twenty innocent people were condemned to death. Some were hanged, and others suffered a horrible end under the crushing pressure of heavy weights.

One can hardly find on the records of human crimes anything more disgusting, more infamous, than this insane systematic persecution of feeble women and tender children.

---

1. Phantasmata, vol. i. R. R. Madden.
2. The repetion of the Lord's Prayer and Creed, was a sure test to discover the followers of Beelzebub. No witch could do so

correctly. If she missed a word, or even if she pronounced one incoherently, she was guilty. Tearlessness was also a good test. Witches cannot shed more than three tears, and that only from the left eye.

3. Charles Mackay, *Memoirs.*
4. Upham, *On Witchcraft.* Drake, *Annals of Witchcraft.*

6

FINANCIAL CRAZES

IF from the horrors of demonophobia we turn to the market place, to the world of business and finances, we are once more impressed by the extreme suggestibility characteristic of the social spirit. The enthusiasm of speculative mania and the abject fear of financial panics are epidemical. Men think in crowds and go mad in herds. The tulipomania of the Dutch, the Mississippi scheme of the French, the South Sea bubble of the English, the financial epidemics and business panics of our own time, may serve as good illustrations.

About the year 1631, the Dutch became suddenly possessed with a mania for tulips. The ordinary industry of the country was neglected, and the population, even to its lowest dregs, embarked in the tulip trade. The tulip rapidly rose in value, and when the mania was in full swing some daring speculators invested as much as 100,000 florins in the purchase of forty roots. The bulbs were as precious as diamonds;

they were sold by their weight in *perits,* a weight less than a grain. A tulip of the species called Admiral Liefken weighing 400 perits was worth 4,400 florins; an Admiral Von der Eyck weighing 446 perits was worth 1,260 florins; a Childer of 106 perits was worth 1,615 florins; a Viceroy of 400 perits, 3,000 florins; and a Semper Augustus weighing 200 perits was thought to be very cheap at 5,500 florins.[1]

An insane mania of speculating in tulips seized upon the minds of the Dutch. Regular marts for the sale of roots were established in an the large towns of Holland——in Amsterdam, Rotterdam, Haarlem, Leyden, Alkmaar. The stock jobbers dealt largely in tulips, and their profits were enormous. Many speculators grew suddenly rich. The epidemic of tulipomania raged with intense fury, the enthusiasm of speculation filled every heart, and confidence was at its height. A golden bait hung temptingly out before the people, and one after the other they rushed to the tulip marts, like flies around a honey pot. Everyone imagined that the passion for tulips would last forever, and that the wealthy from every part of the world would send to Holland and pay whatever prices were asked for them.

The riches of Europe would be concentrated on the shores of the Zuyder Zee. Nobles, citizens, farmers, mechanics, seamen, footmen, maid servants, chimney-sweeps, and old-clothes women dabbled in tulips. Houses and lands were offered for sale at ruinously low prices, or assigned in payment of bargains made at the tulip market. So contagious was the epidemic that foreigners became smitten with the same frenzy and money poured into Holland from all directions.

This speculative mania did not last long; social suggestion began to work in the opposite direction, and a universal panic suddenly seized on the minds of the Dutch. Instead of buying, everyone was trying to sell. Tulips fell below their normal value. Thousands of merchants were utterly ruined, and a cry of lamentation rose in the land.

About the year 1717 a maniacal enthusiasm of speculation seized on the French mind. John Law, a sharp Scotchman, was authorized by the Regent of France to establish a company with the exclusive privilege of trading on the western bank of the Mississippi. Expectation rose on all sides, and thousands of people hastened to invest their capital, which was to be raised with unheard-of profits on the water of that great river. With a large fund in hand and with prospects of getting an unlimited supply of money, the Mississippi Company extended the range of its visionary speculation.

In the year 1719 an edict was published granting to the Mississippi Company the exclusive privilege of trading to the East Indies and the South Seas. The prospects of profit were glorious. John Law, the projector, the ringleader of the epidemic, promised a profit of about one hundred and twenty per cent!

The enthusiasm of the French nation knew no bounds. Three hundred thousand applications were made for the fifty thousand new shares issued by the company, and Law's house was beset from morning to night by mobs of applicants.

The eagerness to be on the list of the stockholders rose to a pitch of frenzy. Dukes, marquises, counts, with their duchesses, marchionesses, and countesses, waited in the streets for hours every day to know the result. Every day the value of the shares increased, and fresh applications became so numerous that it was deemed advisable to create no less than three hundred thousand new shares at five thousand livres each, in order that the regent might take advantage of the popular enthusiasm to payoff the national debt. For this purpose the sum of fifteen hundred million livres was necessary. Such was the eagerness of the nation that thrice the sum would have been subscribed if the Government had authorized it.

The tide of speculative mania rose higher and higher. The French were seized with an insatiable greed for speculation. There was not a person of note among the aristocracy who was not engaged in buying and selling stock. People of every age and sex and condition in life speculated in the rise and fall of Mississippi bonds. The street where the jobbers met was thronged with multitudes of people, and accidents frequently occurred there on account of the great pressure of the crowd. Houses round the resort of speculation——houses worth in ordinary times a thousand livres of yearly rent——yielded as much as twelve or sixteen thousand. A cobbler who had a stall in that street gained about two hundred livres a day by letting it out and furnishing writing materials to brokers and their clients. The story goes that a hunchback who stood in the street gained considerable sums by lending his hump as a writing desk to the eager speculators.

A spirit of furious speculation took possession of the French mind to such a degree that thousands abandoned resorts of pleasure to join the orgies of gambling in Mississippi bonds. The whole nation was in a trance; it was intoxicated with the hopes and expectations of enormous gains, nay——with actual realization of great treasures. The French, however, soon woke up from their trance with a cry of distress; the Mississippi bubble burst, and thousands of speculators were ruined and reduced to poverty and misery.

In the year 1720 a fever of speculation seized on the English mind. The South Sea Company, in order to raise the value of its stock, spread fanciful rumours that all the Spanish colonies would soon be granted free trade, and then the rich product of Potosi would be poured into the lap of the English. Silver and gold would be as plentiful as iron. England would become the wealthiest country in the world, and the richest company in England would be the South Sea Company; every hundred pounds invested ill it would produce hundreds per annum.

Strange to say, people believed in all those fables, and bought shares and speculated recklessly. Business men were in a high fever of excitement. They abandoned their trades and turned to speculation. For a time it looked as if the whole nation turned stock jobbers. Exchange Alley was blocked up by crowds. Everybody came to purchase stock. "Every fool aspired to be a knave." The epidemic grew in vigour and intensity; the mania for speculation became more acute. New companies with schemes of the most extravagant and fanciful nature sprang up on all sides like mushrooms. The share lists were speedily filled up, and the shares grew on wind and water. Business bubbles were raised on all sides, and people were sure to get rich on them.

Verily, verily, there are no bounds to human credulity and folly. People invested their fortunes in such absurd schemes that one who has never experienced the fever of modem speculation can hardly realize the state of the public mind. Thus one of the projects that received great encouragement was for the establishment of a company "to make deal boards out of sawdust." One project was more absurd than the other: "For furnishing funerals to any part of Great Britain"; "For a wheel of perpetual motion"; "For extracting silver from lead"; "For the transmutation of quicksilver into a malleable fine metal." Such were the nature of the projects. Some bold speculator started "A company for carrying on an undertaking of great advantage, but nobody to know what it is." In his prospectus the speculator stated that the required capital was half a million, in five thousand shares of one hundred pounds each; deposit, two pounds per share. Each subscriber paying his deposit would be entitled to one hundred pounds per share. "Man believes as much as he can," says Prof. James, but as a gregarious animal man believes whatever is suggested to him.

The waves of business speculation ran higher and higher, and along with it rose tile stock of the South Sea Company. The shares rose three hundred to five hundred, five hundred to five hundred and fifty, and then made a prodigious leap to eight hundred and ninety, and finally the price of the stock rose to one thousand per cent! The bubble was full blown and burst. People began to sell stock to realize profit. The stock fell. The rush for selling increased. The stock began to sink rapidly. The fall produced an alarm, a panic!

The course of speculation epidemics is to rise to the highest point of heavenly bliss, and then to fall to tile lowest depth of misery; to pass from a state of acute maniacal exaltation to a state of still more acute melancholic depression. The course of the speculation epoch is a kind of social *folie à double forme*. It is this modern social *folie à double forme* that clearly discloses the extreme suggestibility of gregarious man.

A chronological table will show at a glance the uninterrupted chain of European epidemics:

Pilgrimage epidemic,		1000 to 1095	
Crusade epidemic.	Eastern and Western Crusades, Children's Crusade,	1095 " 1270	
Flagellant epidemic,		1260 " 1348	
Black Death and Antisemitic mania,		1348	
Dancing mania.	St. John's dance, St, Vitus' dance, Tarantism,	1374 1418 1470	To the end of the fifteenth century.
Demonophobia, or witchcraft mania,		1488	To the end of seventeenth century.
Speculative mania.	Tulipomania, The Mississippi Scheme, The South Sea Bubble, And business bubbles,	1634 1717 1720 To our own times.	

---

1. Mackay, Memoirs.

7

AMERICAN MENTAL EPIDEMICS

TURNING now to American social life, so radically different from that of the middle ages, we still find the same phenomena manifesting themselves. The social spirit runs riot in mobs, crazes, manias, pests, plagues, and epidemics.

American religious epidemics hallowed by the name of "revivalism" are notorious. A Jonathan, a McGready, a Sankey, or a Moody is stricken by the plague, falls into a delirium, and begins to rave on religion. The contagion spreads, and thousands upon thousands pray wildly in churches and chapels, rave furiously, and fall into convulsions in camp meetings. A revival epidemic has come, rages violently for some time, and then disappears as suddenly as it came. To take a few instances of the many cases of revival:

In 1800 a wave of religious mania passes over the country and reached its acme in the famous Kentucky revivals. The first camp meeting was held at Cabin Creek. It began on the 22d of May and continued four days and three nights. The crying, the singing, the praying, the shouting, the falling in convulsions made of the place a pandemonium. Those who tried to escape were either compelled to return, as if drawn by some mysterious force, or were struck with convulsions on the way. The pestilence spread, raging with unabated fury. Families came in wagons from great distances to attend the meetings. The camp meetings generally continued four days, from Friday to Tuesday morning, but sometimes they lasted a week. One succeeded another in rapid succession. The woods and paths leading to the camp meeting were alive with people. "The labourer," writes Dr. Davidson,[1] "quitted his task; age snatched his crutch; youth forgot his pastimes; the plough was left in the furrow; the deer enjoyed a respite upon the mountains; business of all kinds was suspended; bold hunters and sober matrons, young men, maidens, and little children flocked to the common centre of attraction." As many as twenty thousand people were present at one of these meetings.

The general meeting at Indian Creek, Harrison County, continued about five days. The meeting was at first quiet. The suggestion, however, was not slow to come, and this time it was given by a child. A boy of twelve mounted a log and began to rave violently. He soon attracted the main body of the people. Overcome by the power of emotions, the little maniac raised his hands, and, dropping his handkerchief wet with tears and perspiration, cried out: "Thus, O sinner, shall you drop into hell unless you forsake your sins and turn to the Lord!" At that moment some fell to the ground "like those who are shot in a battle, and the work spread in a manner which human language can not describe." Thousands were wriggling, writhing, and jerking ill paroxysms of religions fury. So virulent was the revival plague that mere indifferent lookers-on, even mockers and sceptics, were infected by it, and joined the exercises of the raving religious maniacs and fell into jerking convulsions of religious hysteria. The following case may serve as a fair example:

"A Gentleman and a lady of some note in the fashionable world were attracted to the camp meeting at Cone Ridge. They indulged in many contemptuous remarks on their way about the poor infatuated creatures who rolled over screaming in the mud, and promised jestingly to stand by and assist each other in case that either should be seized with the convulsions. They had not been long looking upon the strange scene before them, when the young woman lost her consciousness and fell to the ground. Her companion, forgetting his promise of protection, instantly forsook her and ran off at the top of his spell. But flight afforded him no safety. Before he had gone two hundred yards he, too, fell down in convulsions."[2]

In many places the religions epidemic took the form of laughing, dancing, and barking or dog manias. "Whole congregations were convulsed with hysterical laughter during holy service. In the wild delirium of religious frenzy people took to dancing, and at last to barking like dogs. They assumed the posture of dogs, "moving about on all fours, growling, snapping the teeth, and barking with such an exactness of imitation as to deceive anyone whose eyes were not directed to the spot.[3] Nor were the people who suffered so mortifying a transformation always of the vulgar classes persons of the highest rank in society, on the contrary, men and women of cultivated minds and polite manners, found themselves by sympathy reduced to this degrading situation,"[4] The baneful poison of religious revivalism turns its victims into packs of mad dogs.

In 1815 a religious revival swept over the country, and ended in the excesses of camp meetings.

In 1832 a great revival epidemic raged fiercely in this country. An excellent description of this revival is given by Mr. Albert S. Rhodes.[5] I give his account *verbatim*:

"What is usually called 'the Great American Revival' began simultaneously in New Haven and New York in 1832, and does not seem to have been set in motion by any particular individual or individuals, but to have been in a full sense a popular expression. It was in men's minds and in the atmosphere. It broke out and raged like a fire over a certain portion of the country known by the old inhabitants as the 'burnt district.' It was especially felt along the shore of Lake Ontario and in the counties of Madison and Oneida.

"The host that marched in this revival movement had many banners, but were without known chieftains. . . . The corporals and sergeants who marched with the uprising were men of mediocrity (unknown heroes of mobs). These did not make the revival, but it made them. They were of various religious colours, and formed a motley group gathered from the Wesleyan Methodists, Episcopal Methodists, Evangelists, Independents, Congregationalists, and Presbyterians.

"The characteristic signs [of revivalism] attended this spiritual tempest. Ballrooms were turned into places of prayer and theatres into churches. . . . Clergymen who reasoned logically were told that they held the sponge of vinegar to the parched lips of sinners, instead of leading them to the brook of life where they might drink to completion. They met with the treatment unusual in such popular up-heavals——they were pushed aside to make room for the new expounders and prophets, ignorant men full of faith and vociferation, who preached night and day the golden streets of the New Jerusalem and the wrath to come.

"The apple of Sodom grew out of this religious mania; the followers soon became incapable of sin.[6] . . .'And when a man becomes conscious that his soul is saved,' proclaimed one of their spiritual leaders, 'the first thing that he sets about is to find his paradise and his Eve.' The leaders could not find paradises in their own homes, nor Eves in their own wives, and sought their 'affinities' elsewhere. One of their leaders had a vision of an immense throng of men and women in heaven who wandered hither and thither in search of something necessary to their happiness with an expression of longing depicted on their faces. The men hunted for wives, as women did for men. The spirit of yearning for an incomplete joy was every-where visible in these great hosts. The seer have an interpretation of his vision that men and women were wrongly joked on this earth, and that this may be remedied by a proper and spiritual union in the ter-restrial sphere. The interpretation was received with favour, and even with enthusiasm. The man who saw the vision set the example by putting his legitimate wife abide and taking to his bosom the comely wife of one of his brethren. Others quickly followed the ex-ample. . . .The union was popularly designated among them as spiritual wedlock. . . . Old ties were given up. The kingdom of heaven was at hand. Old rules were no longer binding, and old obligations were set aside. Men and women, regardless of marital ties, selected their celestial companions.

"At first such unions were to be of purely spiritual character, but, of course, in the end became sexual. . . . Before long the spiritual union was found to be incomplete, and it assumed the ordinary character of that which exists between man and woman who live together in close intimacy. Men who lived with the wives of others, and women who lived with the husbands of others, produced a strange confusion. . . . Children were abandoned by their natural protectors.

"It resulted in evil still worse. Men and women discovered that they had made mistakes in their spiritual unions, and, after having lived for a certain period together, they separated to make new selections. It soon came to pass that they made new selections in comparatively short periods of time, and the doctrine of spiritual affinity thus inevitably merged into gross licentiousness.

"If the facts were not before us, some of the unions would appear incredible. These were what the French would call *mariages à trois*. The lawful husband and the spiritual one lived under the same roof, in some cases with the same wife, who denied all conjugal rights to the husband in law, and accorded them freely to the husband in spirit; and there are remarkable instances furnished of the husbands submitting to such a state of thins as being in accordance with the divine will. And such examples of degradation, according to the annals of the time, do not appear to have been rare.

"Such were some of the results which the revival of 1832 left behind in the 'burnt district' . . . Such was the revival in its moral aspect. It had still a physical and mental side, which was worse to contemplate, in the number of deluded people who were placed in the hospitals and insane asylums."

About the year 1840 the so-called "Miller mania" broke out.[7] "This delusion originated in the readings, reflections, and dreams of one William Miller, of the State of New York, who came to know about the year 1840 at what time 'the Lord was to appear in the heavens' and the end of all things to come. He soon found adherents—as will the author of any humbug, however palpable—who with a zeal worthy of a better cause set themselves to proselyting. They went abroad preaching their doctrine to all who would hear, and publishing their views to the world through periodicals and newspapers. . . . At the outset they pitched not only upon the year, but the day and hour on which the 'Son of Man should come with power and great glory.' A doctrine like this, solemn and momentous beyond expression, spread abroad with all the rapidity that novelty could lend to it; the zeal of its adherents . . . soon collected around its standard throngs of men and women who hugged the delusion as the announcement of great events, and the support of raptures and glorious ecstasies.

"The beggarly amount of intellect with which its deluded followers were possessed soon yielded to the farce of religious excitement, and long before 'the time drew near when they were to be received up' they forsook their respective callings, closed their shops and stores, left their families to suffer, or abandoned them to the cold charities of the world, attending meetings for prayers and exhortations, 'rendering night hideous by their screams' and by ceaseless prayers and watchings, intending to open in 'the great day of the Lord.'

"The excitement, of which the above brief presentation furnishes by no means an exaggerated description, soon began to produce its effects upon both the bodies and minds of these wretched beings. A pale and haggard countenance, indicative at once of physical exhaustion and great mental solicitude, strange and erroneous views in reference to their worldly relations and affairs, together with their conduct, which showed that the *controlling power of reason was swallowed up in the great maelstrom of Millerism*—all indicated the shock which had been produced by the terrors of this fearful delusion. As the time for the great *dénouement* approached meetings increased, their prayers were heard far and wide around; converts were multiplied; baptisms were celebrated, not by sprinkling, but by immersions which lasted sometimes longer than life. The gift of tongues was vouchsafed, ascension robes of snowy whiteness were made ready, property was freely given away, and on the morning of 'the great day,' with hearts prepared, and decked in robes of peerless white, they went forth to meet the 'bridegroom.' Some, not content to meet him upon earth, actually ascended trees in order first to greet his approach.

"The day first announced passed off quietly. . . . Great was the disappointment of the followers of the doctrine of Miller. Their time for weeks and months had been lost, their business broken up, and their property gone. Yet, to exhibit, as it were, still more forcibly the strength of religious fanaticism (religious suggestion) operating upon (weak) minds, they still clung to their delusion, again 'searched the Scriptures,' and happily found that they had been in error. It was on a certain day and hour of the Jewish year 1844 on which their calculation should have been based, instead of the corresponding year of our calendar. The joyful news was spread abroad throughout the realms of Millerism, and the zeal and fervour of the followers rose higher than before.

"Meanwhile institutions for the insane were daily furnishing new proofs of the mental ravages Millerism was producing throughout the country. Miller maniacs were almost daily brought to the doors of the insane asylums. Worn out and exhausted by ceaseless religious orgies, many broke down completely and became hopelessly insane. Some were already in heaven, clothed with the new bodies provided for the saints; others, like spectres, were hastening to convert to the the faith their fellow-victims to disease; while a third class refused to eat, having no further need of other than 'angels' food.' So strictly did many of the believers adhere to the cherished passages of the sacred Scriptures that they declined to go abroad to respond to the calls of Nature, because, forsooth, we were commanded 'to become as little children,' and hence soiled their underdresses. None slept, or slept but little; all were waiting, waiting in obedience to a divine command. .... Sleep, in fact, was far from their eyes in consequence of the long-continued watchfulness which had been imposed. They had passed the point of sleep; some of them even passed the rallying point of exhausted nature, and sank to rise no more. Scores of the victims to this modern delusion (epidemic) were known by all to be the tenants of madhouses, and it was promulgated far and wide by the most respectful authorities that this was a legitimate result of their misguided views and acts, yet it fell unheeded upon the ears of those for whom in kindness it was designed.

Meanwhile the period approached when the correctness of their last reckoning was to be verified. .... If possible, a more firm conviction of the truth of

Millerism existed in the minds of its followers generally than before; converts to it had increased, and all the elements of prodigious and extended commotion were concentrating preparatory to this event. The scenes which were enacted in view of the fulfillment of this second interpretation greatly exceeded the first. Like the first, it proved to be a baseless fabric of a vision. . . .The epidemic, however, did not abate. The Cry of November 22, 1844, announced the fact that our 'brethren and sisters are not only strong, but much stronger than ever. Our brethren are all standing fast, expecting the Lord every day.'"

Well may President Jordan, of Stanford University, exclaim: "Whisky, cocaine, and alcohol bring temporary insanity, and so does a revival of religion——one of those religious revivals in which men lose their reason and self-control. This is simply a form of drunkenness no more worthy of respect than the drunkenness that lies in the gutter." Prof. Jordan was attacked on all sides by the small fry of the pulpits. But Prof. Jordan was, in fact, too mild in his expression. Religious revivalism is a social bane, it is far more dangerous to the life of society than drunkenness. As a sot, man falls below the brute; as a revivalist, he sinks lower than the sot.

In 1857-58 a great industrial panic occurred in this country. Business was pressed to its utmost limits. The greed of gain became a veritable mania. Commercial centres, cities, towns large and small, and even villages were possessed by the demon of financial speculation. Speculation rose to a fever heat; the wildest projects were readily undertaken by the credulous business public. Finally the crash came. Social suggestion began to work the other way, and the stream of business life turned in the opposite direction. Every one ran for his life, not so much because he perceived danger, but simply because he saw his neighbours running——a stampede, a panic, ensued.

In this morbid condition of the body politic the toxic germs of religious mania, the poisonous microbes of the revival pest, once more found a favourable soil. A fierce religious epidemic set on and spread far and wide. The religious journals of the country gloried in it. "Such a time as the present," writes triumphantly one of them,[8] "was never known since the days of the apostles for revivals. Revivals now cover our very land, sweeping all before them. . . . Meetings are held for prayer, for exhortation, with the deepest interest and the most astonishing results. Not only are they held in the church and from house to house, but in the great marts of trade and centres of business. In New York there is a most astonishing interest in all the churches, seeming as if that great and populous and depraved city was enveloped in one conflagration of divine influence. . . . Prayer and conference meetings are held in retired rooms connected with large commercial houses, and with the best effects (!). The large cities and towns generally from Maine to California are sharing in this great and glorious work."

A Boston journalist caught a glimpse of the true nature of this religious revival. "For the last three months," he writes, "a revival of religion has spread like an epidemic over a wide extent of the country. Prayer meetings noon and night; prayer meetings in Boston, New York, Philadelphia, Chicago; prayer meetings in Richmond, Charleston, Mobile, New Orleans; prayer meetings in town, village, hamlet, North and South, crowded with expectant listeners and accompanied with a copious outpouring of the Divine

Spirit. The whole thing is emotional contagion without principle."

This religious revival then spread to Ireland, where it raged with as great a fury as in its native place, the United States, the country of the revival plague.

"I am unwilling to give the details," writes Rev. J. Llewelyn Davies,[9] "of the kinds of affected which have prevailed. They are painful, and in many cases, to speak frankly, *simply disgusting*." The attacks have so far the character of an epidemic that they have had a singular resemblance to one another. The prevailing symptoms have been a state of perfect helplessness beneath an overwhelming sense of guilt and danger; . . . sudden prostrations, shrieks and cries, cataleptic rigidity, oppression at the heart and stomach, in some cases temporary blindness, deafness, and numbness."

American society oscillates between acute financial mania and attacks of religious insanity. No sooner is the business fever over than the delirium of religious mania sets in. Society is thrown from Seylla into Charybdis. From the heights of financial speculation it sinks into the abyss of revivalism. *American society seems to suffer from circular insanity.*

The friends of revivalism are not unaware of this fact. Thus Rev. H. C. Fish, who made a text-book of revivalism, naïvely tells us: "It is an interesting fact that they [revivals] frequently succeed some great [public] calamity, a prevailing epidemic, financial embarrassment." *The germs of religious insanity require for their development a diseased and exhausted body politic.*

Women in general, and American women in particular, are highly suggestible.[10] The woman's crusade of 1873 may serve as a good illustration.[11] The crusade commenced in Hillsborough, Ohio, on a Christmas morning. After a lecture by Dr. Dio Lewis on the potency of Woman's Prayer in the Grogshop, the response was general. A meeting for prayer and organization was held, the women, led by a distinguished Methodist lady, the heroine of the mob, marched forth on their first visit to drug stores, hotels, and saloons. The crusade mania, like a true epidemic, spread rapidly into adjacent towns, the women visiting saloons, preaching, singing, and praying. Ladies of all denominations joined the crusade. Neither threats nor harsh treatment nor rough weather could check the fervent religious zeal of the female mobs. In many places the ladies suffered severe privations; they were oftentimes kept standing in the cold and rain; they were often offended and ill treated; but of no avail—crusade epidemic kept on raging with undaunted fury. The churches were crowded day and night. Like all things taken up by women, the enthusiasm of this crusade did not last long; it soon died out. Social suggestibility is too strong in woman to permit her to remain long under the influence of suggestions that are out of tile way of commonplace life. Woman can not leave long the routine of her life, the beaten track of mediocrity; she can rarely rise above the trite; she is a Philistine by nature.

Such were, in the main, some of the religious epidemics that befell American society for the brief space of its existence. Who can enumerate all the commercial "revivals," the "business bubbles," and the economical panics closely following in their wake? Who can tell of all the crazes and manias—such, for instance, as the football mania, the baseball mania, the prize-fight insanity, the Trilby craze, the bicycle frenzy, the new-woman pest—that have taken possession of the American social self? Who can count all the industrial, political, and lynching mobs in which the spirit of American society has manifested itself? Their name is legion, for they are innumerable, countless.[12]

Sad and melancholy are the mental aberrations of the social mind, but very painful is it to find that they flow from the inmost soul of society. *Society by its very nature tends to run riot in mobs and epidemics. For the gregarious, the subpersonal, uncritical social self, the mob self, and the suggestible subconscious self are identical.*

1. History of the Presbyterian Church in Kentucky.
2. Gospel Herald. Prof. D. W. Yandell, Epidemic Convulsions, Brain, October, 1881.
3. McNemar.
4. Prof. D. W. Yandell, Brain, October, 1881.
5. Appleton's Journal, December 11, 1875.
6. The sense of guilt and that of regeneration and elevation after conversion are good symptoms of revival mania. Mr. D. Starbuck, to whom my thanks are due for placing at my disposal his rich material on religious conversion, in his article "A Study of Conversion" (The American Journal of Psychology, January, 1897), comes to the conclusion that "revival meetings play an important part in conversion," and that "the sense of sin" and "the sense of elevation" are its main characteristics. What Mr. Starbuck does not realize is the fact that it is not healthy normal life that one studies in sudden religious conversions, but the phenomena of revival insanity.
7. Esquirol, Mental Maladies, English translation.
8. H. C. Fish, Handbook of Revivals. For the use of Winners of Souls.
9. Macmillan, vol. 1, March, 1860.
10. I take here the opportunity to mention the interesting fact of revivalism among the American Jewish women. The revival of acient Jewish customs and the separation from the Gentile world are among the aims of this religious mania. "Those who take part in this revival," a well-known rabbi informs me, "consider themselves superior to other women." This sense of superiority of those who were "saved" is a well-marked symptom of the revival plague. The germs of this epidemic seem to be very active. Although they started their career in Chicago, at the World's Fair, in the year of our Lord 1893, they have invaded nearly every city of the United States. Rich

Jewish ladies form the main body of victims; they are very susceptible to this religious disease. The interesting peculiarity of this Jewish revival plague is that it attacks only women and rabbis.

11. Cyclopædia of Methodism, Bishop Matthew Simpson.

12. While this work was in progress a great economico-political epidemic, the so-called silver movement, was raging over the country. The work was hardly completed when the excitement of the silver mania subsided, but only to give place to a different form of social malady, the speculative "gold-mining mania," the Klondike plague.